MW00617828

Stories

Tommi -
I pray
this will
encourage you
more
to be Him.
in love
Sandy
Parker
3 John 2

Stories

A WOMAN'S JOURNEY OF BECOMING IMPERFECTLY PERFECT

Sandy Renner

Stories

Cover design byFiverr/Rebeccacovers
Interior design byFiverr/Aalishaa
Editing by Pamela Scholtes and Alexys V. Wolf

The opinions expressed by the author are those of Sandy Renner Ministries.

The Fiery Sword Publications
Lexington, South Carolina

Published in the United States of America

ISBN-13: 978-1-952668-09-8

1. Religion / Christian Life / Personal Growth
2. Religion / Christian Life / Spiritual Growth

Table of Contents

Dedication

In memory of Tom and Annie Wheeler

My mom and dad were not perfect people, but they were the parents God chose for me. They gave me life and raised me when they could have done differently. I am grateful to them for giving me the ability to grow up and see the goodness of God.

I love you.

~

Acknowledgements

I want to thank all who has participated in my life's journey, without you, my journey would not be as rich. For anyone I have disappointed in my failures, please forgive me. I hold no animosity toward anyone. I thank God for my parents with all their failures because they brought me into the world and for the most part, they did the best with who they were and what they had. To my sisters, Pat, Barbara, Lucy and Sybil, and my Aunt Barbara, I love you and one day when I get really brave, I will write a book about all of us! That would be a best seller and probably turn into a mini-series!

Pete if you are reading this, and you probably are not, because I know you don't like to read, but please know you were a gift to me. I am sorry we did not honor God and each other the way we should have. We both made plenty of mistakes but look at the legacy we leave this world: our offspring. Nothing can change that.

To my children, Amy, and Jason and Leslie, I love you always and remember it is never too late to be all that God has designed you to be. You all are gifted in so many ways and you are loved by your Heavenly Father. To my grandchildren Clairey, Hunter, TJ, Gabriel, and Elizabeth, you are remarkable, and I love you all. I am honored to be your Meme. God has designed you and you are unique. Never forget who you really are. You are His creation destined to be world-changers!

My sweet little Ariel, my first great-granddaughter. How beautiful you are. You were not yet in our arms when this book was started, but you already had won our hearts. You will carry on long after I may be gone. I pray this book will be a guide to the greatness that is hidden in you. Your rich heritage will be found in the strength of your family and God, your Creator. You do not come from wealth or perfect people, but you do come from a family who knows how to make wrong choices and overcome. A family who will be there when the going gets tough. A family who will fight for you no matter what. You are loved. Your name means 'lioness,' you have the strength of the Lion of Judah, the Messiah. Serve Him. Your great meme is always praying for you. This goes for all my generations who will come after you.

To my newfound family—Veneta Renner, Michael, Lauren, Naomi, Olivia, Paul Michael, Jordan, Haley, Greysen and Landon, Cindy, and George—I want to thank you for accepting me into your family. It's kind of hard to know how to place someone when all the places have been spoken for, you know, everyone is settled into their roles. I don't need a position or title just grateful that you would all share Ray and yourselves with me. I probably am not what you would have expected Ray to bring into the family, but you all have been gracious. I look forward to many years of making family memories with you. I hope this book will give you more insight in who I am and encourage you to be all that God says you can be.

I especially dedicate this book to my husband Ray. You have heard a lot of these stories, but not all, I'm sure. Thank you for saying, "*Hi.*" I know how much cycling means to you, so I am grateful that you chose me, a Bible chick over a biker chic! I know we have challenged each other, but I have enjoyed the challenge, well, some of it anyway. It can't be easy being married to a minister and a prophet. But, it's who I am. I am still enamored with your persevering spirit and energy. Our differences have allowed the

Holy Spirit to change and refine me in many ways. I hope I have deposited good changes in you. I am grateful that God has allowed us to be partners in this journey. I know we have more years behind us than we have in front of us. But, oh my goodness, look at the possibilities. God did not call Moses to be a deliverer of His people until he was eighty years old. Caleb took dominion of his promised mountain at eighty-five! Life in Christ is an awesome never-ending adventure.Are you up for the ride of your life? I hope so. Let's live it to the fullest as we grow the Kingdom of God. I love you.

Last, but certainly not least, I am forever grateful to my spiritual father and mother, James and Jackie Shinn. I could not be who I am in Christ or in ministry without the love and guidance and rebukes you poured into me. Thank you for being a guiding light for me when others were ready to toss me to the wolves, you loved me unconditionally. I love and honor you.

> Come, let's sing to Adonai! Let's shout for joy to the Rock of our salvation! Let's come into his presence with thanksgiving; let's shout for joy to him with songs of praise. Come, let's bow down and worship; let's kneel before Adonai who made us. "For He is our God, and we are His people in His pasture, the sheep in His care (Psalm 95: 1-2, 6-7 CJB)."

Endorsements

I highly recommend Sandy Renner's latest work, *Stories*, a collection of short stories reflecting Sandy's life and spiritual journey. Sandy's gut-level honesty and the sharing of her triumphs and failures make it real in such a way that we can all identify. I've often said that following Christ is not dull, boring, or ho-hum, and Sandy's life as a Christ-follower is certainly no exception. She has experienced many encounters with God and has felt His love and acceptance as a way of living a faith-filled life. Stories is a must read! ~ *Reverend Joe Dillard*

It is difficult to put into words the profound impact Sandy Renner has had on my life. God brought her into my life 18 years ago in the midst of a seemingly hopeless and turbulent period. I was in desperate need of direction. When we initially met, to say we did not care for one another would be an understatement, but, through God's inconceivable orchestration of our connection, we were both transformed by the relationship. Unquestionably, God moved through Sandy to rescue me from destruction by reminding me I am God's beloved who is fearfully and wonderfully made. She poured countless hours into my life and has consistently promoted my spiritual maturity, often through the example of her own life. Sandy's stories are a constant reminder of how God moves through the most unlikely individuals in ways, beyond our comprehension, to further His kingdom. It is a testament to the relentless pursuit of God to enter into authentic relationship with every single person. I have witnessed God move through Sandy to speak into the lives of others and radically transform their relationship with Him and the trajectory of their life. *Stories* will inspire hope and open the eyes of the reader to the depths of the unfailing love and transformative grace the Creator of the universe graciously extends to every person who is open to receive. ~ *Keeley Burgan*

What you see is what you get! This is the Sandy I know and love. You will be captivated and moved in this beautifully written compilation of her life events. Sandy's personal testimonies of Jesus are the life of God breathed into these stories. There was a time when Sandy could quote the Bible back to front until a tragic event took that from her, but it was God's plan for her to share His love in the stories of her life. I don't care who you are or what you have been through in your life, there is a story that Sandy has from her life experiences that you will connect with. In her true-life stories, you will laugh, cry, be encouraged, get angry, experience freedom, know love, and every single other emotion and self-identification lie or truth. I personally know that these stories are anointed by God with the purpose of you knowing Him, His love for you, and how He sees you. Be aware, it probably won't be what you expect—it will, however, leave you with a life changed if you let it. As with many, I affectionately call her my spiritual mom, mentor, and friend. Enjoy! ~ *Heidi M Hunter*

The stories you read here will amaze you to the incredible journey Sandy has been on with our creative, never dull, one adventure after another, incredible God! It's a fact! I experienced a few of these myself, and the day Sandy first visited my pastorate, I knew this person had been on some wild missions with the Lord. *Stories* reminds the reader that following Jesus is never predictable, always beneficial, and worth our life and attention advancing us into seeing how great is our God. ~ *Reverend Pastor Robert Reeves, pastor at Indian Trail UMC*

I've known Pastor Sandy for ten years. After four years of ministering alongside her, together we formed a church ministry known as the *Living Stones International Community*. This has given me a front row seat to witness what God has done with her and to see whence He has brought her. Pastor Sandy has been there, done that, and I'm sure she expects many more God-moments in her future, which will result in many stories to tell. Frankly, the theme of this book fits her well because I've never met a single soul who has a better gift at telling stories than she. I expect this book to be an enjoyment for you, but I pray it challenges you to watch what God does in your life so that you too can have many stories. ~ *Scott R. Cooper, Living Stones International Community*

Sandy is real! Since meeting her nearly a decade ago in the lobby of my office, my life has been forever changed. Today, I am not the same man. I am a changed man with purpose and gifts I never knew I had. Sandy has walked me through two life-altering processes. First, she was instrumental in allowing me to truly understand what it means to be free in Christ. Secondly, she has encouraged and fostered an ever-deepening relationship with God through reading His word with purpose. What she has placed in these pages has the potential to positively change your trajectory in life if you follow through. My sincere recommendation to you is to do what is presented within these pages. Then watch your physical, emotional, and spiritual life change for the better. ~ *Andrew Hass*

To the readers who are getting ready to turn the page and enter into the life of my spiritual momma and mentor, I pray blessings over your life. I sincerely ask the Father above—who has breathed life into each story on Sandy's journey through her magnificent life—to breathe wisdom, understanding, knowledge, and revelation into your life to encourage you and sharpen you on your journey. We are only here for a short time, and the time He has given us is precious. May you know that you are here for a purpose and a plan, and that the Kingdom of God is right in front of you. Sandy has been instrumental in loving me and mentoring me in the ways of God. She has walked hand-in-hand with me for years. God has moved through Sandy to help lead, guide, and direct me. She has taught me about freedom in Christ and has, more than once, walked me through difficult circumstances. This book is not in your hand by accident. Enjoy the stories and glean from her life and be blessed. ~ *Reverend Nicole Hass*

When I see Sandy Renner, I see God! As my dear friend, mentor, and spiritual mother, Sandy has dramatically impacted my life and provoked exponential growth in my life spiritually. There is no question that God's glory rests upon Sandy, and she is truly gifted in more ways than one. As a powerful woman of God, Sandy has an innate ability to tell some of the most fascinating and captivating stories. The stories she shares about her various life experiences are full of purpose and meaning, and God moves through this beautiful, yielded vessel to deliver some very impactful messages. Her listeners are sure to gain a greater knowledge and revelation about our heavenly Father, how awesome He is, what His Word says, and how great His love is for us all. I always feel a desire to draw closer to God, become all He has called me to be, and do all he has called me to do. I can't thank our heavenly Father enough for the blessing of placing Sandy Renner in my life. She is, and will always be, a part of my favorite stories to share with others. ~ *Tanailyn Williams Pernell, Health Promotion Consultant*

In February of 2018, I first said, "*Hi*," to my wife, Sandy. That began an intense amount of time talking to her, getting to know her and who she is in God's Kingdom, seeing and feeling the presence of the Holy Spirit in and on her, and, best of all, getting to hear her many wonderful stories. She had a different story every time we talked. By the way, all this talking was by phone for about a month before we started dating. We lived just over an hour apart. We went out every weekend; one weekend in Rock Hill, South Carolina where she lived, and the next weekend in the Cayce, South Carolina area where I lived. Of course, the long phone conversations continued through the week, and more and more stories were told. She would tell them to me, and sometimes to people we were around. Some stories I had heard several times after just a few months of dating. I never got tired of them. I liked and loved Sandy and her stories so much that I married her in November of 2018, the same year we met. I have heard nearly all of the 100+ stories she has in this book and every one of them excite me as much the tenth time I hear them as the first. Every story is good for ministry. These stories will be applicable to what is happening in your life as well as the lives of your friends and family. They will give you encouragement, healing, and strengthen your faith in God. You will learn that you can trust God and His almighty power to heal and deliver you from any sickness, disease, principality, or whatever is holding you back from a better life filled with the Holy Spirit and His gifts; a life full of joy, peace, and that special unity you have walking with God in His Kingdom. ~ *Ray Renner, Sandy's husband*

Foreword

I met Sandy Renner October 24, 2019 in a God-weird way. Her friend, and now mine, Pastor Robert Reeves of Indian Field UMC, called me out of the blue wanting to obtain a personal copy of *Understanding Kingdom Prayer*. We met, talked a lot, and, during the conversation, he said, "*I'm not saying this is prophetic, but I believe you need to meet a lady named Sandy Renner.*" I agreed to swap phone numbers. By the time I returned home that afternoon, it was around 4 p.m. I thought I would go ahead and call her just to say I did, and, low and behold, with the phone in my hand ready to dial, it rang. It was Sandy. Though I was skeptical, I was also intrigued. That was a Tuesday.

By Thursday, we met at 12:30 for lunch at Zesto's, our famous local burger and chicken joint. If you can believe it, we sat there five full hours talking and talking…well, she mostly talked and I mostly listened! This woman had, by far, the most fascinating stories of any one single person I've ever met in my life. One after the other, boom, boom, boom, came the tales of intrigue and mystery of the hand of God moving in, through, and around her. Three hours in, my back was severely aching from sitting on a hard diner-type bench. But, alas, I hadn't the heart to tell her I wanted to go lie down! Two more hours, and finally her husband called looking for her. That was the beginning of a beautiful friendship.

Fast forward exactly one year, and here I sit typing the foreword to her book, which I am also publishing! From that day until now, October 2020, we have ministered to one another, partnered in a radio broadcast called "*Better Together: Two Girls and a Bible*," joined forces with Robert Reeves with his South Carolina Prayer Academy, and much more. I am fully amazed at the hand of God bringing us together. Sandy and I have, in the past, both been burned by fellow ministers, so we were a bit gun-shy, to be honest. For me, I was optimistically trepidatious moving forward because, frankly, I heard her stories, but did not yet know her character. Knowing other prophets—allegedly—who have been mean and biting with their "*word from God*," I was none too anxious to get aboard another prophet-train. As a prophet, I understand what it is to be bold with the Word, yet God instructs us to be loving, humble, direct, and bold simultaneously. Being around other prophets who were not so loving or merciful citing, "*Prophets are just that way. They can be rude*," act as if rudeness is a God-criterion. It isn't.

I am thrilled to testify that it didn't take long at all to connect spirit-to-spirit with Sandy. I have experienced ministry with her and I've seen her in action. She's absolutely nothing I've experienced before. Direct? Yes. Bold? Absolutely. Humble, compassionate, and kind? All the way! Watching Sandy move in the Spirit of God is a breath of fresh air. Can I understand why some people wouldn't take to her so easily? Of course! Many people have difficulty with someone as forthcoming as Sandy because they're simply not ready to face, albeit sometimes harsh, reality. But, that is an internal issue with those people, not with Sandy. She is one amazing woman of God and I doubt there's another person on planet Earth quite like her. It is my great pleasure and honor to go about the Father's business alongside my friend and ministry partner, Author Sandy Renner.

And, by the way, Sandy has been blessed with an amazing head of white hair what draws people to her. It's one of the first physical attributes about her I noticed. It's striking! Sandy Renner, in a nutshell, is a down-to-Earth gal who listens to the Word of the Lord—both the Bible and His audible voice—and complies with His perfect will. When she misses a step, she doesn't mind telling that too. After all, she is a voice of God in a human container. She is the epitome of humility. God has brought Sandy from absolute poverty and hardship into a loving, God-ordained marriage to Ray Renner, surrounded her with loyal friends, and has granted her a unique gift of hearing Him.

In this book of hers, Author Renner has comprised a group of fascinating tales that will cause any reader to gasp! Take this journey with Sandy through her life and witness how God moved in the most interesting ways. Please, enjoy this book.

Alexys V. Wolf, minister& author
The Fiery Sword Global Ministries
The Fiery Sword Publications
"Better Together" radio show co-host

Introduction

When I started writing this book, I decided to title it *Stories*. After all, that is what this book is about. I tend to be black and white, straight to the point; that's how I roll. God always brings someone into my life possessing the ability to help me see my need to fill in the blanks with some color. This time, that person happens to be Alexys Wolf, my friend and ministry partner.

These stories are true accounts of my life and, more precisely, my faith-journey. However, just the title "*Stories*" can sound a bit generic and not very descriptive. Alexys suggested a subtitle with a bit of an explanation. I agreed, thus "*A Woman's Journey to Becoming Imperfectly Perfect*" became the subtitle. How did I come to use this subtitle? Well, that is a bit of a story in itself. I prayed about the subtitle and just couldn't come up with anything. Seriously, nothing came to mind. When that happens, I have learned that God probably has a plan and I just need to trust and wait for it. That moment came quite unexpectedly while getting my hair cut in Missouri.

I have some good friends in Missouri and I had flown there to do a memorial service for my friend's mother. Every time I'm there, I take advantage of my friend's son's talented scissors. Joshua was cutting my hair and talking, and, suddenly, he said, "*Sandy, you are a woman becoming imperfectly perfect.*" Bingo! I knew that was my subtitle. That describes my life. I am imperfect within myself, no doubt about it. But, because Christ, who is perfect, lives in me, I am becoming more like Him. 2 Corinthians states, *"But we all, with unveiled face, beholding as in a mirror the glory of the Lord, are being transformed into the same image from glory to glory, just as from the Lord, the Spirit."*

I have been told, many times, that I seem to have more stories than anyone. I find that amusing. It's not like I've lived an exotic life. I don't consider myself different than most people I have met in my lifetime. You know—kind of ordinary. I grew up with five siblings ranging in ages like doorsteps. I was sort of in the middle, which is really like no place at all. I was not the oldest, nor the youngest, certainly not the smartest or the prettiest. I think I developed a sense of humor by necessity. When life gets uncomfortable, I tend to crack jokes. Hey, don't laugh—it got me through some tough spots! Something quite extraordinary did happen to me, though, when I was in my early twenties. It happens to a lot of people, but still. I met a man named Jesus! He is extraordinary, so doing life with Him can never be mundane. Even in my difficult childhood, my stories have a link to my relationship with the Lord. However, I would not come to understand that for many years.

I grew up in an alcoholic home. Both my parents drank heavily—though not all the time, —but it was often enough that it overshadowed any good memories, which were few. For many years, as an adult, it was difficult for me to recall any memories. God really has a sense of humor. He used a forgotten memory to bring me to Himself, and I will share that story later. It had crossed my mind to put some of my life's stories in writing, perhaps to hand down to my grandchildren. I had not considered doing it in the form of a published book, yet, here it is!

I am so excited, and yet I am left wondering how this happened so quickly. Where does the time go? I want to leave something of value to my descendants. Not money, mainly because I don't have any. I want to leave them a heritage. The only thing I have of real lasting value is a story. A story compiled of many stories—stories of pain, comfort, sickness, and healing. Stories filled with fear and faith, anger and forgiveness, failures and successes, life and death. Stories filled with how to overcome great obstacles. Stories of how to conquer giants when you are weak and afraid. Stories of mystery. Some of these stories will seem to be impossible to believe. In a world where people, as a whole, have misplaced their identity and there seems to be no real absolute truth. I want my story to help give a sense of hope and guidance to my grandchildren and beyond. I want my life to count, at least, in the journey of life for my offspring. I want my story to inspire my loved-ones to believe God to do the impossible. I want them to believe in something beyond this world. I want them to see that the Creator of this great universe has a plan that gives them the ability to live a life of extraordinary possibilities! Life is short and often scary. It is also an extraordinary adventure if it is guided by a supernatural God. I hope you will not choose anything less than what He has designed for you.

"For I know the plans I have for you," declares the LORD, "plans to prosper you and not to harm you, plans to give you hope and a future (Jeremiah 29:1, NIV)."

My Memories

My stories are not meant to highlight anyone's wrongdoing. They are not being told to provoke blame, shame, or to garner pity. My purpose is to share the goodness of God. Without a test, there is no provision for a testimony. I wish I could tell you that I passed every test, but that would not be true. That is the beauty of grace— God's grace. In the times of my life when I had no understanding that He had a plan for my small, seemingly insignificant life, the Lord of the universe was watching over me keeping me from harm. It would be years before I would come to know Him and, even after, I would not always do it well. He was watching, guiding, and shaping me through all my circumstances, the good, bad, and ugly. All the hard places would eventually be seen as moments of grace and mercy.

I was a small, scrawny, often sickly—but always mouthy—child with mousy brown hair. Nothing about me stood out in a positive way. Who would have ever guessed I was being shaped into a mighty woman of God? Now, if that sounds a bit haughty to you, just read my stories. You will see what a phenomenal God we serve, how He alone could take that insignificant child from the wrong side of the tracks and, eventually, take her to the other side of the world to preach the gospel of Jesus Christ!

I grew up very poor. We didn't even have a car. Walking to town to look at clothing and toys we couldn't afford was exciting. You will see why these stories are a big deal. I hope you can recognize the miracle of a life being shaped out of a nothing beginning and transformed into a walking testimony of His grace. I hope you will begin to look at your own life and see the miracle that you are. I want my grandchildren and great grandchildren and future generations to know they have a legacy. This legacy will live forever, and nothing can take that from them.

> That I may know Him and the power of His resurrection and the fellowship of His sufferings, being conformed to His death; and in order that I may attain to the resurrection from the dead Not that I have already become perfect, but I press on so that I may lay hold of that for which also I was laid hold of by Christ Jesus. Brethren, I do not regard myself as having laid hold of it yet; but one thing I do: forgetting what lies behind and reaching forward to what lies ahead, I press on toward the goal for the prize of the upward call of God in Christ Jesus (Philippians 3:10-14).

〜

The Early Years

Growing up in a difficult home environment, memories are often repressed because it becomes too difficult to function with those unhappy thoughts of fear and emotional pain. For many years, I blocked a lot of memories. Through time and learning to trust the Lord for emotional healing, I have regained some memories, both good and bad. I will share them as needed to show you how these instances were used by God to shape my life.

My family moved from Lancaster to Rock Hill, South Carolina, somewhere around the time I started first grade. We struggled financially. My father always worked. We did not live on government assistance. I am sure my dad did not make a lot of money because he worked in a plant as a color-mixer where fabric was printed. There were six of us children and often other family members, such as my mom's parents and her sister, lived with us for short periods of time.

We lived in the poor section of town where many people, as did my parents, turned to alcohol for comfort. My family seemed to be different in that my dad worked a regular job and we ate regular meals. When they were sober, which was most of the time—the drinking binges seemed more than they actually were—we children were clean and well-mannered. When the drinking binges occurred, mostly on holidays—4th of July, Easter, Thanksgiving, and Christmas—they lasted about a week, which seemed like eternity. Some weekends were also spent in the drunken episodes. Our home-life became extremely different during these binges. I am telling you this to set up a caveat so you will understand why some of these stories have significance.

When parents spend their weekends drinking in the "hood," "slum," or "ghetto," it is not like you see in the movies. Hollywood glamorizes neighborhood drinking like it's one big party, but it isn't that way at all. Our mother did not sit out by the pool sipping on cocktails in pretty glasses, and neither did our father come in from work dressed in a suit to make himself a shot of bourbon to unwind. Liquor was consumed straight from the bottle while sitting on the porch until sitting up became difficult; then they went to the bed where they drank until they became unable to stand. Houses were not cleaned, dishes piled up, food was not cooked, and children learned to fend for themselves. Sleep was interrupted due to cursing, screaming, and often physical fighting.

I have no need to go further into the gory details. You get the picture. We were always aware of Jesus and God. Mom did not take us to church, but she always helped us get ready on Sunday morning. The truth is, Jesus showed up at our house in the form of a woman named Leila Wright. Thus, my story begins.

STORY 3

~

Mrs. Wright

"Behold, I am going to send My messenger (Malachi 3)."

In my childhood neighborhood, strangers were looked at with suspicion. One could not just come in. You had to have an invitation. I guess that is what we were for Mrs. Wright—her outlet into our neighborhood. She started coming by the house to pick up me and my sisters for church. Often, she would take a couple of us home with her. Eventually, I seemed to be the one to spend more time at her home. She had a young girl who stayed with her named "Scoopy," which was not her real name; her real name was Leila. Leila was also Mrs. Wright's first name. Scoopy called her "Aunt Leila." Scoopy's parents and Mrs. Wright had been long-time friends.

Eventually, Mrs. Wright won the right to come and go in our neighborhood. Actually, she would come around on Sunday morning with a box of assorted clean clothes, a gallon of milk, and a box of cereal. Most of the kid's parents were still passed out from Saturday night. Mrs. Wright would go into their houses, wash the kid's faces and hands, put clean clothes on them, and feed them cereal. Her car would be packed. Seatbelts and child car-seats were

5

unheard of in those days. We would descend upon Mrs. Wright's church looking like a bunch of misfit toys. As time went on, all the little raggedy children got to be too much. They were not all bad, but we had our share of troubled children. Many of these children grew up to spend a lot of time in prison. Mrs. Wright solved the issue by setting up an old easel board in our back yard. She would tell us Bible stories and a story called "Barney's Barrel." It was a story of a homeless boy who lived in a barrel.

Several years ago, my friend and ministry partner, Scott, was hanging at my house and talking about things in our childhood. I am the same age as Scott's mother. I started reminiscing about Mrs. Wright and telling him how she was such an influence in my life concerning my heart to teach the Gospel. I started to tell him about the story of "Barney's Barrel" and he told me his mother use to teach that story. I don't know why that was so exciting to me! Silly, I know, but it was like my childhood suddenly seemed normal. I had never run across anyone who knew that story. A few weeks later, after he returned home to South Georgia, I received a package in the mail. It was a complete copy of "Barney's Barrel!" I count that gift among my personal treasures.

Growing up in the environment of an alcoholic home and impoverished neighborhood, getting to adulthood seemed a dim possibility. I honestly never thought I would make it. I had little hope of a future. I know most children dreamed of what they would be when they grew up. I never had a dream, except when I would watch Mrs. Wright stand in her black, shiny high heels and share the Gospel of Jesus Christ. I would find myself thinking, "*Someday, that is what I am going to do. I am going to teach the Bible and have some shiny, black high heels.*" God is good. I do both! Thank you, Leila Wright, for giving me hope.

~

Knowing

"Call to Me and I will answer you, and I will tell you great and mighty things, which you do not know (Jeremiah 33:3)."

I was thirteen years old standing in the yard at lunchtime at the junior high school with my best friend, Libby. It is so funny how kids just seem to know where they belong and where they do not. We just seem to understand social circles without anyone actually explaining it. We were standing around in our little accepted groups when I looked up and saw a group of kids. Of course, I knew some of them from shared classes, this particular group was not like the rich kids, but I guess you would say they were more middle-class. They were not poor like me, but they were a step above. A lot of them were more athletic, football guys. They usually liked cheerleader-types, of which I was not. I guess I was staring because Libby said something and I replied, "See that boy with the blond hair?"

She answered *"Yes, his name is Pete."*

"Yeah, I know, I am going to marry him."

Libby began to laugh and told me I was crazy. She went on to ask, "*Why would you think such a thing? Those people don't associate with people like us!*"

I replied, "*I know, but I am going to marry him. I don't know why I say that, I just know.*"

I now understand that I was hearing something outside of my normal thinking. I did not have a personal relationship with Jesus. What little I knew about spiritual matters certainly did not include things such as spiritual gifts. I still believe, to this day, I was hearing a Word of Knowledge from the Holy Spirit. Many people teach that sinners can't hear from God, but I don't know who we are to think we can put God in such a box!

Later that year, another friend, Sarah, invited me to go to church with her. Upon arrival, we entered the recreational room. There was Pete playing ping-pong with some other guys. As I walked by, he popped me on my behind with the paddle. That was the beginning of our 'dating' relationship. I was thirteen years old.

At age nineteen, we were married. We had two children together. On our thirty-fourth year, we separated. It would be six more years before we actually divorced. The details will unfold in another story later in the book. For many years, I interpreted what I "heard" concerning marrying Pete as God telling me to marry him. But, like a lot of people, I interpreted that by the paradigm I understood. God did not tell me to marry him, just that I was going to marry him. God has a perfect will, a permissive will, and a progressive will. God will work in our choices as long as we submit everything to Him and use it for His purposes. I guess we did not do that as well as we thought.

STORY 5

Beginning

"In peace I will both lie down and sleep, for you alone, O LORD, make me to dwell in safety (Psalm 4:8)."

Young people—nothing can quite compare to youthful stupidity! However, I guess that, without it, truly little would ever get started. Pete and I married July 1973. We went to the beach for our honeymoon. We didn't even have a place to live. Our first day back, we went looking. We found a trailer in a large mobile-home park. We looked at one that was available—it was clean and decently furnished—and we agreed to take it. While Pete was counting the first month's rent and deposit, I had a crazy thought. I didn't have a clue where this came from and, again, it would be years before I would realize I was hearing from God. I still was not yet a follower of Christ. That would come a few years later. Just as Pete finished handing the money to the man in charge, I blurted out, *"I'm not going to live here!"*

Startled, Pete replied, "*I've already given him the money.*"

I said, "*Get it back.*"

"*Where are we going to live?*" he asked.

Pete knew someone from work that had a small trailer and allowed us to rent it. Actually, it was more like a camper. I could sit on the couch and fry bacon on the stove. We did not live there long because we moved to a larger mobile home. This was still in the first year of our marriage and I did not have my driver's license. While Pete was at work, I usually stayed home. This particular day was the day a tornado came through. It didn't seem to be any more than a lot of wind, rain, and lots of lightning. I sat on my sofa and watched as lightning flashed through one window and, seemingly, go out the other window. I got through it without any damage. Later, we heard the storm had caused some damage at the mobile home park where we were originally going to live. We went to check it out later that afternoon. We were shocked to see that the only trailer damaged was the very one we would have moved into. The storm had picked it up and turned it upside down and smashed it flat—it looked like a flattened cereal box! I would have been destroyed with it. God is good.

STORY 6

∽

Jesus is Calling

"… apart from Me, you can do nothing (John 15:5b)."

At this time in my life, I had settled into marriage and I finally got my driver's license. For the first time in my life, I had a credit card, checking account, and car to drive. Life was good. However, something was missing. Maybe I was just bored. Pete worked seven days a week and, in the evenings, he was at his dad's garage helping him. It didn't seem to be a problem for me—he was working and I knew he wasn't doing anything wrong. Little did I know that this was building a foundation of disaster for our marriage. I tried to keep myself busy by going here and there. All that busyness could not hide the fact that something was missing. There was emptiness inside me and I continually dismissed it. I would give myself pep-talks and scold my thoughts. After all, I had everything I needed. I had a good husband and, by this time, we had purchased a home. I decided that the 'something missing' had to be a child. We had been married over a year, so we tried to start a family. It did not happen quickly. It took us two years to get pregnant. But, in January 1977, we had our first child, a baby girl. She was so cute and energetic. Honestly, she did not sleep all night until she was nine years old!

When our daughter, Amy, was about nine months old, my best friend, Terry, suggested we start taking her to church. Terry's husband worked with Pete, so he was gone a lot also. They did not have any children yet. This was in a time when people still dressed up for church and I didn't have any dresses. Terry could sew, so we bought some fabric and patterns and she cranked up her sewing machine. Terry had one of the ugliest dogs imaginable named Baby. Terry kept an old fan sitting on the floor in her hall to keep air circulating. The fan was missing the front grill, so the blades were totally exposed. Amy would start crawling down the hall toward the fan and I would jump up to get her. Before I could reach her, Terry would call out to Baby to get Amy. Baby would immediately grab Amy's diaper with her teeth and pull her to safety. Baby was an ugly dog, but a great babysitter! Once, when we were sewing, I could not find Amy anywhere—I was ready to panic. Terry told me to follow Baby. Baby's bed was underneath Terry's bed. We looked and, sure enough, Baby had taken Amy to bed with her. They were both sound asleep! I guess Amy wore Baby out.

Now that the dresses were finished, we could go to church. No big deal. Go sing some hymns, listen to some preaching, bow our heads while the preacher prayed, throw a few bucks into the offering plate, and go home. I was being a good mommy and our duty to Jesus was done. Little did I know that I was being set up. God was pursuing me, and I thought I was just being a good mother in trying to raise my baby in church.

In church, we did all the church things you would expect to do on a Sunday morning. Yet, something else was happening to me. I felt an emotional pull from somewhere deep inside I could not understand. Being stubborn, I was not about to give into my emotions. Due to the fact I had been raised in a seriously negative emotional environment, I learned to shut my emotions down. It was a running joke that Sandy did not have a heart. I could be very cold and aloof. I was not about to let this church-thing turn me into a weeping mess. During the alter call, we would stand while they played songs like, "*Softly and Tenderly, Jesus is Calling*" and the desire to go to that altar would be so strong in me, I would literally hang onto the pew in front of me until my knuckles were white!

The whole time this was going on, I would remember a girl I grew up with who had gotten saved. She was a nut, or at least many thought she was. I did not doubt her sincerity; I believed she actually had a change in her life. However, she was a fanatic and constantly did crazy things and preached at everyone. The trouble was that she always looked so miserable. I told the Lord, "*If I have to look like that I'm not giving in!*" God had a plan. You will find out what that looked like in the next story.

STORY 7

I Will Fix It!

"Then I heard the voice of the Lord saying, 'Whom shall I send, and who will go for Us?' Then I said, "Here am I. Send me (Isaiah 6:8)!"

I was the family fixer. That was quite a statement. At least I thought I was the "fixer." Every family has one. I don't think it was because I was the smart one, but the bossy one. My sisters would probably agree. In a family that is dysfunctional, there is always at least one in the family who seems to be more confident or cocky than the rest. That would be me! The truth is, I was not confident at all. I really was very insecure and showing a false bravado helped me get through life. At any rate, someone had to keep the herd on the straight path, right?

As I said in the previous story, I was now a churchgoer. Boy, was I about to find out the difference between church attendance and being totally consumed in the presence of Almighty God. At the time, I had no idea of what that would mean or that it was actually possible to be in His Presence. I knew about salvation, Heaven, and hell. I knew that somewhere in the far-off future, Jesus would return, and I had plenty of time to live my life and get "saved" when I was too old to enjoy life anymore. How prideful and stupid could one person be?

I have an aunt, my mother's sister, who is more like a sister because she was thirteen years younger than my mom. Her name is Barbara and I also have a sister named Barbara. In the south, we like to name a lot of our relatives the same name—it keeps us on our toes. Anyway, both Barbara's had been going to church, well, not exactly church as we were accustomed. These events were called "crusades." The leader of these crusades was a man called Prophet James Shinn. It was okay by me that they had gotten saved and now followed Jesus. The problem was, they were not in church as we define church. Oh no, they were coming home with tales of this man touching their foreheads and suddenly they would fall to the floor where they would seemingly feel as if they were dazed and unable to get up. Then, when they got to their feet, this prophet—whatever that was—would prophesy to them. He would tell them how God was going to do great and mighty things with them.

Of course, my great gift of fixing things kicked in and I decided I needed to go see these ridiculous occurrences and expose this Prophet Shinn for the charlatan I was sure he was. I was not sure how I was going to do that, but I would cross that bridge when I got there. People motivated by pride and control do not think they need a plan! Yes, I can see clearly now that I was not moving in God's best interest, just my need to fix something I saw as broken.

I found out that Mr. Shinn was holding yet another crusade the following weekend. It was being held at a local Union hall. Of course, I went in late—no, it was not my strategy, I was always late. Funny how a fixer wants to fix things except they never really fix their own brokenness. I think this is where the old folks would say, "*Clean up your own back yard!*" This was the scene, I quietly walked into a full room, probably at least two-hundred people or more, give or take a few. I found a seat at the back and sat down and watched the show. I quickly spotted my aunt and sister seated at the front. Prophet Shinn was preaching and occasionally praying for some. There it was, the famous touch on the forehead and, boom, they hit the floor! Of course, they had a couple of men to stand behind and catch them so they didn't hurt themselves when they would fall out under the "power." After a few minutes of this, of course, I am rolling my eyes and, under my breath, I am saying, "*O, brother!*" I was sure I was the only one in the building who could see how ridiculous this was. Then, something quite unexpected happened.

Prophet Shinn said, "*There is someone here named Sandy, God wants you up front.*" I was not impressed—the room got quiet. However, my reasoning kicked into high gear. In that crowd, I could not be the only "*Sandy*" as it is a common name. I did not move. He then stepped out into the middle aisle and pointed straight back at me and asked, "*Little black-haired girl, isn't your name Sandy?*" My mind was whirling. Of course, I was still not impressed. I figured out very quickly that, more than likely, my sister or aunt saw me and probably passed a note to the "*Prophet.*" I stayed seated. I guess I thought he would move on. He didn't.

He pointed straight at me and asked, "*Is your name Sandy?*" And, not waiting for an answer, he continued, "*God wants you to come up here.*" This was my big chance to show this man a fraud. With my eyes rolling, and of course I put on my "not impressed" face with a touch of disgust, I walked up and stood with my arms crossed. In my mind, I was thinking, "*Hit me, big boy!*" I fully expected him to touch my forehead and then expect me to go down. I was not about to let that happen. My feet were planted solidly and nothing was going to move me! He messed up my plan of action. He did a crazy thing. He simply looked at me intensely for a moment and walked to the far corner of the pulpit area. With his face in the corner, he waved his hand slightly and, almost in a whisper, he said, "*In the name of Jesus.*"

Something, a power I cannot describe, lifted my feet several inches off the floor and threw me back with a force that should have knocked the breath out of me! There was no way the men who had been catching people could catch me as it happened so fast. There I was, lying on the floor, wondering how I got there. You would think that would cause me to be a believer, but oh no, not me. I was thinking, "*If I can get on my feet, I will figure this thing out!*" The problem was, my legs felt like wet noodles. Prophet Shinn instructed the men to help me up. They walked me over to the place where he was standing. I had regained my composure determined not to let him rattle me again. I still was not impressed. The next thing he said changed my life. I can still remember the entire prophecy. He said, "*I see you as a little girl. You are sitting on a single bed with a half wagon wheel for the headboard. It has on it a faded yellow bedspread with little cotton balls and a lot of them are missing. You are sitting cross-legged, Indian style. You have on a green plaid dress with a white collar. You are about 7 or 8 years old.*"

He went on to tell me a prayer I prayed that day. It came flooding back to me and I remembered exactly what I prayed. I will not share the prayer here except the general focus of it. I was asking God why my life was as it was and for God to get me out of the life I was living. As children, we had bunk beds. At the headboard was half a wagon wheel. I had an old, faded, worn out, yellow chenille bed spread with half or more of the little balls missing. My dress was one of the few I owned. I had my school picture made in that dress and it was exactly as he described.

After he finished talking, he did the famous forehead touch. Again, I hit the floor. The difference from the first time was not in his manner or administration. The difference was me. Suddenly, my awareness was not this man or my need to be in control. I became aware that the God of this universe was aware of me. Small, insignificant, broken me. I was undone.

After I stood to my feet, the man of God began to quote a Scripture concerning the plan God had for my life. I did not know the Scripture, but I became familiar with it in the days to come. *"Before I formed you in the womb, I knew you, and before you were born, I consecrated you; I have appointed you a prophet to the nations,"* reads Jeremiah 1:5. I never recited the "sinner's prayer," nor did I have any idea what a prophet was. Nations? I grew up without a car. I went to Texas at sixteen, but nations? It was more than I could comprehend. Yet, I came off that floor a brand-new creation in Christ Jesus. That I knew without question!

I was in my mid-twenties at that time. I found out later that my Aunt Barbara and my sister Barbara were storming the gates of Heaven for our family. They decided they were wearing themselves out and started praying smarter, not harder. They had the crazy idea to start praying for the one who was more stubborn than the rest. Me. All I can say is, *"Thank you!"* At this writing, I am sixty-six years old. I am still learning how to be a Christ-follower. Nations? Since turning sixty, I have been to India and Kenya twice, and Honduras. I believe my future years will be greater than my former. We serve a mighty God! He never gets old and you are never too old for Him to move through!

STORY 8

∽

Light in the Darkness

"But indeed, as I live, all the Earth will be filled with the glory of the LORD (Numbers 14:21)."

I had only been saved a short time, less than two years. I knew just enough about this new journey to understand how little I actually knew. I was on the fast-track of learning about this lifestyle, especially concerning the Holy Spirit. My son was not yet two years old and still sleeping in his crib. My husband often worked the third shift and slept during the day. We kept our windows blocked from light so that sleeping in the daytime would seem more normal. This made our bedroom very dark at night. I was sound asleep and was woken suddenly. I lay very quietly, I thought, perhaps, the baby was stirring. I did not want to get up, so I stayed still hoping that, if it was the baby, he would go back to sleep. It only took a few seconds to realize that it was not the baby that caused me to awaken so suddenly. There was a feeling in the room. A presence. I instinctively knew it was not evil. It was intense, weighty, and consuming. I somehow knew it was the presence of God. I don't know how I knew, I just did. It was fearsome. I wanted to hide. Not because I was afraid of something dreadful happening to me, but because neither my physical body nor my natural mind were prepared to be in that holy presence.

With as much ease and the least amount of movement possible, I slid off the bed and crawled into the closet. This was not a walk-in closet. It was an older home, so the closets were small. I pushed my body as far back into the corner as possible. There was a blanket on the closet floor and I used it to cover my head. I know that sounds a bit extreme. It was already pitch black and, if it was God, well, that would be a no-brainer! I sat with my knees pulled up to my chest. I guess I was trying to be invisible. Suddenly, there shone the brightest light out of nowhere! The light was not from this world. It was brilliant, yet clear and soft all at the same time.

What happened next was beyond anything I could even think possible. I still had the blanket over my head, my eyes tightly shut. I was afraid to move. I saw two huge hands holding a bucket. The bucket seemed to be like a galvanized metal bucket, but it was almost translucent. The hands tilted the bucket until a substance began to pour out. The liquid was thick like honey, clear and golden at the same time. It shimmered unlike anything I had ever seen. It poured and poured until I began to wonder if it would ever stop. As suddenly as it began, it stopped. At that time, I heard a voice, loud and clear, yet it was only a whisper. I knew it was God. He said, "*There will come a time when I will pour My glory upon this Earth and you will see it.*" Just like that, it was over. I still could not move. I stayed in that position inside the closet the entire night. I have caught glimpses of His glory, but I know there is a greater measure of His power and glory the world is yet to experience. I believe it is very near, I can almost feel it!

STORY 9

~

Quit Being a Baby

"But when the heart is sad, the spirit is broken (Proverbs 15:13b)."

In the early years of my spiritual growth, a lot of it was accomplished sitting at my Aunt Barbara's kitchen table. She, my brother, and I would drink coffee and share what we were learning about God, the Bible, and the Holy Spirit. We were all fairly new in our faith-journey. My aunt is thirteen years older and my brother eight years older than me. My brother went to be with the Lord in 1981 at thirty-four years old. I miss him very much. This particular meeting probably happened somewhere between 1979 and 1980. I guess I had blocked a lot of my memories of my childhood. It would take the work of the Holy Spirit to heal me and that is what started on this particular day.

We were talking about dreams and my aunt had been studying how to interpret them. As each of them shared a dream, I remembered one I had many times through the years. In the dream, I knew that I was there, but I never saw myself. I was moving toward a sound. It was a baby crying. I knew the baby was distressed. It cried relentlessly. I moved closer to the sound. I thought if I could just get to that baby, it would be okay. As I approached, I saw a wall. It was made of rough, unpainted wooden planks. It had a strange, small window that was attached at the top with leather hinges and pushed out from the inside at the bottom. There was a string hanging down on the other side at the bottom. This was so you could pull it and close the window. The crying grew louder as I got closer. Just as I got to the wall, I woke up.

It was the same every time. It always left me feeling alone and scared. When I finished telling my dream, I looked at the other two who were staring at me in total disbelief. I shrugged my shoulders and asked, "*Why are you looking at me that way?*" They looked at each other as if they were not sure what to say. Finally, my brother said, "*You cannot possibly remember that.*" He went on to explain what I had described as a dream as being an actual event. Remember, he was eight years older than I.

He began his story:

"*When I was around eight years old,*" he said, "*you were less than a year, maybe around eight months old. Mom left me to take care of you while she went off. I do not remember where Patsy and Barbara—my two older sisters—were and Dad was working out of town. Mom was gone for a couple days. I can remember being there at least one night by ourselves. We lived in the country where neighbors were far and few. I remember you started crying. I suppose you were hungry. I could not find anything I thought you could eat except some apple butter. I fed it to you. That did not end well because you pooped all over the place. It ran out your diaper. You had it all over you. You just kept crying. I was scared and didn't know what to do. I started trying to clean you, but how much could an eight-year-old do? I was crying by this time. Just when I felt hopeless, a woman who lived a good way off came walking by and heard our cries. She came in and*

*cleaned you and took us home with her until mom got back.
The really strange thing is that we lived in a house just like
you described from your dream. Even the window. You could
not possibly remember that. You were just a baby."*

When he finished talking, I looked at my aunt and she was
shaking her head in agreement. She said, "*The baby in your dream
is you. I don't know exactly why, but I believe God has allowed you
that dream for a purpose.*" I guess I was a little stunned. How could
my mom do that? All of a sudden, I felt something leave me. I had
no understanding of it at the time, but I knew I would never have
the dream again, and I never did. My aunt and brother prayed
for me. God healed something in me that day. He has continually
healed me in so many ways. I realized later that God delivered me
from the spirit of abandonment. He will heal you too. You must
release any unforgiveness and trust God to help you.

Father God, thank you for healing my emotions. I ask You, in
the powerful name of Jesus, to touch someone through this testimony of Your grace. Show them that they do not have to carry that
pain and unforgiveness. You want to heal their heart if they will
just receive Your goodness. Amen

Trust and Obey

*"Each one must do just as he has purposed in his heart,
not grudgingly or under compulsion, for God loves a
cheerful giver (2 Corinthians 9:7)."*

I have heard it said, *"God loves a cheerful giver, but He will take it from a grouch."* However, that is not true. First, God does not need our money. Giving is for our benefit and it serves to provide for the purposes of God. I have found that giving our money is one of the hardest things we have to learn. It is funny to me how we will trust God enough for salvation, but when it comes to the offering plate, that is a whole different story! It is often said, *"When God has your pocketbook, He truly has your heart."*

This is a story of God teaching me to give without having to understand why. If you are reading this book in sequence, you will recall the story where I talked about Prophet James Shinn. I got saved under his ministry. He and his wife, Jackie, became my spiritual parents. Their son, Tim, played the drums at the crusade. Jackie played the organ. When I first met them, Tim was between the ages of ten to twelve years old.

One night at the crusade meeting, the Lord spoke to my heart to give Tim fifty dollars. I was horrified—I was not about to give a ten-year-old kid fifty bucks! You must remember, this was around 1979 and fifty dollars was a lot of money, especially for a ten-year-old. No sir, I was not about to be that irresponsible. However, I knew I had heard from God and I really wanted to be obedient. I was going to give the money, just not to that kid. I took the money out of my purse and took it to his mother, Jackie. She said, "*Thank you, I'll get my hair done.*" I felt rather good. Then the Lord spoke again, "*I told you to give it to Tim.*"

I still could not bring myself to give that much money to a ten-year-old kid. So, I did the next best thing. I took out fifty more dollars and gave it to James. He thanked me and put the money in his pocket. I hoped that would be sufficient to God because I was running out of money. The only reason I had that much was because we had gotten a tax refund and that was my share to do with as I wanted. I had fifty dollars left. I had plans for that money. Shopping! God had a different idea. Not really different, He was still stuck on Tim getting that money. I could not get away from His instruction. Finally, I relented. Boy, it was hard to take that money to that kid.

I found Tim and handed him the money and explained the Lord wanted him to have it. Tim began to cry. When he stopped crying, he told me how he had laid away a drum set and only needed, you guessed it, fifty more dollars to finish paying for it. He had just prayed that morning for God to send him the money. That taught me a valuable lesson. Your obedience may be God answering another person's prayer. I left there happy—broke—but happy.

Sandy Giveth and Sandy Taketh Away

"So, take care how you listen…(Luke 8:18a)."

This is going to be a noticeably short story.

My Aunt Barbara and I were attending a meeting one night. We had never heard this particular preacher. I was still a young believer but had been really studying the Scriptures. I knew just enough to be dangerous! This preacher did something a bit odd, but, oh well, I tend to be a bit odd myself. He took an offering before he preached and I gladly gave my ten dollars. He did some goofy things during the sermon. He cut his tie into small pieces and threw them into the congregation. This seemed to excite most of the crowd. It was supposed to show how anointed he was. When that seemed to be a crowd-pleaser, he threw a small cup of water into the air showering folks on the first row. I was sitting far enough back that I missed the baptism.

I understood that I was fairly new at this game, but I knew enough to see this was a show. Now let me give you a disclaimer here. I have had God tell me some strange things and I have witnessed God moving in ways through others that, while I may not understand, there is a sense that God is in it. It is called "discernment" and you grow in that through knowing the Scriptures. I discerned this was bringing glory to himself and not to God. The preacher thought he should have gotten a larger offering, so he passed the plate again. When it got to me, I quickly took back my ten dollars and stuck it into my pocket. My poor aunt was horrified!

She asked, "*Did you just take money out of that offering plate?*"

I replied, "*Yes, I am not going to support just anything.*"

The moral of this story is, listen to God. It does not mean you must have a prophetic word, two angelic visits, and the sound of a trumpet to give an offering. Just be sensitive to how you steward all that God has given you.

STORY 12

~

God Kisses

"May he kiss me with the kisses of his mouth! For your love is better than wine (Song of Songs 1:2)."

Just every once in a while, you remember something that happened to you that seemed like a dream, but you find out it actually happened. Such was the case as I was sleeping one night. This was still in my early years of getting to know the Lord. I woke out of a sound sleep. I lay quietly for a moment thinking one of the children may have been awake. All was quiet. Suddenly, I felt a cool breeze brush against my forehead. It was ever so slight and yet I could feel its lasting effect even after it passed. There was no fan running nor was there a window open and I only felt it on my forehead. Strange. I went back to sleep.

A couple days later, my aunt and I were attending a service. I did not know the man leading it, but, during ministry time, he called me to come up front. He looked at me and said, *"A couple nights ago, you woke from a sound sleep. You felt something brush your forehead. That was God. He leaned down and kissed your forehead."* He had no way of knowing as I had dismissed it and did not feel the need to tell anyone. I would later learn this man was moving in a gift of a word of knowledge through the Holy Spirit. It was sweet to think of my Lord kissing me. Yet, He is my Father and fathers kiss their children.

Dear Lord, today someone needs to feel Your touch. Show them how much they are loved by You. Amen

STORY 13

❧

Oh God, Please!

"Therefore, I say to you, all things for which you pray and ask, believer that you have received them, and they will be granted you (Mark 11:24)."

One of the hard lessons you learn as a young believer is how to pray by faith instead of fear. I am sure you have been there. You know, you feel desperate and you somehow have to figure a way to get God to see your desperation. You take a lot of your prayer-time explaining to God why He needs to put the managing of the universe on hold to take care of your crisis! This was the case with me in the early stages of my faith-journey. Just as I was really getting to know how to walk in this new lifestyle, a lot of changes were happening in my life. My daughter was around eighteen months old and I was expecting another child in three months. It was my birthday and my husband came home from work. The last thing I wanted as a present was the news he brought with him. As soon as he entered the door, I knew something was terribly wrong. He said, *"Happy Birthday. I got fired."* I stood there with a small child hanging onto my shirt-tail and my abdomen extended with another one and said the only thing I knew to say.

"Whatever you need to say, go back, say it, and get unfired!"

Of course, that was not what he needed to hear at that time. After calming and getting over the initial shock, we started to look at options. His dad also worked in the same plant as Pete. They were both mechanics. When Pete's dad found out they had unjustly fired Pete, he packed his tools and left. He just quit and walked out with his son. Pete's dad had a small garage, which he ran after work, and it became an opportunity for Pete to help him to run it full time. Of course, this afforded Pete a way to earn income; at least it kept us afloat for a while. That was the foundation for the real story. I am going insert a short story before I get to the real point, so you can see how God moves in the midst of our crazy places of life.

As I said, I was pregnant and very hormonal! Pete was working in the garage with his dad. One day, I stopped by the garage to tell Pete something. His dad came out to the car to tell me Pete had gone to pick up parts. Before I could get out of there, I burst into tears and left. Pete's dad was a quiet man; he only said what he meant and meant what he said. We probably could use more people like him today. He was a man of integrity.

> He could be funny without trying. Theron—Pete's dad— walked up to his house and said to my mother-in-law, *"That girl was down there crying."*
>
> *"What girl?"* Essie—Pete's mom—asked.
>
> *"That girl, the one that is married to Pete."*
>
> *"You mean Sandy? Her name is Sandy, Theron!"* Essie said.

Ignoring Essie's correction, he went on to ask, "*What is she crying about?*"

"*Well, let me see. She has a small child, she is pregnant, they are broke, and her husband does not have a real job. Gosh, I don't know why she would be crying!*"

Theron replied again ignoring her sarcasm. "*If she needed money, she should have said so.*"

Essie told me this later. After a while, I drove back to the garage and Theron came out to the car to tell me Pete was not back yet. Then, extending his hand, I could tell he had something clinched in his fist.

He said, "*Here, take this. I'll have you some more tomorrow.*" He handed me a handful of wadded up bills. He turned and walked away. That is who he was.

Now, back to the main story.

The first job Pete found was simply God intervening in his life because the man with whom he was employed was a man who loved Christ and was instrumental in Pete receiving Christ. This is where I wish I had kept a journal because, no matter how hard you try to keep timelines straight, life gets messy with so many twists and turns, so I can't remember exactly how many years passed between each situation. But that is not the important part. Pete worked that job for a short time and went to work in a new business that lasted a few years. We made friends with a couple, Rodney and Sherry, which would last many years. That place of business shut down and, although I was working, we needed that second income. Again, Pete supplemented our income by working in the garage. Our friend, Rodney, went to work at a tire manufacturing plant. Pete put in an application, but they never called him.

One day near Christmas, we were seriously in need of money. I started praying. I remember that prayer and it went something like this, "*Okay God, this is what we need. Pete needs for the folks at General Tire, where they already have his application, to call today. We also need one thousand dollars to pay some bills and buy our children something for Christmas. In Jesus mighty name. Amen.*" As God is my witness, it was not five minutes later when the phone rang. The lady on the other end asked to speak to Pete. I told her he was not home. I just had a feeling it was General Tire. Before that thought was complete, she informed me she was with Human Resources at General Tire! I told her the phone number at the garage and assured her it was okay for her to contact him. I could hardly wait for Pete to call me. It was not long, and he was pulling into the driveway. He came through the door and immediately said, "*You are not going to believe what I am going to tell you.*"

Before he said any more, he handed me a check for one thousand dollars! He went on to say, "*The check is from Ed. I had done some work on his daughter's car about a year ago and she never paid me. I just let it go. Ed has been too good a friend to let it come between us. But, this morning, Ed overheard his two daughters arguing. The daughter, whose car I had fixed, had been partying away her money and the other daughter scolded her about blowing her money and that she should pay me what she owed. Ed came to the garage and asked me if she owed me money. I told him not to worry about it. He kept on until I had to give him a figure. I told him it was near a thousand dollars and he wrote me a check. Oh yeah, they called from General Tire and I have an interview in the morning.*"

Seriously! Prayer answered just like that! It was not because I was that great a Christian. God was teaching me how to trust Him. God is good!

Father, today someone is reading this and wondering if You could possibly be that caring about their needs. I know You *are* that caring. Show them. Not to prove Yourself, but that they might know You. Thank you for all the miracles you bring. Amen

❧

Run, Devil, Run

"Are they not all ministering spirits, sent out to render service for the sake of those who will inherit salvation (Hebrews 1:14)?"

Some of my stories, no doubt, will cause some of you to wonder if I am either a liar or just plain crazy. I have interacted with many different denominations and found that some of them, while teaching Jesus Christ, tend to stay away from the parts of the Bible that talk about demons, angels, and the manifesting power of the Holy Spirit. I have some understanding of why they do this, but these stories are not to prove someone wrong. They are simply stories of my faith-journey. All one has to do is read the Bible and see things that cannot be explained outside the supernatural. It happened in the early church and it is still happening today. I pray you do not get caught trying to prove it wrong. Just take it as a testimony of God's goodness. After all, He is supernatural!

This event happened in the early part of my faith-journey. I was at my Aunt Barbara's house. You will read about her a lot in my stories because she was, and still is, an important part of my life and walk with the Lord. It was late, probably around midnight, and I had to go home. She walked me out to say goodbye. I paused for a minute before getting into my car. I was standing by an evergreen tree about seven feet tall. Beside her house was a narrow dirt road with woods on the opposite side from her house. I saw a tall, dark figure coming toward me at terrific speed. It was every bit as tall as the evergreen, if not taller. It took him hardly any time at all before he was steps away from me. All this happened so quickly. At the moment the figure was steps away from me, I felt a presence walk up beside me. I did not see it, but it was as real and as present as a person. I even felt it brush my arm! At the very moment I felt this presence, the dark figure turned on a dime and darted back across the dirt road into the woods. The presence that stood beside my left side did not leave. I didn't tell anyone about this until later. The next Wednesday night at church, a man got up and pointed at me and said, "*Sister Sandy, a few nights ago, an angel of the Lord walked up and stood on your left side. He is still with you and will be for two weeks.*"

I could literally feel his presence! I was not aware of the time he left. I just realized, at some point, that I did not feel him at my side anymore. I know the angel was sent to protect me from that evil force that night. Thank you, Lord, that you appoint Your angelic hosts to help us.

STORY 15

~

Help, I Peed My Pants!

"For our struggle is not against flesh and blood, but against the rulers, against the powers, against the world forces of this darkness, against the spiritual forces of wickedness in the heavenly places (Ephesians 6:12)."

If you had trouble digesting the previous story, you might want to skip this one. On the other hand, what do you have to lose? Come and take a walk on the wild side of the spirit realm. I had only been saved for about six months and my spiritual father decided I was ready to get my feet wet in the ministry of deliverance. I had no idea what deliverance was. I trusted James, yes, the same James that is the prophet who called me out. As I stated previously, he and his wife, Jackie, became my spiritual parents. James instructed me to fast and he would come pick me up in three days.

For the next three days, I let neither water nor food in my mouth. I had never fasted, but I wanted to do it right. When I got into the car with the others, James asked me if I fasted. I told him about not having food or water for three days. He felt so bad; he just assumed I understood not to do that on the first go round. He made me eat something light. I didn't have a clue what I was supposed to do. My Aunt Barbara and Jackie went with us. All I knew was this man had told James that his wife was calling on demons. It all sounded pretty spooky to me, but I trusted the people I was with. I thought to myself that I would only have to pray. James was the man of power for the hour. Up to this time, with the exception of the dark spirit in the previous story, I had never seen a demon.

We arrived at their house and I noticed, right off, they had roaches. I did not see any demons, but I did see the roaches. This started the "*pocketbook ministry*" for Jackie. She did not do much with deliverance ministry at that time, so she held our purses so the roaches could not crawl into them. We got into a circle and boy was I praying! Then James looked at me and said, "*Go ahead, Sandy.*" I must have looked like a deer in headlights. I thought, "*Go ahead with what?*" James ignored my look of horror and said again, "*Go ahead, obey the Holy Spirit. He is talking to you.*"

About that time, I saw the strangest and most horrifying scene unfold. Above our heads, I saw creatures forming in thin air. They were something like mutated, deformed creatures and they were flying toward me. I literally peed my pants. I was terrified. I ran to the bathroom and was trying to pull myself together and dry my jeans when my aunt came in. She assured me I was not crazy. She had seen them also. She told me to trust James and the Holy Spirit and go back out there and continue. I went back out to the living room. Don't ask me why. I don't understand why, except I trusted that James was teaching me to hear from God. I knew better than to argue, so I listened for the Holy Spirit. I did not hear a voice, but, all of a sudden, I turned and pointed my finger in the face of the man. With a voice I did not know I had, I said, "*You are a liar from hell. It is not your wife calling forth demons, it is you! I see you coming out of your body into the air and calling forth demons to terrorize your wife!*"

I need to stop right here and tell you that I had never heard of astral projection—an out of the body experience. The whole time I am talking to this man, I am wondering who it was speaking out of my mouth. Then I saw his wife in a vision. She was pinned down by fear on her bed and these horrible demons in the form of mutated creatures were continually flying at her, terrorizing her. The man had been fooling around with all types of interaction with demons and the supernatural of darkness. I would like to tell you he repented, but he did not. His wife did get free from the fear that had been tormenting her.

That was my first encounter of that sort. I thought everyone who does deliverance experienced that, but I promise you, that is not the norm. I still do deliverance and seldom run into that realm of the demonic. Mostly, deliverance is about inner healing and not that scary or weird at all.

~

Running To and Fro

"Then I looked and I heard the voice of many angels around the throne and the living creatures and the elders; and the number of them was myriads of myriads, and thousands of thousands (Revelation 5:11)."

One day I was sitting on my sofa. There were three windows behind me facing the front of the house. The house has a long porch. There were always a bunch of kids at my house playing with mine. I liked it that way. At least I knew where mine were. I caught a lot of movement out of the corner of my eye. Thinking it was the kids, I kept doing what I was doing. The movement continued and I realized there was no noise. Now, any mother knows that noise comes with kids, especially kids with movement. I turned to look out the window and was shocked at the sight!

On my porch were literally hundreds, if not thousands, of spirits, ghosts, or whatever you would call them. They were running back and forth, many running through each other. They did not seem to be aware of where they were. They seemed to have no real purpose, not looking around, just moving continuously and fast. Then I heard the voice of the Lord, not audible but clearly, *"I just wanted you to see the spirit world. It is a very busy place."* We may think that strange. We tend to only believe what we can see or touch with our natural senses. I have come to understand that the spiritual realm is more real and will outlast this natural existence. I think God would like us to be comfortable with the spirit realm. After all, He is a Spirit!

STORY 17

Bad Habits

"But there is nothing covered up that will not be revealed and hidden that will not be known (Luke 12:2)."

When I received Christ, I did not fully understand that growing and changing would come through process. I, like many other new and not so new Christians, always want to help God fix us. That did not work out well for Abraham and it will not work out well for us. God does not need or want out help. That might surprise some of you, however, it remains true. What He does want is our cooperation. He is the only one that can change us at the very root of our problems. I have learned that most of our insufficiencies do not come by way of choices or learned behavior. It is true that these things influence our lives, but most of our problems come from a heart-issue and this, in turn, influences our choices. That, my friend, is a God-sized problem.

When I came into relationship with Christ, I had smoked about eight years. I was also a heavy smoker, mostly due to staying home. Not working gave me too much free time. When you work, you have to limit such habits due to time restraints. I decided it was time for me to get sanctified. I needed to look like a Christian. I decided to quit smoking, but, because I rarely smoke outside my home, a lot of people were not aware that I had such a bad habit. Of course, my Aunt Barbara knew. It seems funny now that we both would sit for hours with our coffee and cigarettes while studying the Scriptures. Strange how it never stopped the Holy Spirit from teaching us truth!

I told my pastor and he was surprised I smoked, but he said he would be in prayer for me. I had decided I would quit smoking, but I would not tell anyone other than my pastor and aunt. I had reasoned that, if I failed, it would not make God look bad. How stupid can one person be? I thought God needed me to protect His good name. Unbelievable! Still, being young in the faith, I would go to any gathering that I could find to learn more about this newly found faith-journey I was on. I heard of a service being held in a local union hall. Actually, it was the same building where I received Christ. You have to remember, this took place around 1977 or early 1978. There was not a lot of interaction in worship services between black and whites. It happened a bit more in charismatic circles than traditional denominations—I am thankful that has changed. I also am grateful I was in the arena where it was not unheard to be in a service with other races.

I had been three days without a cigarette and the withdrawals were ridiculously strong, but I stayed the course. I found out the time of this meeting at the union hall and I had no idea who would be there. I walked in and the place was fairly full. Everyone, and I mean everyone, was black. I was the only white person in the room. I was so hungry to know more about Jesus that I did not care so long as they did not care. They didn't seem to mind, so I took a seat at the back. The lady minister was already into her message. I would get to know her well over the next few years. Sister Tina—she was quite a character, but she knew how to hear from God. There she was with her head covered and her feet bare. I found out later that she felt that is how God wanted her to preach, so she did. I came in quietly so as to not disturb her. Of course, I stood out like a sore thumb. The minute I sat down, she stopped dead in her tracks and pointed at me and said, "*Little black-haired girl, come up here.*"

I thought to myself, "*Everyone here has black hair!*" I got out of my seat and stood in front of her.

She looked me up and down. The whole time she was saying, "*Umm, huh.*" She looked at me as if she could see straight through me! Then she held up three fingers and said, "*Three days ago, you decided to stop something. God did not tell you to do that. Now, you go back to that thing. God has an appointed time for you and, when He does it, it will be for His glory and not yours!*"

I stood there without a word. I was thinking, "*Is she saying what I think she is saying?*"

She looked at me with surprise and said, "*I am saying exactly what you think I am saying!*"

"*Oh my God,*" I thought, "*she can read my mind!*"

I still did not understand the gifts of the Spirit. I learned quickly about the gift of the word of knowledge. That is a gift given by the Holy Spirit where a person empowered by the Holy Spirit knows facts that they do not know through natural means.

She waved her hand at me as if she were shooing away a fly and said, "*Go on now, do what God told you to do.*"

I turned and walked out the door. As I was leaving, I heard her say to the crowd, "*You nosey people, you are wondering what the thing is she has to do. It is none of your business.*"

I left there and stopped at the first convenience store I saw and bought a pack of cigarettes. Two weeks later, I was headed to my church. We were having a revival and the speaker was a Spirit-filled Jew. I had no idea what that meant, but I was going to find out. The church I attended was in a town about twenty miles from where I lived. I was always late during that time of my life. God was still working on me.

I got there after the service started. The small church was bursting at the seams. I managed to find one seat open at the very back. The Spirit-filled Jew preacher was just beginning his message. I have no recollection of his message, but what came after changed my life.

He said, "*There is one person in this room that God has told you that you have an appointed time of deliverance. Now, I know how you Pentecostal people are, if there is a blessing, every one of you will want to run up here. I know who this person is, so if you come up here and it is not you, I will send you back to your seat. You know who you are.*" No one moved. My heart was beating out of my chest and my hands were sweating. It was so hard to get my feet to move. No one except my pastor and aunt knew about my smoking. I knew he was talking to me. Finally, I managed to get to the front.

He looked at me and asked, "*Where are they?*"

I knew what he was asking. "In the car," I replied. "*Go get them.*"

I thought to myself, "*My God, how hard does this have to be?*"

I was about to learn something that some believes never learn. I went to my car. This was still in an era where you could leave your car unlocked and the keys in the ignition. Just as I opened the door, I heard a voice say, "*You better run, they are going to humiliate you.*"

The voice was soft and sweet—comforting. Then I heard another voice. "*You can run, but there is freedom on the other side.*" This voice, too, was soft, sweet, and comforting.

You're probably wondering what the difference was. That is the role of the Holy Spirit, the teacher of truth. I just knew that the voice that told me to run was demonic. It wanted me to feel as though I had no choice. The other voice was that of my heavenly Father. He always gives us choice.

"I call Heaven and Earth to witness against you today, that I have set before you life and death, the blessing and the curse. So, choose life in order that you may live (Deuteronomy 30:19)."

That day, I learned that you cannot go only by *what* you hear, but *how* you hear. Both voices can sound the same because the devil shows up as an angel of light. You must learn the character of God. I had the cigarettes in my hand and I went back to stand before the man of God.

I held them out to him, and he said, "*I don't want them, throw them in the trash.*"

I did and he asked me, "*Do you know why God wants you to quit smoking?*"

Of course I did. I began to explain the reasons, "*It is harmful to your body, which is the temple of the Holy Spirit. It is a bad witness to others.*"

He replied, "*All that is true, but that is not why God wants you to quit. Every time you kneel down to pray, you hide that part of your heart from God. He wants your whole heart.*"

By this time, I was crying. I was so overwhelmed at the love of God. The preacher touched my lips and I felt something leave my body! Then he said, "*There is a beam of light from the throne of God straight into your heart. Whatever you ask you will receive it.*"

I left there wondering what I will do when I get around other smokers and if I would get fat. There was no need to be concerned. Not only did I never crave a cigarette again, I lost five pounds!

After that blessing, I prayed, "*God, never let me forget what it was like to be a slave to cigarettes and help me never to be judgmental towards others.*"

I have a hard time with Christians who used to smoke and now, when they see someone light up, they get so self-righteous. Chill out, you did not mind it when you were the one blowing smoke! Give grace.

Father, You are so faithful. I know many people struggle with addictions. You alone have the power to set them free. I pray that many will experience Your love which is true deliverance. In the name of Jesus. Amen

~

Jewelry

Writing this section is so funny to me. When I was a small child, I would go to church with my maternal Grandma. She belonged to a denomination that believed it was sin to wear jewelry. As a matter of fact, they did not believe you could do much of anything that God approved. It seemed like everything we did; God was surely going to get us! I want to say this very clearly. We have been taught many things that have little to do with God, but everything to do with religion. Do this, do not do that. I don't think any true believer deliberately taught us wrong on purpose. In being a teacher of the Word of God, one of the problems I have found is that we can only teach on the level of revelation we have. A lot of people just continue to recycle the same teaching they have received without studying it for themselves.

One of the biggest and worst problems many have is not understanding the true boundaries between the Old and New Testaments. I personally love the Old Testament. Some New Testament believers think you should only read the New Testament. How sad because we need the whole Word of God. You just have to understand what benefit the Old Testament has. We have to be careful not to mix the law with grace. Under the New Covenant, it is only Jesus. Not Jesus+. This means Jesus paid the full price for our redemption. There is nothing we can do to earn His free gift. There are things we do to violate and frustrate His grace. We have this insane need to rely on the goodness of God and, at the same time, ask God to judge those with whom we are not in agreement. Mixing the old and the new only brings confusion and says to the world that there is no absolute truth. In this short section, I am going to share a few stories that span a few years. God is such a good, good Father.

STORY 19

Robyn

"Then all whose hearts moved them, both men and women, came and brought brooches and earrings and signet rings and bracelets, all articles of gold to the Lord (Exodus 25:32)."

For several years, my Aunt Barbara and I followed the ministry of Perry Stone. He held two major conferences each year. One was in Georgia and the other in Tennessee. Attending these two events on a regular basis, over time, gave us the ability to form friendships. People from all over the United States came and many came consistently. This was instrumental in developing relationships that would last for many years. I met a lady named Sharon from Missouri and got to know her over the course of a few years. She came to these conferences on a regular basis. It is strange how you can see a person only twice a year and feel such a strong bond.

Sharon and I were on the prayer team for Perry Stone, so we would spend time before each service in prayer. This particular year, she told me she had brought three ladies with her from Missouri. She asked if I would come to their room after the morning service and minister to them. I said I would be glad to. At the prayer time that morning, I spotted a woman I could not recall seeing before. She was tall and beautiful. She stood out of a crowd, and, at first, I just thought it was her physical appearance. Then the Lord began to speak to me about her. She was standing alone, so I walked up to her and told her my name and she told me hers. Just first names—nothing more at first. Before I could tell her why I was approaching her, she reached up and unclasped her necklace. She handed it to me and said she felt she was supposed to give it to me. I have never seen another one like it. It is a cross with gray-ish-blue stones and each stone is jointed so that each piece moves on its own. She owned her own boutique and said she could never find another exactly like it. I thanked her and I still have it. I left with the word the Lord had given to me for her.

Later after the service, my aunt and I went up to Sharon's room to meet these other ladies. It was quite a surprise to find the lady who had given me the cross necklace standing there! My aunt and I prayed with the three ladies. Sharon has since gone to be with the Lord, but my relationship with these three ladies has remained. I have continued to grow a relationship with Robyn, especially. I go to Missouri at least once a year and continue to minister to her and her family. I consider her one of my best friends. The other two ladies I do not get to see very often, but still love them very much. So, if you are reading this book, Doris and Brenda, I love you! This was the beginning of the Lord sending me people to give me jewelry.

❦

Two Strangers, Two Gifts

This story also took place at a Perry Stone conference. I was just walking around speaking to people before the service started. Outside the room where services were held, there were booths and tables set up where you could purchase ministry products such as books, study materials, and jewelry, among other things. This lady came up to me. I had not met her before, but she told me her name and, of course, I introduced myself. She immediately told me why she wanted to talk to me. She said, "*I saw you walking around and the Lord told me to take you out to the tables and let you pick a gift for me to purchase for you. But the Lord was clear it had to be a piece of jewelry.*"

I told her how much I appreciated that, but it was not really necessary. She insisted and said she had to be obedient. We walked out to the table and I picked out a bracelet. She told me to get what I wanted and she would be glad to pay for it. I said the bracelet would be fine. She purchased it and told me to be blessed. At the next service, another lady approached me. I had never met her either. She held out a small bag and said the Lord had instructed her to buy me a gift. Surprised, I opened the bag and it was an identical bracelet I had picked out that morning. I was not quite sure why I got two of the same bracelets, but I thanked her and went on about my business.

Later that day, while discussing this with my aunt, I shared my question of why I had gotten two identical bracelets. She said that God often would confirm His word through two or more witnesses. She also explained that God would reveal to me the reason in His own time. She was right. He did many years later.

~

No End to His Provision

*"Let the favor of the Lord our God be upon us; and confirm
for us the work of our hands; yes, confirm the
work of our hands (Psalm 90:17)."*

Through the years, I have had people walk up and pull their bracelets, necklaces, rings, and watches off and give them to me. It always took me back to the first time when Robyn, from Missouri,
gave me her cross in 2004. I thought about it many times and, in
this next story, I will share with you why God chose to bless me in
that manner. I have learned it is never just about us.

In 2006 I got involved with a ministry where I was to learn
what it really meant to walk in faith. In that year, major changes
were taking place in my life. I left my husband of thirty-four years,
which I will talk about a bit later in this book. This sent me on a
journey I never expected to travel. In the Gospel of John, Jesus was
telling the disciples that it was important that He go away so that
the Holy Spirit could come. Please do not think that I am com-
paring leaving my husband to Jesus' agenda; I am simply making
a point that, sometimes, one major event takes place in our lives
that sets us up for another major life changing event. Such was

the case in moving out. Being fifty-two years old and the fact that I made a minimum wage brought its own challenges. Within a few months of leaving home, I changed cars, jobs, friends, and churches.

Through a process, I became acquainted with Chuck. He was the pastor of a church that was meeting in homes. It was not long before we realized God was doing something unique. It is important for me to lay some foundation about my relationship with this ministry and its people. They would become a major part of my life and God's agenda for what He was doing. Although I am no longer a part of that ministry, we have remained friends and they are a huge part of where I am today in the Lord and ministry. You will see how many of my stories have a foundation intertwined with them. They not only were ministry partners, but very much a family to me and my granddaughters. I am forever grateful for their obedience to the Lord and their participation in my life. The ministry name has been changed, but I still refer to it as *Christ Fellowship*.

I was in a season of learning to walk by faith in finances. I was not working a regular job. I did not have an income. God took care of me largely through the ministry of *Christ Fellowship*. I would later become part of the staff and receive an income. I had been invited to speak at two women's conferences. One was in South Carolina and the other in North Carolina. I was looking through my clothes and realized that I had not bought anything new in quite a while. Most of my clothes looked tired and a bit dated. So, I prayed and asked God for His provision for a couple of new outfits for these conferences. I am not one to be extravagant in buying clothes, actually I am very practical. But, still, I wanted to look nice. It was only a few days after asking God for new clothes and I got a phone call from a friend. It is worth mentioning that I had told no one about my need. I learned through walking out this faith-journey not to go around poor-mouthing. That is not trusting God. There are times when you must share your need, but you must do it only with someone God has placed into your life that will agree with you in prayer. Man is not your provider, God is.

My friend Robin—*not* Robyn from Missouri—called and said she was supposed to take me shopping for a couple new outfits to wear to my conferences. Yeah, God! It is so cool when you get that kind of answer from God! Long story short, we went shopping and picked out two outfits. One was black pants with a yellow shirt. The other was a color combination I have never worn. Pretty, but not something most people would see me in. The pants were brown and the blouse was a mix of brown and turquoise. The weekend came for me to go to North Carolina. It was about a two-hour drive and I did not want to be late. I dressed in the brown and turquoise combination. I was getting low on time. I got into the car and was going to pick up my friend Carol. The Lord spoke to me very clearly, "*I want you to change into your other new outfit.*" I thought, "*For real, Jesus?*" I am going to be late. Nevertheless, I went inside and changed my clothes. Dressed in the yellow and black combination, I picked up Carol and we were on our way.

We arrived to the church in time and there were only a few cars in the lot. The church was my spiritual parents' home church. Pastor Judy met me at the door and immediately began to apologize. She said that, when she planned this event, she did not know that a large percentage of the ladies had bought tickets to a concert on that date. I assured her it was okay; I was not bothered by the amount of people. She was obviously embarrassed. As it turned out, there were only eight women there and that included Carol and I. Pastor Judy had a couple of her ladies to share their testimony and then we took a short break. We had some finger-food and drinks. As in most women conferences, there is usually a drawing for gift bags. I could tell Pastor Judy was still struggling with the low turn-out. I think it was funny that there were exactly eight gift bags on the table! She could not have, in her wildest imagination, planned that. That spoke volumes to me that God was up to something and Him telling me what to wear had something to do with it. Just before we started to draw numbers for the gift bags, a very pretty young lady named Stephanie jumped up and stated that she would be right back. She came back and handed me a gift bag. She explained, "*I made this for you. I prayed and asked God what color and I thought these are the colors He told me to use. But I was not going to give it to you because I was afraid you would not like the color combination. When I saw your outfit, I thought maybe I did really hear from God.*" I opened the bag and there was a beautiful yellow and blue necklace and matching bracelet!

Now I understood why God told me to change into the yellow blouse. Not only was He blessing me, but He was teaching Stephanie how to hear Him. That, my friends, is how God rolls! But, this story had more blessings to be told. All the bags had been claimed and, as God would have it, my number was last. There was only one bag left so, unlike the other ladies, I did not have a choice. Pastor Judy picked up the leftover bag and said she needed to explain something about this particular gift before giving it to me. She started laughing and had to take a moment to settle down. She said, "*I am laughing because I had no idea there would only be eight women here and that you would get the last bag. The truth is, and you will have to trust me, I am not making this up. I picked out this gift just for you. I heard the Lord tell me very clearly to purchase this particular color for you. When I showed it to Jackie—my spiritual mother, Jackie told me that it was not a color she had ever seen you wear. But I really believe I heard from God.*"

She handed me the bag and I pulled out a necklace and a pair of earrings. Do you want to guess what color they were? Brown and turquoise! They perfectly matched the outfit I was going to wear. I was speechless! Seriously, I have served God a long time and have witnessed many strange occurrences, but you mean to tell me God goes jewelry shopping? This was turning out to be such a God-inspired conference. I was no longer concerned about the size of the turn-out. It was time for me to preach. We headed back to the sanctuary and, on the way, I asked God a question I had asked a few times since this whole jewelry thing began.

"God, why do you continue to give me jewelry?"

To my amazement, He replied, *"I like decorating my tabernacle and you are my tabernacle."*

I cried.

You would think that would be enough for a single event. There is more to come. I finished my message and Pastor Judy got up to take an offering for me. Honestly, I did not want an offering as I had already been blessed beyond measure. Besides, not counting me, there were seven other ladies and two of them were on Social Security. But people of faith do not look at the circumstances and Pastor Judy is a woman of faith. She said, *"Okay, I was a little worried when I saw how few people came, but I know that God spoke a specific amount that Sister Sandy is to receive, so I am writing a figure down so we will see."* She took the offering and I had no idea what she had written on the paper. I must admit, I was a little nervous, not for me, but I did not want Pastor Judy to be embarrassed. I do not know why we think we have to protect or explain God.

Usually, the church leaders write the speaker a check from the church account, but she explained that, because it was so few, she would just hand me what was given. Two checks were written to me. She gave the paper with the written the amount and gave it to someone to read. I cannot remember the exact amount, but it was an odd number. I know it was four hundred and some odd dollars. The offering was exactly that amount! Of course, my first thought was that Pastor Judy put in enough to cover it. When I looked at the offering, I saw that Pastor Judy had not covered it. God will always perform His Word.

You would think that was enough for God to do in one conference, but He always has more than enough. Pastor Judy's husband and my spiritual father came in at the end. I could see that James had a word from the Lord, I know him well enough that I know the look. I asked him if he had something he wanted to share. He looked intently at me and said, "*God said to tell you, 'It will never end. Stop waiting for the other shoe to drop, because, it will never end.'*" I am sure everyone was wondering what he was talking about, but I knew what he meant. Several days before, I was inquiring of the Lord concerning His provision. I still had trouble believing that God would provide for me indefinitely. I kept waiting for the other shoe to drop and the giving through others to stop. I stood in front of that small group totally unglued. Our God is not subject to the things that limit us. He is not limited by our economy or our resources. He is only limited by our inability to trust Him. He has a way of moving even when He is training us. Never judge what God may be doing in the supernatural by what you see and understand in the natural. You might miss something!

STORY 22

~

Give it Away

"Freely you received, freely give (Matthew 10:8b)."

"No, no, no, God you don't understand!" I wanted to scream, but I kept quiet. I was in a church service with my spiritual father, James Shinn. He had been preaching, but called me up to minister to people. If you read the previous stories, you will see how selfish I was being. Isn't it strange how good God can be to us and we still don't get it? This story took place after God had blessed me so many times by others giving me jewelry. There I was, standing in the pulpit, and God was telling me to give away my ring. The ring was given to me by a lady I had never met before. This stranger walked me out of a conference and bought the ring for me. I loved that ring. It was not expensive. It was a band with Hebrew letter cutouts. It said, *"I am my beloved's and my beloved is mine."* It is a Scripture from the Song of Songs. I was standing in front of a young woman and the Lord told me to give her my ring. I told the Lord I would be glad to give her money.

"*Give her the ring,*" He said.

That is all I could hear. I explained to God that this girl was a little bit on the heavy side and my ring would not fit her.

"*Give her the ring.*"

"*Okay, already!*" Only in my mind did these words take place.

I took off the ring and explained to the young lady about God wanting her to have it. She said, "*I am too fat for that ring!*" I told her to wear it on a chain. It was never about her getting the ring, it was all about me giving it up. The following Christmas, a friend bought two rings with the same message on them and gave them to my two granddaughters to give to me. God's people are the best people and He is a good, good Father!

STORY 23

Friends

"Two are better than one because they have a good return for their labor. For if either of them falls, the one will lift up his companion. But woe to the one who falls when there is not another to lift him up (Ecclesiastes 4:9-10)."

The next several stories are about a few individuals who have impacted my life on an ongoing basis. These people are not the only ones God has placed in my life, but there are too many on which to write a particular story. If I were to do that, I would have to write a separate book. You will see others mentioned within the stories that make up my life. God has placed people at every station of my life. He always brings the ones for His purpose and my benefit just in time. I hope I have benefited their lives as well. God is not about us being the lone-ranger and everything being about one person. He designed us to be in relationship with Himself and with others. I am so grateful for the people He has placed in my faith-journey. Every one of them has been an important part of how God has shaped me. Whether positive, negative or both, every one of us plays a part in God's design.

I heard a minister say that every successful ministry needs three things: a butler, a baker, and a pharaoh. This is patterned after the story of Joseph in the Old Testament. A butler opens doors. A baker knows how to put things together, and a pharaoh finances the assignment. I have seen God put all these in action throughout my life. I am so grateful. If you are reading this book and your name is not mentioned, and you have been one of those people, remember, God is keeping the records. He will not forget.

John 15 tells us that Christ is the vine and we are the branches; we are to bear fruit. That is our mandate. I pray my fruit will bear more fruit. Every one of you that has been a part of my faith-journey will participate in my fruit. Many of you have helped me sow the seeds of the Gospel. Others have helped me fertilize the soil by your giving support, both spiritually and financially. A lot of you have often been the pruning process. Some of you have been all three. My prayer is that I have not just been a recipient, but also a baker, butler, and a pharaoh for others because that is how the Kingdom of God rolls!

STORY 24

Shelly

"A friend loves at all times...(Proverbs 17:17)."

When I first started *Christ Fellowship*, Crystal, the pastor's daughter, approached me and asked if I would mentor her friend Shelly. I said I would be glad to and told her to give Shelly my number and have her to call me. I learned early in ministry that it was fruitless to call people at other's request. If someone would not make a phone call on their own, it usually means they are not ready for change. It would be two years later when Shelly finally got around to calling me! We would occasionally see each other at church because we went to different home-groups. She would always find a way to escape talking to me.

We began our crazy journey of me trying to mentor her and her trying to let me without her letting down her guard. Well, you can imagine how that went. It was an up-and-down, hit-and-miss, confusing, and often frustrating adventure. During the process of getting to know Shelly, she told me about Crystal giving her my phone number—Crystal had written my number on a scrap piece of paper and given it her. Shelly laid it on her dresser. It lay there two years! She said she would not even touch it. She would dust around the paper, but she could not bring herself to throw it away. Shelly had been an atheist, but Crystal never gave up sharing Jesus with her. Shelly gave her life to Christ at a "Women of Faith" conference. She only attended because her brother had given her a ticket for her birthday. You never know what God will use to get someone to the place He can speak to them. Today, Shelly is a phenomenal teacher. She has a unique way of presenting God's Word. She has become one of my dearest and most trusted friends. Be encouraged. If you, as a believer, have a friend that is stubborn, do not give up sharing Christ. Love them and be Christ-like. Live as Christ and only use words when necessary.

Scott

"Go therefore and make disciples of all the
nations…(Matthew 28: 19a)."

I was spending the weekend at a Christian retreat in the mountains of North Carolina near Brevard. I had been there several times. I always sat in a different spot in the dining hall and not usually with the group or persons with whom I had come. I found that was a good way to meet new people. We tend to stick with what we know and limit our outreach. I really do not like playing the safe way. With every new person you meet at *Living Waters*, the usual two questions you get asked are, *"Where are you from and where do you go to church?"*

This particular meal in 2010, I found myself sitting next to a young man. He was in his 30's and I am old enough to be his mother. Actually, his mother and I are the same age. He did not know anyone there and he sat in the only empty chair and that happened to be beside me. Talk about a God set-up!

He looked over at me and asked, "*What do you do?*"

I responded with a question, "*Don't you want to know where I am from and what church I attend?*" I will never forget his answer. After getting to know him so well through the years, I found out this is the real Scott.

He said, "*No, I don't really care. I just feel like you do something different than the norm.*"

I told him I was involved with a ministry called *Christ Fellowship*. I went on to explain that we were trying to figure out what the five-fold ministry of Ephesians 4:11 would look like working as a team and not just individuals doing their ministries alone. He seemed interested and said he would like to come visit and see how that works. I invited him to come anytime. Scott is from Thomasville, Georgia. That is about as south as you can get in Georgia before you find yourself in Florida. I was living in upstate South Carolina at the time. He went on to explain that God had him on a track of living totally by faith. He had been a worship leader and was doing very well in a rather large church until God required him to give it all up. When I say all, I mean everything—job, salary, home, material goods, and even his car.

I asked him how he got to the retreat and he told me his only possession was his motorcycle. I told him to ride his motorcycle to South Carolina. He explained that he had no money for a hotel or food. I promised him I would see to it that he would have somewhere to stay and we would feed him and give him gas money. In short, he did, and I kept my word.

After we finished our meal, Scott asked me if I would be interested in doing some ministry with him that evening. I was good with that. On his way in that morning, he had helped a group of ladies from Georgia unload their car and they wanted him to pray with them. This would also become a God-appointed time for me. This is where I met a lady named Lynn. She would speak into my life many times, of which I will share through several of these stories. Later that day, Scott asked me to walk down the stream to the waterfall that ran behind the houses. It was autumn and the leaves were beautiful. Scott was taking some pictures for his website.

> When we came to a stopping place, I asked a question I had been wondering, "*If you have nothing, no money or means, how do you afford a cell phone?*"

> He laughed and explained, "*A minister that stays at my mom's house sometimes when he is in the states, along with another ministry, provided the phone and the monthly bill.*" He went on to tell me this man was from New Zealand.

> I asked, "*Is his name Craig Marsh.*"

> Scott's mouth fell open and he asked, "*You know Craig Marsh?*"

> I replied, "*Actually, I just met him a couple weeks ago. I had lunch with him in Columbia, South Carolina through an invitation of a pastor friend.*"

Seriously, what are the odds? I am from South Carolina and Scott is from Georgia and we meet in the mountains of North Carolina and we both are acquainted with the same man from New Zealand! Meeting Scott was simply God-appointed and it started a new chapter in my life. Scott has traveled to many nations sharing the Gospel. This was going to be a catalyst for prophecies to come to pass where I was told I would go to other nations. Since meeting

Scott, we have traveled together to India twice, Kenya twice, and look forward to many more international opportunities.

In 2014, we started a church with Scott as the lead pastor and president. It is a fellowship of believers who have a Kingdom-mindset and are not interested in just doing church. We have never been about growing into large numbers, although we are not against it. We are more concerned with allowing God to change us as individuals so we can impact the world for change. Our church's name is *Living Stones International Community*. We, through the leadership of Scott, helped a new church start in Kenya by giving guidance to its leadership and encouragement to its pastors.

God has appointed times, places, and people for our lives. I do not want to miss anyone of them. You do not have to try to make these things happen. Just submit yourself to His will and cooperate with Him even when you do not understand what He is doing. Trust Him. Scott says this about patience, *"Patience is the ability to trust God without complaining when you do not understand what He is doing."*

Lorrie

"Most beautiful among women…(Song of Songs 1:8)."

Chuck—mentioned a few chapters back—and I were teaching a seminar on deliverance where we had approximately twenty men and women in the class. We took turns and it was my turn to teach. I always take a quick look around my congregation just to get a feel of the people I will be speaking to. Often, God points out certain ones for different reasons. I spotted this woman right away. Throughout the seminar that day, I could hardly take my eyes off her and I knew God was highlighting her for a reason. Her name is Lorrie. She had such a regal look about her that day. It was not just the way she wore her hair; it went much deeper than that. I just knew she would become a significant part of my life.

Sometime later, we were invited to spend a weekend on top of a mountain with a group of women. This was just before a group of us from *Christ Fellowship* was to go to India with Scott. It would be my first overseas trip. Lorrie was also going. We did not know each other well at this time. During ministry time, Lorrie came over and told me that she and I would be a team God would use.

We would be like salt and pepper. While each can stand on its own, they always work best together.

At the writing of this book, we are in great turmoil in America. Racial tension is at an all- time high. This is being driven by darkness and wickedness in high places. It is necessary to mention here that Lorrie is a black woman and I am white. There we have it: salt and pepper! I always caution people not to assume she is pepper because of her skin color or that I am necessarily the salt because of my being white. It is obvious that we work well together and we often are interchangeable in being salt and pepper.

Together she and I have been to India twice, Kenya twice, and to Honduras once. I cannot even imagine going overseas without her. I would feel as if a part of me would be missing. There may come a time God will send me somewhere overseas without her, but I would miss her more than I can imagine. I value her as a minister and a friend. I have four biological sisters and love them dearly, but I consider Lorrie every bit a sister. Scott, Lorrie, and I are a team of leaders in *Living Stones International Community*. Because of Scott's leadership in Kenya, the three of us work well as a team and have a strong influence there among other pastors. Lorrie truly has a heart for people of all races. I do not look at her as a black woman, I see her as a woman of God. I trust her with my life. It would be awesome if everyone could have a partner in ministry like Lorrie. She is a regal queen in the Courts of God. That is what I saw in her the first time at that seminar and I have seen her carry herself with great humility in that royal priesthood.

STORY 27

Holly

"But in all these things we overwhelmingly conquer through Him who loves us (Romans 8:37)."

I met Holly through my relationship with Scott. She and Scott had been friends for quite a number of years. Holly has a disorder called *Spinal Muscular Atrophy*, SMA for short. She was diagnosed at fifteen months old and was not expected to live past the age of three. God had other plans. Holly has been in a power chair most of her life. She has extremely limited movement and needs help with all the things we take for granted. Basically, she can only move her hands and head.

Most people would have given in and allowed the situation to define them. Not Holly. Not only did she finish high school, but she was valedictorian of her graduating class! She went on to college and now teaches at the University of North Georgia. Holly has written and published books. She has her own publishing company called *Spiritfire Publishing*. I think the only thing she has not accomplished on her bucket list thus far is to drive an 18-wheeler truck, but hey, her life is not over yet!

I met her at a time when I needed someone to illustrate my first children's book. I haven't mentioned that she is also an artist. We became good friends quickly. I could write a whole chapter on her, but, for the sake of space, I will weed it down. Our relationship grew, so, by the time my granddaughter who lived with me grew up and decided it was time for her to move out, I invited Holly to live with me. I did not particularly want to live alone and Holly, for obvious reasons, did not need to live alone. I became her caregiver out of necessity. It was not planned, we just did life together. It was a give-and-take situation. Holly helped me as much as I helped her. I don't know how we ever got the idea life is supposed to be settled into one thing for twenty or more years. Life in the Kingdom of God is constantly moving and we must learn to move as God directs. Holly and I had a lot of fun. Holly often pushed me out of my comfort zone. She is so gifted and highly motivated. We lived together in my home in York, South Carolina. Through a process, she and I moved to Cayce, South Carolina. What happened after that is another story, one that will come later in this book. I wanted to give you an idea of who Holly is because, like so many individuals, she is such an important part of my journey.

STORY 28

Clairey

Clairey is my oldest granddaughter born in 1996. From the first moment I saw her, I knew that she and I would have a special bond. I have four grandchildren. My daughter, Amy, has two girls, Clairey and Elizabeth. My son, Jason, and my daughter-in-law, Leslie, have two sons, TJ, and Gabriel. I want to make it clear that I love all my grandchildren. They are all special to me for different reasons. At the writing of this book, Clairey just gave birth to my first great granddaughter, Ariel. TJ is attending Clemson University, Gabriel just graduated high school, and Elizabeth will graduate in 2021. I will talk about Clairey and Elizabeth more than my grandsons, not because they are more important, but because Clairey lived with me from the age of twelve and Elizabeth stayed with me the majority of the time from the age of five. Clairey has an unusual spiritual awareness and the stories I will share with you will be about those God-moments.

Speaking in the French

"Now I wish that you all spoke in tongues…(I Corinthians 14:5a)."

God has such a sense of humor. Spiritually, my background was of the Pentecostal persuasion. Meaning, speaking in tongues was a natural part of my understanding. However, God loves to stretch us beyond our comfort zone. I was still in my first marriage and Amy and Clairey lived with us. God had placed—more like tricked—me into a Southern Baptist church. Two things are important to note about this denomination. First, their doctrine does not allow women to be in ministry where it involves teaching men, and second, the gift of the Spirit of speaking in tongues is, at the very least, not practiced openly. The Lord had instructed me to start a Bible study for women and that is what I did. It was either held on a Tuesday or a Thursday night at my home. Clairey was around five years old at that time and, on Bible study night, she had visitation with her dad. Her grandmother would pick her up and bring her home. I always instructed her to come in quietly because we probably would be praying to dismiss about that time.

This particular night, we had a lady named Tami sitting in the hot-seat while we, as a group, gathered around her praying. She was getting ready to fly for the first time and she was going on a mission trip to Russia. Clairey loved Ms. Tami. While we were praying, Clairey returned from her visit. She came in very quietly and stood between me and another lady named Sue. We were all praying and, suddenly, I heard someone softly praying in a language and it was not English. I opened my eyes and saw Sue almost toppling over as she leaned closer to Clairey to listen. It was Clairey praying in tongues! No one had ever prayed with her to receive that gift. She was speaking so softly and fluently. It was one of the most beautiful tongues I have ever heard. We finished praying and no one said anything until later. Sue told me much later that she was always very skeptical where this gift was concerned, but, when she heard Clairey praying in a language of the Spirit, she became convinced that it was real.

I did not say anything to Clairey because I didn't want her to take any credit for God's gift. It seemed as if she was not aware that she did something out of the ordinary. My husband at the time worked the third-shift and the next morning, when he got home from work, he asked how the Bible study went. Before I could answer, Clairey spoke up.

She said, "*Guess what Poppy?*"

He asked, "*What?*"

She replied, "*I was speaking in the French!*"

He looked at me for an explanation and I shrugged my shoulders and said, "*It sounded like French!*"

~

Angels Singing

"And the four living creatures, each one of them having six wings, are full of eyes around and within; and day and night they do not cease to say, "HOLY, HOLY, HOLY is the LORD...(Revelation 4:8a)."

Clairey had gone with her dad's mom to visit. She had only been gone a short time when I received a phone call from Brenda, the grandmother. She sounded a bit upset and said she was bringing Clairey home. I asked if something was wrong and this was her reply:

> Clairey was in the back in her car seat—she was about five at the time—and I was just talking to her when Clairey said,
>
> *"You need to be quiet Nanny."*
>
> I scolded Clairey, *"It is not nice to tell your grandmother to be quiet."*

"*I know Nanny, but I am listening to the angels sing.*"

Thinking she was just making up a story, I went along with it. "*Well, what are they singing?*"

"*Oh, they are not singing in words we know. But I can understand them.*"

I was sort of amused and asked her, "*Okay, what are they saying?*"

Clairey said, "*The angels are flying around God's big chair and they are saying, 'HE is, HE is!'*

I thought I would just go along with her, so I asked, "*You mean, He is good, He is great or what?*"

Clairey then said, as if everyone should know, "*HE just is!*"

Brenda finished recounting the conversation with Clairey and said to me, "*I am bringing her home; she gives me the heebie jeebies!*"

I looked this up later and found out that, when God says in Scripture, "*I AM,*" it really means in Hebrew, "*He is.*"

STORY 31

∾

Pajamas

"Therefore, I say to you, all things for which you pray and ask, believe that you have received them, and they will be granted you (Mark 11:24)."

After my first marriage ended, it became necessary for Clairey to live with me. This caused Clairey and me to create some new traditions for holidays. Clairey decided that one of those traditions would be for us to wear our pjs to a local Waffle House on Christmas morning. We would pack a few gifts and ask the Lord to whom we were to give them. Clairey began this tradition by working odd jobs such as cleaning for other people to earn the money to buy matching flannel pjs. Christmas morning, we dressed in our flannel pjs and took our little gifts to the Waffle House. It is surprising how many people eat out on Christmas morning.

One particular Christmas, Clairey had bought us red pjs with big, white polka dots. Needless to say, we stood out.

We had to wait in line, so I turned to the man standing behind me and asked, *"How are you this morning, young man?"*

He answered, "*I wasn't doing very well until I got here. My mom died this past year and this is the first Christmas without her.*"

Feeling his sorrow, I replied, "*Holidays are difficult when you lose someone. I am very sorry and hope your day gets better.*"

He went on to say, "*I came to see my daughter, she works here. Seeing you girls in your red pajamas just makes me feel better!*"

I laughed and replied, "*You calling me a girl makes me feel better. To be honest, I felt a little silly wearing my pjs out in public at my age.*"

At that time, a table came open and we were next to be seated. We had just gotten settled and Clairey said, "*We are not supposed to sit here.*"

Before I could reply, another table came open and the man behind us in line was headed toward that table. Clairey intercepted him and asked if we could trade tables. His face lit up! He thanked her and explained that he was hoping for the table we had gotten because that was in his daughter's section, but he did not want to make a fuss. We got a lot of stares, but most were good-humored. We sat down and our server came to get our drink order. She was so busy that she hardly stopped while taking our order.

Clairey said, "*She is the one we are supposed to give our gifts to.*"

Finally, the server came over and apologized for running past us. I assured her it was fine. I told her that, when she got a minute, to come over because we had something for her, but to take her time. A few minutes later, she came over and, taking a deep breath, she said she had a minute to stop. Clairey gave her the two small gifts and the server began to cry. Between her tears, she explained how busy they had been and that she was glad because it kept her mind occupied. She had to leave her two children on Christmas morning because she needed the hours. She also explained that every one of the servers and kitchen staff had received a gift from someone except her.

God is so attentive to us and, most of the time, we miss it. That particular Christmas morning, God was mindful of the man who was sad because of missing his mother and it was no small thing for him to sit in his daughter's section so he could at least see his family. I am thankful that Clairey was sensitive to the Holy Spirit about changing seats. God was also mindful of the severe feeling of being alone and left out. Through us, He gave her gifts. That is the goodness of God!

STORY 32

∼

For the Love of God!

"Moreover, I will give you a new heart and put a new spirit within you…(Ezekiel 36:26a)."

My daughter, Amy, married at the age of eighteen to a man about whom her dad and I were absolutely not happy. We knew it was not going to be good, but she had a right to be as wrong as anyone else. That marriage was short-lived and Amy came home to live with us with a two-week-old baby. Her name is Clairey. They continued to live with us and Clairey was about five years old when this event happened.

I disliked her dad and there was no love lost—he did not like me either. The sad part is, I more than disliked him; I actually hated him. There, I said it. I know how ugly that sounds. After all, I was a Believer in Christ Jesus. Still, I hated him. I knew that was wrong and I sincerely prayed about it, but I could not or would not turn it loose. He had caused a lot of pain to our family. One thing I was very adamant about was I never let anyone, including myself, talk negatively about him around Clairey. He was her dad and I knew it would not serve her well to hear those things. I had seen how that worked in other's lives.

This particular day, Clairey's dad called and wanted to speak to her. I called her to the phone, but I always stayed near to monitor the call. Of course, I could only hear her side of the conversation and it went like this:

Clairey, *"Hey Daddy."*

Pause.

Clairey, *"Hey Daddy, do you want to talk to my Meme* (that's me)?"

Pause

Clairey, *"Daddy, my Meme loves you!"*

I have to stop here and tell you the horror I felt when I heard her say that. The problem is she kept repeating it and then she went on to say, *"Daddy, my Meme loves you, do you love my Meme?"*

She just kept asking that question! I was horrified. But then it dawned on me how horrified he must have been. I promise you, he hated me as much as I hated him. The more Clairey talked, I began to imagine his shock and what the look on his face must have been. I started laughing and, as I laughed, something began to leave me. In the midst of that laughter, God delivered me from hatred for this man. I still was not crazy about him, but I found myself able to pray for his well-being. I no longer had hatred in my heart. Laughter can be good for the soul. Thank You, Jesus, for teaching us to love through You!

STORY 33

∿

High School Graduation

"Is anything too difficult for the LORD (Genesis 18:14)?"

Wow, Clairey grew up so fast! After my separation from my first husband, Clairey came to live with me and we saw God provide for us in so many ways, but I guess we all have areas of faith in which we have to continue to grow and Clairey's faith surpassed mine many times. It was Clairey's high school graduation. She came to me one day and said she had been praying and believing God for six thousand dollars for graduation so she could buy a good used car.

I laughed.

I explained to her that even rich kids did not get six thousand dollars. She said she knew because her friends had laughed at her too. Yet, she still insisted God would send her six thousand dollars. Like all high school graduates, cards began to come in and most had money in them. Great! She got cards with money from people she had never met. She got money from people all the way from California, people she did not even know, yet they were acquainted with me or other friends. She started getting sums of money in the amounts of hundreds and thousands of dollars. When all was accounted for, she got $6,005.00! She said she knew God would do it! Father God help us to have unfeigned faith in You. Amen.

~

Money Mystery

"Ask, and it will be given to you, seek, and you will find…
(Matthew 7:7)."

I have shared the pajama story and this is connected to the ongoing tradition of wearing our pjs to the Waffle House on Christmas morning. Clairey always bought our matching pjs by making money, usually by cleaning my sister's house. This particular Christmas season, Clairey was out shopping with a lady from church and three other kids her age, also from our church. The girls had spent their money and Clairey had not yet bought our pjs. She usually spent about fifty dollars. She said she went behind some racks and prayed asking God to provide the fifty dollars to buy the pjs. One of the other girls asked Clairey to see if she had some change. They all were spent, but wanted a cold drink, so they all started searching their purses for change. When Clairey opened her purse, there sitting on top of everything was a fifty-dollar bill! She went to the lady who had brought them shopping and asked her if she had put money in her purse. The lady told her no, because she would not do that for her if she could not do it for all of them.

Clairey is convinced that God supernaturally put that in her purse. I believe that also. If you have trouble buying that story, then what will you do with the stories of miracles we find in the Bible? *"Now faith is the assurance of things hoped for,"* states Hebrews 11:1.

Braces

"Therefore, humble yourselves under the mighty hand of God, that He may exalt you at the proper time., casting all your anxiety on Him, because He cares for you (1 Peter 5: 6-7)."

When Clairey was twelve years old and still living with me, she was, and still is, a beautiful girl. Her major flaw was her teeth. They were very crooked and this caused her a lot of embarrassment. Kids can be very cruel and they made fun of her because of her teeth. This was in the first stages of God teaching me how to walk by faith in finances. I did not have a job in the normal sense—I will talk about that later. I literally had to trust God for everything. God works through people. Being twelve years old is already a vulnerable time in a young girl's life. Adding that on top of living with me instead of her mom because of difficult circumstances did not help. She was dealing with a lot of broken emotions. We had been praying about her teeth.

One night, I went in to say goodnight to her and found her crying. I thought it was about her mom, as it was often the case. When I asked her what was wrong, she told me she was embarrassed about her teeth and she needed to get braces. I agreed and said we would simply have to pray because I did not have five dollars, let alone five thousand. I guess neither of us had the faith to believe God would actually send us the money. We prayed and went to sleep. The next morning, I woke up late and jumped out of bed while calling Clairey to hurry so she would not be late for school.

Please hear me—I am not spiritual in the early morning when I get busy! I had not had my coffee yet. All I had on my mind was getting Clairey to school on time. God began to speak.

He said, "*You have been praying in unbelief.*"

Being spiritual as I can be early in the morning, I replied, "*Nuh-uh!*"

He went on to say, "*You believe I can give her braces, but you do not think I will.*"

I knew He was speaking truth, ha, that is a no-brainer as that is all He can speak! I asked, "*What do You want me to do?*"

"*Repent for your unbelief and do not ask Me for braces again, but thank Me for them. Tell Clairey to do the same.*"

Clairey was ready for school by this time and I called her to sit for a minute. I told her what God said. I prayed, "*Lord, I repent for my unbelief and I thank You for the braces You will give Clairey. Amen.*"

Clairey prayed, "*Lord, what she said. Amen*" Real spiritual we were. We left to go to school. I told no one about that morning. Around two o'clock that afternoon, I received a phone call from a man who will remain anonymous. The conversation went something like this:

> The man, "*Sandy, my wife and I have been praying for quite a while about paying for braces for Clairey, but only this morning in prayer did God release us to do it. The only thing we require is that you never tell anyone about who is paying for it. We would not tell you except we need your cooperation. Take her to the dentist and we will pay the cost.*"

> I was beyond flabbergasted! "*Do you know what those braces cost? She will need top and bottom.*"

> He said, "*It does not matter, we will take care of it.*"

> I was curious so I asked him, "*What time did you hear from God?*"

> He answered, "*Around 7:30 this morning.*"

I was in tears. While Clairey and I were half-heartily repenting for our unbelief, God was speaking to someone to pay for the braces. His grace is overwhelming! I made an appointment with the orthodontist and that was very interesting. The orthodontist did his evaluation and told me what the process would look like. He went on to say, "*Most of our patients are twelve and thirteen years of age, but Clairey is very unique. She is not only beautiful physically, but she has a classic model's face structure. She seems to be beautiful on the inside as well.*"

I knew that, but I am her grandmother, so I am probably prejudiced. He sent us back to the lady to make arrangements for payment. She gave me the options and asked if I wanted to put it on a credit card or pay by check, or they would set up a payment plan.

I informed her I did not have a credit card and I did not have any income. I could almost read her thoughts. She was wondering what I was doing there without a plan of payment. She was trying to find the words to ask tactfully. I interrupted her thought process and told her how another person was paying for it. She was curious, so she asked me how that came to be, so I told her the story.

She started crying and, about that time, another office worker came in and the first lady said, "*Tell her that story.*" She started crying also. The doctor came in and saw his two assistants crying and asked why. I then had to tell him the story. It was easy for me to see he was not a believer nor did he understand faith. He responded by saying, "*This is the craziest story I ever heard! Someone just called you up and said they would pay for it without knowing what the cost would be? This needs to be on Oprah Winfrey or something!*" I just laughed.

The cost was just over five thousand dollars and, true to the man's word, he and his wife paid the total cost. I have never and will not ever reveal those peoples' identity. But God keeps the book of remembrance. A few days later, I asked God why He did that for Clairey. I actually knew a few girls her age that had a closer walk with the Lord than Clairey at that time. He explained, "*Where I am taking you, it will require you to walk by faith and Clairey will take this journey with you. She cannot go on your faith; she needs her own faith.*" I have seen God give Clairey an increase of faith in times when mine wavered. I am so thankful and pleased to have her as a granddaughter. She has a strong anointing on her life and it is up to her to live it, but God knows what she needs and He will see her through.

~

Elizabeth

"...a little child shall lead them (Isaiah 11:6)."

Elizabeth is my youngest grandchild. She and my oldest grand-child, Clairey, are sisters. They have different dads, technically making them half-sisters. I only tell you that because they have different last names and they are slightly different in skin color. Elizabeth is bi-racial. Her father is black and her mother, Amy, is white. Neither one of these facts makes her half of anything; nei-ther does it make her mixed.

Clairey and Elizabeth, as well as all of us who know them, con-sider them sisters, period. When Elizabeth was born, I was in the room and did not know that she was bi-racial. Her dad was not present. It was a shock. It was clear, from the moment she came into this world, that she was different. It took a while for us to adjust. But, I want to make this clear. We loved her then and we love her now. She is as much mine as any other grandchild I have. I know many people describe children who are born of parents of different races as "mixed." I hate that terminology. It lends to the connotation that they are somehow not whole. That is why I do not say she and Clairey are half-sisters unless someone asks about their last names being different.

Elizabeth is whole in every way. She has struggles like everyone else. She was not quite five years old when she and her sister came to live with me. Amy lived with Pete, my ex-husband and her dad. There were lifestyles that created an unhealthy environment for the girls and they came to live with me. Elizabeth was so young when she came to live with me and it stirred a lot of confusion within her. She was unaware of the things that caused me to remove them from her mom. She did not understand why she could not be with her mom. I am not telling this story to make anyone feel guilty or to make my daughter look bad. We all make choices that have consequences and it costs us more than we anticipated.

I remember when Elizabeth was born and, because I did not know my daughter was involved with a black man, it was a shock. As I prayed about the situation, the Lord said to me, "*I gave her to you because she is going to need a strong woman who knows who she is in Me to help her to know who she is. Many are going to try and define her, but you will teach her to know who she is.*"

I think my grandson, TJ, said it best. TJ and his brother, Gabriel, and Elizabeth were playing on the floor one day. Elizabeth was around five, Gabriel was about six, and TJ was about eight. Elizabeth blurted out, "*Y'all know I am black!*" TJ looked at her with a puzzled look on his face and replied, "*No you are not, you are our cousin!*" Wow! Would it not be wonderful if we could simplify our differences that easily? Through Elizabeth, God has taught me some principles that have helped me rightly divide the truth.

Once, when I was trying to explain to Clairey why is was not a good idea to date someone of a different race, I told her that dating is "running interviews for marriage." Building a successful marriage is difficult enough. When you stack on serious differences such as racial, religious, educational, social, and economic backgrounds, it almost surely sets you up for failure.

Clairey listened and then she asked a question that changed the way I evaluated this particular subject. "*Well, Meme*," she said, "*Then who is Elizabeth going to date?*" I was stunned! I realized I had been using the wrong standard of measure. I was evaluating a situation with what I consider common sense and human wisdom. Everything I said was true in the understanding of man. But, as Christ-followers, we are to measure everything by God's standard. So, I did what I should have done in the first place. I prayed and used the standard of the Word for the answer. God impressed me with His wisdom and said, "*Submit your life to Me and look for the one who does the same. Then you will know who your mate for life should be.*"

I once heard a minister speaking to a youth group say, "*You run after God as hard as you can. While you are pursuing Him, look at who is running alongside you doing the same. That is who you should consider as a life mate.*" Race or any of that other stuff will play a vital role in your marriage as we have to mature in Christ, but the main thing to look for is a partner who is in step with you in your faith-journey. Sometimes it is good for older people to learn from the younger people.

❧

Taking Over

"Take courage, stand up! He is calling for You (Mark 10:49b)."

During the time Clairey and Elizabeth lived with me, we had fellowship in our home on Sunday mornings. Everyone, including the children, was expected to participate, whether it was insight into the Scripture or following the leading of the Holy Spirit—yes, children hear from the Holy Spirit too. This particular morning, we had a couple visitors; two guys around Elizabeth's age, somewhere around twelve and fourteen years old. During the ministry time, I felt like the Holy Spirit wanted to minister to these young men. This is where I was not listening very carefully to Him.

I did not wait to see if someone else was supposed to go to them, I just went. I had just gotten started when Elizabeth came over and, immediately, told me that she would take over. And takeover was exactly what she did! She began to talk to them and they were listening. She was boldly bringing correction to their thinking and attitudes. They were receptive to her because of several factors. She was their age and she spoke their language—you know, teen talk. They listened and received because she had the anointing of the Holy Spirit on her to minister. Those two young men went away knowing that they had been touched by the Holy Spirit. Seeing Elizabeth in action also allowed them, and us, to see that God can and will move through anyone who will be obedient.

Father God, give each of us the ability to take over any situation through Your leadership. More now than ever, help us to take courage and stand up! Amen

Leadership

"Come you children, listen to me; I will teach you the fear of the LORD (Psalm 34:11)."

During the time I was a part of the ministry of *Christ Fellowship*, we had several homes in which we gathered in small groups on Sunday morning. I held one in my home. Our main agenda was to encourage others to read the Scriptures and learn how to hear the Holy Spirit as individuals. We did this by picking a book of the Bible. Each day, we would read a chapter, write what stood out to us, and then explain how we felt it was applicable to our personal faith-journey. When we gathered on Sunday morning, we had a focus chapter. Each person, including the children, was encouraged to share their insight.

Elizabeth stayed with me on weekends during school and most of the summer. She was around ten years old. It was winter and snowing on this particular Sunday morning. I felt it was in the best interest of safety to cancel the fellowship. We had a couple friends staying with us. Some of us were sitting around in our pjs drinking coffee.

Elizabeth came into the living room and looked around. She asked, "*Are we not having fellowship this morning?*"

I replied, "*No, it is snowing so I called it off. I don't want anyone to risk getting hurt in this weather.*"

She looked at me as if I had suggested we should all defect from the faith! With her hand on her hip—she was famous for doing that when she took a stand on anything, she asked, "*How many people do we need to have church? We have five people. Is that not enough?*"

I felt a little put out that this ten- year-old kid was calling me out. Me! The preacher! Imagine that. But she was right and I knew it. "*Okay then, we will have fellowship. You can be the facilitator and lead it.*"

"*I will,*" she stated with confidence. "*Everyone, get your coffee and your Bibles. It is time to start.*"

She jumped right into the role of a leader. She even sat where the leader would normally sit. All eyes were on her. I think everyone was a little amused at the whole incident. I know I was curious to see if she could pull it off. In a voice of authority, she ordered us to turn our Bibles to the book of Proverbs. She then asked for prayer requests and directed who should take each request and pray for that need. After prayer, she led the discussion on what we got out of the Scriptures. She ended it with prayer. She handled herself like a true leader. Pastor Chuck, aka PC, would have been pleased with her. His heart was to develop a way of doing church where anyone could lead, not just the leaders. I believe he has been successful. Dare to be like Elizabeth. Be bold. Follow the Holy Spirit and take charge!

Then I said, "Alas, LORD GOD! Behold I do not know how to speak, because I am a youth."But the LORD said to me, "Do not say, 'I am a youth,' Because everywhere I send you, you shall go, and all that I command you, you shall speak. Do not be afraid of them, for I am with you to deliver you," declares the LORD (Jeremiah 1:7-8)."

Signs, Miracles, and Wonders

"God also testifying with them, both by signs and wonders and by various miracles and by gifts of the Holy Spirit according to His own will (Hebrews 2:4)."

In this next section, you will read accounts of things only God can do. I want to make it clear that these stories are not shared to elevate me or to make me look super spiritual. These signs, miracles, and wonders, as well as gifts operated by the Holy Spirit, are to establish Himself in any ministry to bring others to Himself. These things were done for me to build my faith in Christ and that, through the testimony of His faithfulness, others will learn to trust Him. He provided everything I needed so that the ministry to which He has called me would be able to function for the sole purpose of the Kingdom of God and for the benefit of the Body of Christ.

Some of these stories will seem to be simple blessings; others will be hard for many to believe. I am not sharing to impress anyone. I am only sharing the goodness of our Father in the process of becoming a vessel of honor to Him. I still have a long way to go, but I am moving forward and trusting Him to guide and change me as He sees fit. Life in the Spirit is an adventure and I do not intend to waste it.

There is an old hymn with the line, *"It gets sweeter and sweeter as the days go by, oh what a love between my Lord and I, I keep falling in love with Him over and over again."* As you read, you may think this walk of faith came easily—it did not. There is a price to pay. What is the cost? Jesus said it best in Luke 9:23, *"And He was saying to them all, 'If anyone wishes to come after Me, he must deny himself, and take up his cross daily and follow me.'"* I would like to tell you I have done this perfectly, but that would be a total lie. I have rebelled at times and certainly disobeyed, and I have fallen short many times. Still, His grace is sufficient and His mercy endures. Repentance is the key. Allowing Him to change your heart as you retrain your thinking in accordance to the Holy Spirit, freedom will develop within you. You will transition from pitiful to powerful. This life will cost you everything, but the benefits are out of this world! Nothing really belongs to us. It belongs to Him. We are only stewards of this Earth and all the fullness He gives.

> Not that I have already obtained it or have already become perfect, but I press on so that I may lay hold of that for which also I was laid hold of by Christ Jesus. Brethren, I do not regard myself as having laid hold of it yet; but one thing I do: forgetting what lies behind and reaching forward to what lies ahead, I press on toward the goal for the prize of the upward call of God in Christ Jesus (Philippians 3:12-14).

A Real Pain in The Neck

"It is still my consolation, and I rejoice in unsparing pain, That I have not denied the words of the Holy One (Job 6:10)."

Life is a funny thing. You sort of put your life on autopilot and go through your daily routine—at least until something comes around the corner and plows over you! You lay in the wake of the disaster and wonder what happened. In 1999, little did I know something so severe was about to happen to me that my life would dramatically change.

I was working at Celanese and had been for seventeen years. It was a fiber plant and the job was manual labor. I worked swing shifts and, for those of you who are not familiar with what that means, I worked on the third shift, the night shift. I worked seven nights with two days off followed by seven nights on the second shift—afternoon till evening, two days off— sometimes these days off were not consecutive—then I worked seven days on the first. After this rotation, we were off for four days.

I was forty-five years old. Two of my friends and I began to see that two things were happening. Our job was changing and we felt like the company was headed toward closing its doors. Meanwhile, the workload was increasing. We were picking up a lot of weight and not getting any younger. We decided to go back to school. I had dropped out of high school before graduating, so I had to finish that step first. It was strange going back to school at my age. I had been out of school twenty-eight years! After finishing high school, I enrolled in some college classes. I decided I would work toward a Medical Office Assistant Degree. It was the quickest curriculum to get through. I didn't have a lot of time to waste at my age. I was healthy. I walked six miles every day besides keeping a house and family going as well as helping my daughter raise her baby who lived with us. My life was fast paced and the last thing I needed was an invisible bulldozer plowing through my life!

In the spring of 1999, I was attending classes five nights a week plus working and getting ready for my son's wedding in May. I started noticing that I did not feel like myself, but who would with a schedule like mine at my age? I passed it off as being tired. I didn't really have any significant symptoms, so I pushed through. One night, in my class of medical terminology, the teacher asked me to stay after class for a minute. It is so crazy, I felt like I was being sent to the principal's office! Mrs. T was a nurse as well as our instructor. She said she wanted to address two issues; the first was my choice in curriculum. She had talked to some of my other teachers and discovered that my grades were well above average. I knew I had gotten good grades on my tests and so forth, but I honestly did not think of myself as smart. Going to school during my growing-up years was a struggle. Our home-life was a test of survival and school was simply something we had to get through. At any rate, Mrs. T was convinced I should go for something more challenging in the medical field, a nurse or medical practitioner. Ha, I thought she was mistaken!

The next thing was almost as surprising as her educational evaluation of me. She said that she had noticed I did not seem myself. She went on to ask if I felt alright and if I had seen a doctor. I did admit to her that she was correct in her observation. I told her that, while there was nothing specific I could put my finger on, I did not feel like myself. She told me to keep an eye out and come to her if she could help in any way.

Not long after this discussion, a couple of weeks before my son's wedding in mid-May, I was on the third shift. No one really feels great working the night shift since our bodies were designed to work during the day and sleep at night. I really wish I had kept a journal because the timeline gets a bit fuzzy, but you will get the general sense of the timing. It was within the first few nights of that shift that I developed a serious headache. That, in itself, is not abnormal. Most people have headaches on the third shift, but I could not pass this off as an ordinary headache. By the time I finished working on my machine and headed for the quiet room—that is what we called our break area because the floor we worked on was very noisy, the pain in my head became extremely intense. It felt as if it balled up in the back of my head and that ball traveled down to my neck and suddenly it felt as if a bomb went off in my head! I walked into the break room and tears were streaming down my face. The intensity of the pain did not last but a few seconds, but the pain became a strong, dull ache that stayed with me for years.

My friend, Pat, was sitting at our table and saw my face streaked with tears. She immediately wanted to know what was wrong and I told her what I had experienced. Of course, she tried to get me to go to first aid. I was having no part of it. I did not trust the company to watch out for my best interest and I really did not like doctors anyway. I was very stubborn and told no one else about the incident, not even Pete. I worked several more nights with that dull, ever-present headache. The last morning of the third shift was a turning point. I really felt terrible. I wasn't really dizzy, I just felt hazy, like I was in a fog. I got lost going home. For the life of me, I could not find my way. I had lived in the same house for twenty-five years and lived in that town all my life. It took me an hour and a half to find my house. I walked in and Pete commented he thought maybe I had gone to eat breakfast with some of the girls. I did something I rarely ever did. I broke into tears and told him I had gotten lost and explained what had happened earlier in the week. He said with a voice I hardly ever heard from him, "*You are going to the doctor now and that is all there is to it.*"

I did not argue.

This began a new and terrifying journey for the next five years. I went through several types of doctors: neurologists, cardiologists, orthopedic specialists. They couldn't figure it out. I did not fit the proverbial box. No joke, I never did. I had brain scans, CAT scans, MRI's, X rays, ultrasounds, tests on my heart, etc. Finally, they sent me to a neurosurgeon. He found through myelograms, which was very painful, that every disc in my neck, with the exception of the very top one where your head sits and is able to turn, had ruptured. Much later, they found evidence of a stroke. These ruptured discs, along with bone spurs, were causing a lot of intrusion into my spinal cord.

The stroke, by most standards, was mild, but it still interfered with my motor skills. My eyesight was very poor due to all the pinching in my spinal cord. I could not turn my head and any movement in my neck was very limited. Words that used to be a normal part of my vocabulary now were missing. Conversation was difficult. That is devastating when you are in ministry; my gift was communication. Reading became a thing of the past. I could hardly keep enough thought process to make sense of a sentence. I did not read a book again for four years. I could not read my Bible. The bones that once held up my head were now so compromised that it forced the large muscles in my back and shoulders to work overtime to support my head. This caused me to look like the hunchback of Notre Dame, which, in turn, limited the use of my arms. They literally froze at my side. I could not fix my hair or clean my hind parts. Well, enough of that. You get the picture. I was a mess! I have always been so independent, but I was about to go through some life-training in many areas.

I want to stop here and assure you of something about which many people get confused. God did not do that to me to teach me a lesson. God does not put sickness or disease on people. Think about it this way: we teach that God is love and He is a good Father. Then we want to turn around and teach that God is going to get us and punish us, what kind of father would do that? God does correct us, but that is not the same as punishing us. There are many reasons we get sick and this book is not for the purpose of teaching that principle. I never once thought God did that to me. I certainly do not have all the answers, but this is one thing about which I am sure. He is love and love does not inflict us with pain or disease. An earthly father that loves his children would never do such a thing and God is far better equipped to love us unconditionally. Enough said. The next few stories will be about specific events throughout this process. You will see God's protection, and, more importantly, the things He taught me through this.

The Journey

"Be gracious to me, O LORD, for I am pining away; Heal me, O LORD, for my bones are dismayed (Psalm 6:2)."

I was in real trouble. The doctor immediately put me out of work. I guess I thought this would be short-lived. I am of the mindset, *"Just get over it!"* Before the neurosurgeon would consider surgery, he wanted to try everything possible. He told me that surgery would change my way of life. I went to physical therapy and that proved disastrous. It works well for most people, but it only made my condition worse. Next came the shots. It was not a fix, but a pain management. I was to have a series of three injections in my neck, each two weeks apart. I got to the pain management center and was prepped. I was only supposed to be there about thirty minutes or so. They do this routinely, so no big deal. Well, it turned out to be a big deal. They offered to sedate me, but I hate medicine and I also have a high pain tolerance. Because the doctor said it would be very uncomfortable but would only last a minute for the needle to go in, I opted out of sedation. I thought I would get out quicker without sedation. I was wrong.

I sat on the side of the bed with my arms and head stretched out face down on top of a table. It was supposed to only take a few minutes. I was warned to stay perfectly still as they were putting needles into my spine. To make a long story short, forty-five minutes later with sweat pouring down my face and pain unimaginable, the doctor standing over me kept saying over and over, "*I do not understand, I just do not understand. The needles will not go in.*" That is not what you want to hear from the doctor who is putting needles in your spine! Why it took him multiple times to figure out what was happening, I have no idea. I just stayed still and prayed to get through it. He finally gave up and left the room.

The nurse was cleaning me and I was able to raise my head. I had blood all over and, on the table, there was a small box with used needles spilling over the top. I was very shaky and asked the nurse how many times he had stuck me. She said she had lost count. I went home where I spent a night in horrible pain. Needless to say, it was unsuccessful. My daughter tried to count the puncture wounds. She counted about thirty that she could see clearly. Two weeks later, I was scheduled for another injection. I had no intention of doing that again. The doctor called for me to come in early to discuss a different procedure. They would put me under Fluoroscopy. This would give them the ability to guide the needle in while watching. Apparently, my discs were so compact that there was very little space between them. This is why the first procedure was so difficult and he kept running into my bones.

This was a different doctor and different procedure, so I consented. The doctor told the nurse to put an IV in my arm. She questioned him because, according to her, they never do that for this procedure. He looked at her as if to say, "*Don't question me,*" so she complied. It turned out to save my life. So, the procedure began and he talked to me assuring me he could see clearly why the other doctor could not get in. The spaces were so small that there was no way he could have gotten in without a visual. He said

I would feel the stick of the needle, and I did. He said I would feel the medicine as it went in, and I did. All was okay, but, as the medicine began to flow through my neck, I started to feel strange. I began to feel foggy. Suddenly, it felt as if someone had removed my throat and I could not swallow. I tried to tell them, but no sound would come out. My body started going numb and I was drifting away. I knew I was dying. I could hear the doctor and nurse, but it sounded as if they were far away. I could hear her tell him my blood pressure was dropping very fast.

I could hear her tell him, "*We are losing her!*"

He said with some panic in his voice, "*This is why I insisted on an IV, don't ever question me again!*"

He went on to tell her how much medication to give me intravenously. It was very strange that, while I could hear everything going on, I was extremely aware that I was dying. I felt calm. I had no fear of dying. I did not see a light like some reports about a near-death experience, but I heard a voice clearly. I knew it was God.

He said, "*You can stay, or you can go. It is up to you this time.*"

In my heart I knew that I had to stay. Pete and Clairey were in the waiting room. I was only supposed to be in and out—it was a normal, everyday procedure. Clairey was around five years old and I knew that, if I died on that table, she may never recover from that trauma. In my spirit, I replied to the Lord, "*I will not die today. You may take me at any other time You choose, but not today.*" Immediately, I felt life returning. I was in that clinic for about four hours. I was hooked up to all types of machines to monitor my vitals. A nurse came in to give me some pain meds. I was in horrific pain. It felt as if two elephants were stomping on my neck, but I refused the meds. I was dry-heaving constantly. I was as sick as I could tolerate and was not about to take something that could, potentially, worsen my condition.

Then the nurse leaned down and whispered, *"If you tell anyone what I am going to tell you, I could lose my job. I don't blame you for not taking any medication with the condition you are in. I cannot explain what happened in there. I have done this for years and I have never seen anything like this take place."* I was supposed to have another injection in two weeks, but that was not going to happen. The doctor called for me to come in for a consultation. He explained that, because my spaces were so small, the injected medicine was the correct amount, but it spilled over onto my spinal cord and caused temporary paralysis.

I really didn't buy it and neither did my primary doctor who sent me to a bone specialist. I told the orthopedist what happened with the injections. He listened and, because he only had my word for it, he had to be careful of his response; he was not about to trash another physician on my word. The specialist said, *"If this happened just the way you said, and I am not saying you are not telling the truth—I have only your word and no official reports to look at—I will tell you this. You should be, at the very least, in a wheelchair, probably for life. In reality, if what happened is what I suspect, according to what you are telling me, you should be dead!"* He then went to the next office leaving the door opened and called my doctor. He was very stern and told my doctor that he should take charge of his patient's well-being and manage my case.

After that, there was no more physical therapy, no more injections. Surgery was now the only option left for me. It had been about a year since that first explosion in my head and I was now facing surgery. The neurosurgeon I was seeing was one of the best in the country. He was with a team of doctors where each one of them specialized in a different part of the spine, especially concerning the neck. He told me my case certainly was not the worst patient case he had, but mine was the worst with no explanation. The type of injuries I had in my neck were only found in serious sports injuries, or being hit by an 18-wheeler, or falling out a window from a tall building. None of these things were my issue.

It was a year after the initial doctor's visit when they found the stroke. I had a minor interruption of blood flow deep in my right side of the brain that affected my left side. My neck issues were so dire that they just thought all the other symptoms I was experiencing were due to the strain on my spinal cord. This was also a freak occurrence; I had no medical reason for a stroke or the ruptured discs. The doctors were baffled by my case. The neurosurgeon conferred with some of the other specialists in his practice and he wanted me to talk to one of them.

I asked him, "*Is he smarter than you?*"

Dr. Henegar laughed, "*He is one of the brighter crayons in the box.*"

He brought the other doctor in to talk to me and his opinion was to fuse all the ruptured discs at one time. His reasoning was because it was going to happen sooner or later. He left the room. I looked at Dr. Henegar and asked if he agreed with the other doctor. He said he preferred not to do them all at once. He did say that, eventually, it would have to be done. He went on to explain that it would drastically change my life and thought it would be too hard for me to adjust being as active as I was.

I asked, "*If I were your mother, or sister, what would you suggest?*"

He replied, "I *would say fuse the worst one and take it one step at a time.*"

"*You are my doctor and I trust you. We will do it your way,*" I replied.

He explained to me what that would look like. I would have an incision in my throat and they would take a piece of bone from my hip to fuse my disc. I would have to wear a large brace collar for twelve weeks at all times, while sleeping or showering, and during the day. Oh joy! During the course of my treatment, the scans showed that my neck was bent the opposite direction. In other words, my neck was bent backward. No wonder I was always different!

Surgery time! The only time I had ever been in the hospital, up to this point, was the two times I had given birth and the time when I was twelve years old and had my tonsils out. This surgery went very well. Dr. Henegar said it should help relieve pain. Besides fusing the disc, he had to remove two bone spurs that were jutting into my spinal cord. He manually manipulated my bone structure so that it was bent a bit more in the right direction. The pain never left. I expected the pain to be present as I healed, but it never let up. I could not read because my eyesight was too affected. Wearing that brace was very restricting. I could not turn my head or lower it. Of course, that was what the brace was for, to stabilize my neck.

There were some good things happening in the process of all this negativity. Although I taught the Bible and lived it as best as I knew how, I had no compassion for people. I felt like everyone should handle crises the way I did. "*Just get over it!*" was my motto of life. When I saw someone suffering from sickness or difficult places in life, I did feel sorry for them, for a moment, but I did not have true compassion. During the time between the stroke and having the first surgery, my niece graduated high school. I went to graduation, of course, and we, as a family, went to eat at an Italian restaurant. It is funny now—it was not then—but I kept walking sideways. Someone would have to gently guide me back in line. Once we got inside to our table, I started to sit down and missed my chair. If that had happened when I was in my 'normal' state, I would have laughed at myself, cracked a joke, and it would have been over, but no one laughed. They all knew I was having a lot of problems with my motor skills.

Have you ever noticed how stroke patients seem to cry for no reason? There are medical explanations for it, but, during this episode of my life, I learned other causes. I did not cry. I would get so angry that I would lose control. When I missed that chair, I went berserk! I turned over chairs, swiped the dishes off the table, and food went flying. I could not stop myself. I was a raging maniac! I remember my oldest sister, with tears in her eyes, stating, "*That is not my sister.*" She was not denying me; she just recognized that I was not the person she knew.

The reason, or at least one of the reasons stroke victims cry, is because they still know what they want to say, what they need to express, but they cannot articulate what is really going on inside them. I was still me and I knew what was going on around me, but it seemed as if I did not exist any longer. Someone I did not recognize now controlled my actions. Through this entire experience, God taught me compassion. Now, I can usually spot a stroke victim easily and my heart breaks for them. That was God at work in me and it has caused me to be a better person and minister.

The first surgery on my neck was in late 2000. It was a difficult year, but it had its great moments too. Shortly after the initial onset of my neck and stroke issues, my son got married. I went shopping to buy my mom a dress for the wedding and the Lord spoke to me and told me that, whatever I bought for her to wear, that is what I would bury her in soon after. The wedding took place in May of 1999 and my mom died in September of that year. We buried her in the lavender suit she wore to the wedding. The following May, my first grandson was born. I am so thankful that, although I was having serious health issues, I was well enough to be present at his birth. I actually got to be present at the birth of all four of my grandchildren. Today, my first grandson, TJ, is a grown man and attends Clemson University. I am very proud of him. Life is strange, even in the midst of turmoil. The good times present themselves and disrupt the negative. That is how it should be. Even Jesus said we would have troubles in this world, but we can still have joy!

Trust

"But as for me, I trust in You, O LORD, I say, 'You are my God (Psalm 31:14).'"

As I said in the previous story, my first of three neck surgeries took place in 2000. In the next five years, I would go through two more surgeries and many changes. Everything we go through in this life, good and bad, gives us opportunity to grow. We can use these times to make us bitter or better. Life is all about change. While my body was going through dramatic changes, my spirit-man was being reshaped as well. I have learned that God does not waste anything. He uses all our circumstances to mold us if we allow Him. Everything is a choice. Maybe we do not get to choose everything that happens to us, but we have the power to choose how it will change us.

I realize that some circumstances are harder to overcome than others. It is really funny how one life-event leads into another season of change. At the time of my mother's death, I was in between churches. I should stop for a moment and take you back a few years, actually more than a few; about twenty years would be more like it.

I mentioned in earlier stories about my brother, aunt, and I would study the Bible together. In November of 1980, my father died. He was really a good man, a hard worker. He always supported his family and I guess he did the best he could, all things considered since he had his own demons to battle. Five months later, in April of 1981, my brother died. It was very hard losing both of them so close together.

During this time, the church I had been attending was falling apart, mostly due to several of us being led by our flesh instead of bringing correction to one another the biblical way. These three major events happened at the early stages of my faith-journey and were really a deterrent from God's purpose in my life and others. It is amazing to me how none of these things rock God off His throne. He has a plan and all He needs us to do is keep a repentant heart and a willingness to continue. Often, what we see as a place where something is broken, it becomes a place to quit. God, however, sees it as a catalyst to the next season. Such was the case in these two deaths and my church's demise. My first pastor, Marvin, he helped shape me by teaching me how to hear from God and move in the gifts of the Holy Spirit.

After the church fell apart and my brother and father dying, I drifted. The book of Hebrews warns us against drifting and neglecting our salvation. I am so grateful God does not give up on us as easily as we give up on Him. It was in 1982 when I went to work at Celanese. I was trying to adjust to not having a church, a brother, or a dad. I was now a working mother of two young children. I was starting to realize that my marriage was not what it should be, but, like many others, I simply kept doing what I knew to do and hoped it would work out for the best.

Eventually, I got back into church, but never quite settled. Fast forward again to where we were earlier in this story.

I was in between churches when my mother died, so I did not have a pastor. My sister, Lucy, had been attending a Southern

Baptist Church, a fairly large church in our area and the pastor was an old high school acquaintance. Actually, Pastor Jerry had been a friend of Pete's in high school when neither of us knew Jesus. Pete had heard Jerry was the pastor of that church and wanted to visit, but I was having no part of it. My reasoning was that I was Pentecostal and they were Southern Baptist, and we had nothing in common. Don't worry, God had a way of getting that self-righteousness out of me!

Remember, it was at this time when my neck had crashed, mom died, and my sister Lucy asked about allowing Pastor Jerry to preach mom's funeral. I said it would be fine. I thought it would kill two birds with one stone. We had someone we were familiar with to preach mom's funeral and Pete would get to hear him and shut up about going to this Baptist church. Problem solved. Ha! I was in for a rude awakening! Pastor Jerry did a great job and, I have to say, the ladies in the church were wonderful. They prepared and served meals for our family. The decent thing to do was to show up at that church and show our appreciation. This is what I told Pete the following Sunday morning after mom's funeral, "*We are going to that Baptist church. We are going to thank Pastor Jerry and give a nice offering and then we are leaving, and I do not want to hear any more about going to the Baptist church!*"

Sunday morning, we went to church. We thanked the ladies for their excellent service and sat down. A man name Ken, whom I had met somewhere, came up to us and invited me to go into the prayer room with him and some others. They always prayed over Pastor Jerry before the morning service. I declined and he continued pressing me to come with him. I had been very hurt in my first church and really did not want to get personally involved again. The problem is, ministry is like the mafia, once you are in, you can never really get out! The whole time Ken was talking to me, my heart was telling me, "*No, no, don't go,*", yet I found myself getting out of my seat.

On the way to the prayer room, I reminded myself that I was Pentecostal and, therefore, they did not pray the way I did, so I needed to stay in the background and keep my prayers quiet. Needless to say, keeping quiet and staying in the background are not my strong suits. We went into this small room filled with people. Pastor Jerry was sitting in the middle of the room. I tried to do what I intended. I stayed by the door thinking maybe I could escape if need be. At that time, Pastor Jerry reached through the small crowd, took my hand, and pulled me toward him. He asked me to pray. Oh my, I really tried to pray their way.

The next thing I knew, I had my hands on his head and began praying in the Spirit—in tongues. Folks, that is not cool in a Southern Baptist Church! At any rate, as hard as I tried, I prayed loud and long. It was a strange experience, even for me. I know that we have control over how we behave and the Holy Spirit never violates our will, but the sense that God was actually doing something beyond my understanding was overwhelming. I felt a bit like Paul when he got knocked off his donkey! Of course, he had choice; however, it probably did not seem as if he had any. I was so lost in the Spirit, meaning the Holy Spirit was on me so heavily that I felt as if I were in another dimension. I remember opening my eyes and I could see lights of different colors bouncing all over the room. I am sure no one else saw it, but some of them were experiencing something out of their comfort zone. One young man seemed to be plastered against the wall.

He was shouting, "*Oh God, oh God.*"

During this episode, the Holy Spirit was showing me some things about the pastor. Finally, everything got quiet, including me. People started leaving the small room. Pastor Jerry stood at the door. I was the last to leave. He stopped me and I figured he would ask me to leave and not return. He did ask me what any self-respecting Southern Baptist minister would:

"Can you interpret that?"

I replied, *"No, but you can!"*

His face was still a bit pale, *"I was afraid of that. I am going to tell you something, I have never told anyone."*

I laughed, *"You mean you have never told anyone to leave your church before?"*

"No, I mean I am going to give you freedom to do what you are here for."

I started walking away as I replied, *"Be careful what you give me, I just might take it."*

I got back to the pew where Pete had been sitting. He was standing holding my purse and Bible. He said, *"Do we need to leave? Everyone could hear you!"*

"Not yet!"

When I sat down, I could feel the stares. I heard the Lord speak to me, *"You are going to stay for a season."*

I explained to the Lord, *"I am not a Baptist."*

He said, *"Neither am I, but you are staying."*

I did, for a bit over seven years. It was difficult at times, but wonderful things took place there. During my time there, God got me out of my "Pentecostalism." He taught me how to use the gifts of the Spirit without everyone knowing what I was doing. He showed me a more natural way so that it could be accepted. It was a fairly large church and I made a lot of good friends, many with who I am still in relationship today. The people in that church helped me through the years of surgery and difficulties concerning my neck issues. They were there for me; they cooked meals, cleaned my home, visited me, and chauffeured me when I could not drive. There were two very special people for whom I will always be grateful: Earl and Nancy. They were at every procedure and surgery. Their daughter, Angie, once left her vacation to bring me a pillow to the emergency room in Charlotte, North Carolina. I had to go to the emergency room after leaving the hospital because my throat was closing up due to the swelling. The emergency room was so busy that they ran out of pillows. I had a huge neck brace on and two large incisions in my throat. Lying flat was not the best position. Angie was called and she brought me a pillow. I always referred to her as my "pillow angel."

~

Living and Dying

"Christ will even now, as always, be exalted in my body, whether by life or by death. For to me, to live is Christ and to die is gain (Philippians 1:20b- 21)."

I talked briefly about my first neck surgery. Somewhere around 2004, or early 2005, the doctor felt I needed to have a surgery where the incisions would be in the back of my neck. It would not be to repair, but rather to clean some debris from around my spinal cord. In doing this, he hoped to relieve some of the symptoms I was having. He also hoped to put off the inevitable "big" surgery that would eventually have to take place. He scheduled the back-of-the-neck surgery. It was, by comparison, an easy surgery. He had to cut through a lot of tiny nerves. This resulted in the feeling of worms crawling. It really is remarkable how God has designed the body. I do not understand how a "big bang" could do that! While healing, these tiny nerves were working to reconnect to the severed ends. It felt like worms crawling. It was horrible! It felt as though it was itching, but scratching was useless. This lasted about six weeks. The surgery was a failure. It did not help my condition.

Dr. Henegar told me that it was a matter of time until it would become necessary to do the surgery he had tried to avoid. He informed me that he would have to depend on me to let him know when I could not go any further in the pain and difficulties I was experiencing. He also told me this surgery would change the quality of my life. I would not be able to work and do normal everyday duties, even driving would be difficult. He would have to fuse my entire neck and place a bar with screws the entire length of my neck. He said that, when it was time, he would go into more detail.

Over the next six months, the pain got worse and everyday life became harder to handle. I mentioned this briefly in a previous story, but I want to give you a short recap of where I was physically. I was unable to read for four years due to my compromised spinal cord. It really messed with my eyesight. I could not drive because I could not turn my head. For a lot of that time, I could not raise or lower my arms. The strength in my neck was greatly affected. Because my neck bones were so weakened, they could not hold up my head. The main muscles in my shoulders and upper back took over, which affected my bodily functions. I was a serious mess!

Even in that state, the grace of Almighty God was sufficient. I could still teach Sunday school. It is funny now how I functioned. Because of the stroke, words would escape me. My friend, Tina, would sit on the first row. She knew me so well and my style of teaching that she would immediately fill in the blanks for me. How awesome is our Father? One particular Sunday morning, I was teaching on the peace of God. While speaking, I heard the voice of the Holy Spirit speaking to me. It is important for you to understand that I was in a Southern Baptist church teaching an adult class of men and women—God can be a rule-breaker! The people in my class loved me even though I did things out of their comfort zone. I stopped teaching while holding up my hand, *Please give me a minute, the Holy Spirit is speaking to me.* Of course, they were used to me doing the weird stuff.

The Holy Spirit told me to call my doctor on Monday morning and tell him I needed to schedule my neck surgery. I would need to have the surgery within the next two weeks. He also gave me strict orders to not allow the doctor to tell me the negative possibilities of the outcome because the outcome was not his business. The Holy Spirit did tell me that Dr. Henegar was the best man for the job and he had been picked by God to take care of me. Dr. Henegar had already told me earlier that this surgery would be difficult and would, more than likely, put extreme limitations on what I would be able to do physically for the rest of my life. He also said that this surgery could be life-threatening.

Monday morning, I put in a call to Dr. Henegar. His secretary said she would have him call. Within an hour, he returned my call. I told him what I had been instructed to tell him and, of course, he wanted to know why I felt I needed the surgery within two weeks. *"Dr. Henegar, I do not expect you to understand this, but this is what the Holy Spirit instructed me to do. I am in more pain and it is getting more difficult, but I am not sure why the time is two weeks. I just know the voice of God and I trust Him."*

"Well," he replied, *"I have to trust your judgment. I will bring you and Pete in early this week to go over the details of what this surgery might entail."*

"That won't be necessary. The Holy Spirit said the outcome is none of your business. He went on to say that you are the best man for the job. I am interested to know how much you have to cut me. You can tell me that now."

"I guess that is as high of a recommendation as it gets," Dr. Henegar laughed.

He went on to explain that I would have two fairly large incisions in the front of my throat and I would have a lot of swelling and bruising. At that point, I told him that was all the detail I needed. He said he would have his assistant call me with the surgery date and details. The surgery was set within the next ten days. Over the next week, I found out why the Holy Spirit had told me to do it within the next two weeks. Just a couple of days later, after setting the date for surgery, I was at home alone. I simply turned my head a bit to the right and everything went black. I did not pass out, but I became disoriented and lost my vision. I crawled as I felt my way to the bed and lay there until it passed—about forty-five minutes. I felt a little weak, but continued with my day. I did not mention it to anyone. A few days just before surgery, I was getting ready for my uncle's retirement dinner when it happened again. This time, it was worse and lasted over an hour. I still did not tell anyone. I spent the next few days preparing for surgery.

STORY 44

A Day of Miracles

"This I know that God is for me (Psalm 56:9)."

2005 was the year of a major turning point in my life. Although I had two other surgeries on my neck, this was the big one! The attending nurse was preparing me for surgery when Dr. Henegar came in to tell me what would be taking place in the next hour.

"Sandy, how many pastors do you have?"

I knew there were a lot of people in the waiting room, so I asked him, *"How many are out there saying they are my pastor?"*

He laughed, *"Somewhere between twelve and fifteen."*

Of course, I knew that, while they may have been all pastors, they were not really *my* pastors. I told the doctor to send Johnny Shaw in. Johnny Shaw was the youth pastor at my church. He was a quiet, humble man. Everyone loved him. It was kind of funny; I really never had a lot of interaction with Johnny. It was a fairly large church, so I was a bit surprised when I found out he was out in the waiting room. Johnny was ushered back to pray for me before they took me to surgery. He is such an unpretentious man. He began to explain why he was feeling a bit awkward. He said he could never pray as well as me or some of the other pastors. I told him I did not want him to pray like anyone else. This is what he prayed and I have never forgotten the simplistic beauty of what he said, "*Breathe in grace and blow out mercy!*" Still, today, when I am unsure of how to pray in a situation, I use that prayer.

It was show time!

The surgery took almost five hours. They fused every disc in my neck except for the one that had been fused in the first surgery and the top disc that turns your head. They placed a bar with eight screws down the front of my neck to brace and strengthen my neck. I had two significant incisions in the front of my throat. They were trying to get me off the table as soon as possible and working in such a tight place that, when they put the bar at the top, they tore my esophagus. Finally, I was taken to the recovery area. As I woke up, I could barely get out a raspy whisper. Certainly, that was to be expected. I had a torn esophagus, two large incisions, and a lot of swelling and bruising. My throat was swollen, even with my chin. I could feel something in my throat. The attendant with me was awesome and very reassuring as I tried to tell him there was something in my throat. He assured me that there was nothing there. He explained to me that I was feeling the swelling.

I knew it was more than that. I had not eaten since noon the day before because anesthesia makes me extremely sick. The last thing I needed to do was start vomiting or dry heaving with incisions in my throat. I tried to cough it up. I put my fingers in my mouth and, from the top of my throat, I pulled a string of carrot out. I had eaten seafood and coleslaw the day before and the coleslaw was chopped very coarse. The medical attendant looked at me with total shock. He immediately called Dr. Henegar while putting the carrot string into a small container. Dr. Henegar came down to recovery and I could tell he was a bit annoyed. He is a busy man and had other surgeries that day. The attendant held up the small vial and Dr. Henegar looked at it with disbelief.

"This is impossible! If that had been in her throat during surgery, she would have choked to death before we could have stopped it!" The doctor was obviously perplexed.

The attendant explained, *"That is why I called you. I watched her pull this from her throat."*

The doctor left instructions for the attendant to watch my vitals carefully and call him if any problems arose. I was finally taken to my room where I began to get a little sick from the movement. The nurse took my blood pressure. It was higher than it needed to be. She wanted to have me moved back downstairs to recovery. I told her. *"No, I do not want to move again because it caused me to be nauseated."* She was obviously in the last stages of pregnancy and seemed a bit stressed. I asked her to turn off the overhead light and leave the room for a few minutes and I would get my blood pressure under control. I am sure she was wondering how I was going to do that. She told me she was not supposed to leave me alone and, because I had just gotten out of surgery, she really should send me back to recovery. I guess my insistence was strong enough. She finally consented to leave the room. After she had turned out the light and left the room, I got very still and began to quietly pray in tongues. Within minutes, she was back and took my blood pressure. It was normal.

I was scheduled to stay in the hospital seven days, but, by the next day, I wanted to go home. Of course, the doctor said, *"No."*

That afternoon, I told the nurse my throat was closing. I could not even get water to go down. She tried to tell me it was just the swelling, but she looked at it anyway. She went, straight away, to the nurse's station and spoke to a female doctor who was making her rounds. I could hear her explain to the doctor with urgency in her voice. The doctor who was not part of my doctor's practice looked in my throat and called Dr. Henegar and explained that my throat had, indeed, closed. He authorized her to give me a shot of steroids to open my throat. The medication acted quickly.

I rested a few minutes and got up to brush my teeth and freshen up. I was not supposed to be out of bed. Dr. Henegar came in and admonished me for being out of bed and insisted I get back in it. He said he needed to talk to me and Pete.

Dr. Henegar sat down and began, "*I have to apologize to you, Sandy. I nearly let this go too far. Did something happen in the last two weeks that you did not tell me?*"

I felt a little uneasy because I had not told anyone about the two times my eyesight went black or becoming disoriented. I told him about those episodes.

"*That explains some of what I saw as I was working on you,*" he said. "*Every disc in your neck was so compacted that it had pinched your spinal cord till it was doubled over! I don't understand how you are still alive or, at the very least, not paralyzed in a wheelchair. On top of that, how we missed that carrot string in your throat, I don't know. That should have caused a serious problem. I do not understand how you have survived.*"

I simply held up my finger to point toward Heaven, I whispered, "*God.*"

128

I then asked him if I could go home. He said that he would feel better if I stayed a week, but, if no more problems arose, he would let me go home on the third day. The next day, I went home. However, that proved to be a wrong decision. Later in the evening of my first day at home, I felt my throat closing up. Pete called the doctor and he instructed us to get to the hospital at once. We were preparing to leave and I silently prayed for someone to show up to pray for me. We opened the door and there stood a man named Marvin from our church. He prayed and we left. Let me give you some serious advice. Never go to the emergency room during a full moon! I am not kidding. Every weird person in town must think that is where the party is. The emergency room was full. The waiting room did not have an empty seat. Because I had just had major surgery three days before, they took me back immediately.

There I received another shot of steroids and, because of the recent surgery, they had to take some x-rays to check for blood clots. The test came back and showed a spot in my lungs. It was not a blood clot, but it was something that had to be watched over the next few months. I had mentioned in the story just before this one about my "pillow angel." It was during this hospital visit that Angie brought me that pillow. That may seem a small thing, but when you are in serious pain and you have a neck brace on with incisions in your throat, a pillow is a God-gift! I was released. I went home and began another leg of my journey.

Fight for Life

"You have armed me with strength for the battle
(Psalm 18:39, NLT)."

Surgery and being put to sleep takes its toll on a person's body. I guess we all think that, once surgery is over and healing progresses, we will be back to normal. It is not always that easy. Dr. Henegar had warned me, all through the process, that my life would be very different after the last surgery. Early in the process, he informed me that, once it got to the point of having to fuse all the discs in my neck, I would no longer be able to do many everyday things.

The muscles in my neck had not yet gotten the memo concerning the bar in my neck. They were still trying to do the work of holding up my head. I was unable to move my arms very much. I could not touch my head or lower them enough to go beyond my waist. This left me unable to fix my hair or clean the lower parts of my body. I was extremely weak. I could not stand, sit, or lie down for any length of time. My body was so stiff that I had to constantly move, which was not an easy task. The pain was horrific. I refused to take pain medication until I just could not stand it any longer.

I could not read. My eyesight was poor. I constantly felt like I was in a fog.

Before this whole neck thing happened, I was extremely active. I worked a full-time job, walked six miles a day, and went to school at night. That was besides doing ministry and keeping up with housework. A few years later, I had to be evaluated to see if I was able to return to work. I spent eight hours doing all sorts of physical and mental testing for endurance and dexterity. The lady administering the test told me that, if she went solely on the results of the tests, she would have determined me to be a much older woman who sat on the couch eating junk food all day. I had lost that much ground. The moral of this story is, don't put your faith in the physical accomplishments, but rather the eternal. At the same time, I probably would not have survived at all had I not been in good physical shape.

I knew that, if I were to ever start living again, I would have to push beyond where I was. Friends had sent me dozens and dozens of cards. I could not read a book or my Bible. I had Pete hang all the cards on the walls at my eye-level. They were on every wall in every room. I would stand in front of each card and focus my eyes to read the encouraging words. Most of them had Scriptures on them, so they became my Bible. Others had funny sayings and that became my entertainment. I would always look at the names of the senders and silently pray for them. This was my prayer life. They were short enough I could comprehend them. Those cards actually were my therapy. It is sad that, in today's world of internet, we no longer send cards. I would go to the kitchen table and walk around the edges and wipe with a dish cloth. The edges were all I could reach. My family would tell me to sit down and they would do it. Cleaning the table was not my objective, staying active was. I was determined to not give up!

Pete had taken a couple of weeks off work to stay with me. I could not eat unless someone was with me. I would get choked very easily. I could not take a bath alone because I was so weak. However, life goes on and he had to return to work. He worked at night, so he would help me eat and get ready for bed. My son had offered to stay with me at night, but I told him I would be fine. Everyone knew that I could not talk on the phone because I could hardly speak above a whisper. I had also asked not to receive flowers because I am so practical. I would rather have something that would last. I got a lot of gowns and pjs and several sets of the Bible on cassette tapes. That really dates this story; most of you probably do not remember using those!

Pete returned to work and I was propped on the couch. I thought I might fall asleep when, all of a sudden, the air seemed to get heavy. I felt as though something was covering me like a blanket. I recognized it as being spiritual. Fear—irrational, terrifying fear—settled on me. Fear without cause makes absolutely no sense in the natural. That's because it is not natural, it is demonic. I fought it the way I taught others to fight fear. I prayed. I listened to the Word on tape. It was not working. In my understanding, I knew I was fine, but fear is beyond normal reasoning. I felt vulnerable and alone in the battle. Then God showed up! Not in spirit form, not an angel, not a mysterious voice out of Heaven, but the ringing of the telephone.

I picked up the phone and, in a raspy whisper, I said, "*Hello.*"

My Aunt Barbara was on the other end, "*Sandy, don't try to talk. I just wanted to tell you that I will be there tomorrow to spend the day with you. Bye.*"

I stood there holding onto the receiver—this was in the day when we used land lines—as if it were a life raft. Tears ran down my face. It was just a phone call, right? No, it was deliverance! The minute I heard her voice, the fear that had overtaken me just moments before left as quickly as it came. I prayed and gave thanks to God. I asked Him why fear left the moment I heard her voice. He said, "*She abides in me and I abide in her.*" I once heard that "*abide in Christ*" means you are comfortable in His presence and He is comfortable in yours. The enemy of our soul is not comfortable in peace.

> "By this we know that we abide in Him, and He in us, because He has given us of His Spirit (1 John 4:13)."

STORY 46

❧

Lost and Found

"Restore us to You, O LORD, that we may be restored; Renew our days as of old (Lamentations 5:21)."

During the years of illness, I lost many abilities, but God gave back to me everything I needed. One of the things I did not get back was the ability to quote Scripture. Seriously, before the stroke and my neck injuries, I could quote most of the Scriptures, chapter and verse. I lost that ability and asked God to restore it and He said, *"No."* He told me He never liked my doing it because I trusted my ability more than I trusted the Holy Spirit. OUCH! He also said it makes other people feel inferior and God is never into elitism. God is not against us learning to quote Scripture; He is against us being prideful. I was prideful. He would get a lot of that out of me in time.

Even in our dysfunctions while we are growing, changing, and maturing, God gives us love-nudges all the way. One of the sweetest things He did for me happened at a Perry Stone Conference. As I said in a previous story, I could not read for about four years. I could read a very short paragraph, a single Scripture, if I could focus my eyes well enough. But, to read a book or study the Bible was just not possible. My Aunt Barbara and I had attended Perry Stone conferences many years. This time, our husbands went with us. It was at the end of my healing process from my last surgery. We attended the partner dinner where numbers were drawn to see who would receive the gifts. One of the gifts was a large basket filled with all Perry Stone's newest books. I silently prayed and asked God to give it to me. My number was not drawn but my husband's was and he hates reading! I had a lot of catching up to do.

∽

God's Glory

"And in that day, you will say, 'Give thanks to the LORD, call on His name. Make known His deeds among the peoples; make them remember that His name is exalted (Isaiah 12:4).'"

Years after all the tests, multiple doctors, therapy, injections, brain scans, MRI's, CT Scans, Myelograms, and three neck surgeries resulting in five incisions in the neck and throat, a titanium bar with screws, not to mention the tremendous pain and loss of strength, I am still here! After all this, it was a slow climb to freedom. One day, I was going to visit a friend in the hospital in Charlotte, North Carolina. I was looking for his room and passed by a group of doctors. I really did not look at them and walked past them.

I heard someone say, *"Mrs. Starnes, Sandy! Is that you?"*

I stopped and realized it was Dr. Henegar. He was looking at me with utter amazement. He exclaimed, *"You look amazing!"*

Dr. Henegar is a very handsome, much younger man than me. He was not trying to be cute. He was very sincere. He also was not a talkative man; I always found him to be very serious and focused.

"Thank you. I feel great."

He asked how long it had been since he saw me as a patient and I told him over ten years. He then admitted something that I found surprising, knowing him to always be extremely professional.

"I probably should not tell you this, even though you are not currently my patient. I really did not think you would live. I certainly thought that, if you did live, you would more than likely be bound to a wheelchair," he said.

It was startling to hear this from him. He would never overstep proper protocol as a doctor as he has great integrity. He was amazed at my appearance and ability to function.

He went on to say, *"I cannot believe how well you look! How did you overcome so well?"*

I simply held up my forefinger toward Heaven. He smiled, something I did not see him do a lot as my surgeon, and said, *"That is what you always said."* God is faithful. You may not see the results right away, but stay the course, keep the faith, learn in the process what God may be doing in you. Trust Him. He loves you.

"Yet those who wait for the LORD will gain new strength; they will mount up with wings like eagles, they will run and not get tired, they will walk and not become weary (Isaiah 40:31)."

STORY 48

~

Endings

"Truly, truly, I say to you, unless a grain of wheat falls into the Earth and dies, it remains alone; but if it dies, it bears much fruit (John 12:24)."

There comes a turning point in every person's life. Truth be told, there is probably more than one turning point, but at least one of these turning places are more significant that all the others. This is a story where I have to choose carefully what and how I tell it. I do not have a need to cause any pain or embarrassment to anyone. The problem with new beginnings is that it also means an ending to something else. For me, a new chapter and major turning point in my life also created a new beginning and an ending in my family's life.

I will spare you the details. I know that, for many of you, you would like the details, but divorce is painful and there is no way to do it well. There is always a story behind the story. There is her side and his side and, somewhere in the middle, is the complete truth of the matter.

I would like to skip this story altogether; however, it must be told for the purpose of making sense of all the events that got me where I am now and all the provisions of God. Pete and I married in 1973. We met when we were thirteen years old, and, as we grew older, we continued to date. Pete graduated high school—I quit in the tenth grade—and turned nineteen shortly thereafter. We married in July and I turned nineteen in August.

Some of the details are sprinkled here and there in previous stories. Some might wonder why I would include so much of my former marriage when I am now in a different marriage. Much of my life was involved with Pete, so there is no way it can or should be ignored. We were married for thirty-four years when I left home. There wasn't any one thing I could say that brought it to a close. It is a compilation of many small issues, and then there are the major things that happen in the course of a lifetime. We tend to ignore so many of the small problems and continue without properly dealing with them. In so doing, they grow into monsters.

This might be a strange way of writing a story and a different approach to summarizing a lifetime. It may not even be proper writing, but it is my story, so I will take some liberty. I will give a timeline of major events in our marriage. We got married, as I said, in 1973. In 1977, Amy was born. In 1978, Jason came into the world. This is when I first really became aware that something seemed to be missing. I dismissed my feelings of emptiness. I didn't believe in fairytales and I had everything I needed. Just before Jason was born, Pete came home from work and announced he had been fired from his job. Seriously? You have to understand that Pete worked seven days a week and was never late; he never laid out of work. I was eight months pregnant with a child twenty-one months old. This was no time to get fired. It was a stressful time for both of us, but we got through it. This was also the timeframe I became born-again. In 1980, my dad died on Thanksgiving night. Five months later, my only brother died at the age of thirty-four. The following year in 1982, I went to work at a local fiber plant. I only intended to work a year to get us ahead. I stayed for eighteen years. Life goes on.

There is no way to condense all the daily events into story form. Besides, every family has life to deal with. We were no different. In 1994, two extreme events took place. Pete's dad was diagnosed with cancer already in the last stages. He did not want treatment and we kept him home. The company Pete worked for shut down, which actually was a blessing. Financially, we were okay. I encouraged him not to pursue other employment because it gave him the time to stay with his dad. This would be a help to his mom and he would get to spend the last days of his dad's life with him. The other huge event took its toll on our family, friends, and marriage. Our daughter ran away from home. She left with a guy who we had forbidden her to see. I didn't know where she was for two weeks. It was hard to concentrate on anything else. I lost it. I mean, I really lost it. I could not eat. I had to finally take a leave of absence from work. I could not stop crying. This was a strange place for me as I had always been the strong one, nothing really shook me.

Amy had left her family at a time when we really needed to pull together to get through Pete's dad's ordeal. I will not go into the details because I do not want to magnify Amy's wrong choices. She was seventeen years old. Amy's decision brought many emotions to the surface in everyone who knew us. I found myself dealing with my own pain and insecurities and, all the while, trying to defend her to others. What she did was wrong and I was not defending her bad behavior, but I was not willing to throw her away. I will not recount all the details of those next two years; because it won't well serve anyone.

Have you ever swum in the ocean? On the surface, it can look just like it always does, waves always building and moving toward the shore. You can't see what is happening below the surface, yet there are all sorts of life forms swimming. For the most part, they're harmless, but try to swim out of danger and the ocean carries you out further from shore. It is in control. That is how I felt when Amy left home—helpless and out of control. The next two years would have a lasting impact on us as individuals and as a family. Pete's dad died a few months after Amy left home. He was buried on my dad's birthday and, at the time of his funeral, my mom was having surgery. It was, at the very best, a tough day. The battle raged on. It was like that undertow; you get out of it and get to shore, but it takes all your energy. Underneath the surface, though, it leaves its lasting mark on your emotions. It magnifies the weak foundation inside you. Everything is shaken and some of those places, no matter how hard you try to ignore them, they will not go away. It chips away at you until there is nothing left onto which to hold. I am not saying that Amy is the reason Pete and I eventually separated, but it was one more major event that revealed what was already lost.

Two years after Amy left, she returned home with our first grandchild. Clairey was two weeks old when she came to live with us. It is ironic that, in the midst of such pain and suffering life brings, it is mixed with great times. Fun vacations, birthday parties, celebrations of high school graduations, grandchildren— we experienced all these things and tried hard to allow it to be enough. Yet, the nagging disappointments of events not properly dealt with will discolor the good times. You are never really prepared for the last straw. That last straw usually is an insignificant occurrence. Sometimes you can't even identify the last straw.

Clairey was born in 1996. In 1999, all the discs in my neck crashed and I had a stroke. That was also the year my mom died. In 2000, our first grandson, TJ, was born, so stinking cute with his dimpled cheeks! 2001 brought the arrival of our second grandson, Gabriel. He was one of the funniest kids, always making us laugh. Then, 2002 brought a big surprise as Elizabeth burst on the scene! She was our fourth grandchild.

I loved Pete, at least as much as I could understand. In hindsight, I realized I had no idea what love was supposed to be. Pete was and is a good man. He never did the big stuff. He did not cheat or mistreat me in any way. We just did life together as well as we knew how. But, inside me, there was always something missing. There were certainly things Pete could and should have done differently—the same was true of me. I almost hate to say what actually happened because it seems so much like a cheap excuse. In the past, I have said that we just grew apart and that's partly true. However, I think it would be more accurately said that we grew in different directions.

I often teach how most Christians don't deliberately take a sharp turn away from their faith, but rather, they drift. You know, at first, we just find reasons not to go to church and then some of the other things that are a part of our faith-journey start becoming less and less important to maintain. Before you realize it, you are distant in relationship to Christ. You never meant for that to happen, it just does. We, as humans, tend to not evaluate effectively where we are in relationships. This happens in marriage. Life gets busy, major events take place, and we don't stop to evaluate how those things are affecting us emotionally. We simply push it down into what I call our "emotional trash compactor." Pretty soon, that compactor gets filled to overflow and it comes out at a most inconvenient time.

This happened to my marriage with Pete, he thought we were fine, and I pretended that it was just life and I needed to get over it. The problem was that I wasn't sure what the 'it' was. There was nothing to put my finger on and say, "*This is it!*" It was a lifetime of disappointments, frustrations, and unresolved issues. This happens in every marriage. There is a line from an old movie that starred Paul Newman which goes like this, "*What we have here is a failure to communicate.*" That is the crux of the breakdown of every relationship: a failure to communicate. More accurately, it is our failure to communicate effectively. We pack it down into our emotional trash compactor and when those painful memories get stirred up, they erupt! All that unresolved anger gets mixed up together with the current issue and the argument is contaminated with the past failures.

This all seemed to climax in a time where several major things were going on. Our marriage was at a crucial point. No matter how hard Pete and I tried, we simply could not put the brakes on to stop the downward spiral. I had been having some female problems which caused me to bleed for a year. It was going to require me to have a hysterectomy. Pete's job was on the verge of closing down due to the company closing which caused us to have to make quick decisions because our health insurance was through his employment. The hysterectomy was scheduled. What should have been an hour and a half surgery turned into a four-hour ordeal. My uterus had grown six times its normal size and was a difficult process to remove it. I came through it.

My best friend, Lou, was losing her battle with cancer. Just two weeks after my hysterectomy, Lou decides she needs to have a famous TV minister to pray for her healing. She had a dream concerning this man praying for her and was convinced it was from God. Maybe it was, but she was thirty-four years old and had a five-year-old son. She was desperate. The problem was this minister was going to be in Indiana the next week. Lou knew her time was near. I did too. She had already told me she wanted me to be the minister at her funeral. Actually, the Lord had already given me the Scriptures to use when the time came.

Remember, I had just gone through this surgery when Lou informed me, she, and I, were going to Indiana. I reminded her that I had just had surgery and could hardly walk. She said in true Lou fashion that she did not care! Her dad was going to pay our way, but I had to go with her. I could hardly walk, and Lou had to use a wheelchair because she was too weak to walk far. She also needed assistance to get up and down. This meant I would have to pull on her, not a good idea for someone who just had a hysterectomy. Another problem was Lou had to have fluid drained off her liver, and as awful as that was, I thought it would be my saving grace. I thought surely, we could not travel with that situation. However, in true Lou fashion, she had that resolved. She would go into the hospital a few days prior to our trip and have a tube inserted and I would get to drain it while we were gone.

She got the tube done, and she made final arrangements for us to fly to Indiana. The day before we were to leave, Pete and I had a full day of running errands. We went to Charlotte, NC to pick up our glasses and had a great lunch. Later, after returning home we began to talk. For the first time in our marriage, we really talked and listened. We both poured out our hurts and disappointments. Things we had held in and issues we knew existed but never dealt with. We both repented to God and to each other. We probably talked more that day than our whole marriage. I am sorry to say it came too late. I thought that maybe it could be a start, but I still didn't feel the way I needed to in order to work it out. I did not have a plan to leave at this point. Honestly, leaving was not on my radar screen. I already had too many issues at hand to deal with. I still had not regained my strength from surgery and now had to take a trip with my best friend for a last-ditch effort to find hope for her. I already knew her death was not far off, and quite frankly, I was afraid the trip would be too much for her. I was terrified she would die on the trip.

My hormones were raging due to the hysterectomy, between that and knowing my marriage was at the point of no return, I had never been so sad in my life. I felt truly alone and scared. My emotions were in turmoil, I knew I had caused a lot of hurt in Pete, I was a blubbering mess! It was only the goodness of God that got me through that trip. She never got the prayer from the minister she desired. We returned home. I went home and things between Pete and I got worse.

I had agreed to do a revival some weeks prior to my surgery and our trip. It was too late to cancel. Pete became increasingly hostile as I became more emotionally distant. I was not sleeping and between trying to deal with exhaustion, unbalanced hormones and my best friend losing her battle, I had to get away. My oldest sister had built a house out in the country about fifteen miles from my house. She built it even though she still lived and worked in Virginia. She expected to retire early and that did not pan out. I had the keys to her house and asked if I could stay for a few weeks. I told Pete that I needed to get somewhere quiet where I could prepare for Lou's impending funeral and study for the revival and get some much-needed rest. He agreed. I never thought for one minute that it would become permanent. I had every expectation of staying until I returned from Missouri then I would go home and try to work out our differences.

I took the books I needed for study and enough clothes and personal items for my trip. I left home on June 28, 2006. Lou died a few days later. Her funeral was the first funeral I ever did. It was very difficult. She had worked for the local phone company besides being a worship leader at several churches, so she was well known. The church was packed. News travels fast, especially bad news. People from the church I had attended and the people of the church where I was, were all there. They had all heard that I had left Pete. They forgot to tell the whole truth, that I only left for a short while. At least that was my intention at the time. Hostility filled the atmosphere. Everyone was angry with me. Because of dealing with my marital issues, it would be a long time before I could even grieve the loss of my friend. It was hard to keep my emotions in check. I felt like a stone statue as I spoke about Lou.

A week later, I drove to Missouri and did a week-long revival. My friend, Carole, went with me. She was one of very few who stood by me during that time. I will always appreciate her for that. On the way home from Missouri, I just knew I was not going to return home. I did not plan it that way, I just knew I was not going back. I called Pete, before I could tell him, he said it for me. He said he knew that I would not return home.

STORY 49

Beginnings

"Though your beginning was insignificant, yet your end will increase greatly (Job 8:7)."

I was fifty-two years old when I left my home and marriage to Pete. I made eight dollars an hour without benefits. That is crazy! It is okay for you to think it, I thought it myself. What was I going to do? It was a blessing to have my sister's home to live in. She was a tremendous help to me. I would live there for a year and a half before getting my own home.

It was not all easy. I was in the middle of great change. I had never lived on my own. I not only left my husband but my granddaughters as well. I missed them more than I can say. I worked three jobs most of the time that first year. I changed churches and changed jobs. I lost friends, many of them could not understand what I was doing. I suppose many thought I left for another man. I guess after being single for over twelve years, that notion played itself out. Everything was different. Holidays were painful. I am sure Pete suffered during that time as well and I get no pleasure from that.

I could go into a lot of personal detail, but these stories are not for the purpose of showing who was at fault. These stories are to share my journey of becoming who I was meant to be. They are to show how God changed me and is still changing me. I want to show how remarkable God's provision was.

When I left home, I worked for a small fire extinguisher business. Shortly after I left, I decided to change cars. I had an SUV and decided to get a smaller car. My sister's house was out in the middle of nowhere and gas was eating me alive. I went to the Hyundai dealership and test-drove an Elantra and decided to purchase it. The salesman asked me to come to work for him. I laughed and told him I knew nothing about selling cars. He said I would work upstairs in the internet department. I figured I may as well change jobs; everything else in my life was changing. Besides, I would make a little bit more money and I would have insurance benefits.

I'm sure this is not true of all car dealerships, or at least I hope it is not, but, spiritually, that was the darkest place I have ever been. There were some Christians working there, but the overall atmosphere was saturated with selfishness. The name of the game was money. It was a dog-eat-dog world. On my first day at work, I found out the job was to call people on the phone to promote car sales. Ugh, I hated that! About half-way through the morning, the sales manager called upstairs and asked me to come to his office. He explained that a woman was coming in to purchase a car, but she would only deal with a woman salesperson. He said he understood I had never sold a car, but he had observed that I was a people-person and he would put an experienced person with me. I told him that I would not lie to this woman to sell a car. Kenny was the lucky salesman put with me to help sell this car. The lady and her husband came in and decided on a vehicle to purchase.

The lead manager was standing with us as we were talking over details when the lady asked a question, "*I know that*

Sandy is in training, but she will get the commission off of this sale, correct?"

Everyone was silent for a split second, and the manager spoke up, *"Of course, whatever it takes."*

I looked at Kenny and the look on his face told me how he felt. I spoke up immediately, *"No sir, it is not okay for me to get the commission. Kenny has to do all the actual work. I am in training and not qualified to do the paperwork. The commission should go to Kenny."*

It felt as if the air had been sucked out of the room. I am sure the manager was thinking of ways to kill me. After all, I had just questioned his authority. We all were pretty sure we had lost the sale and I was pretty sure I would be looking for another job. After a long pause, the customer walked over to me and reached out to pick up my necklace. My friend, Lou, had bought it for me. It was a small replica of the breastplate of the high priest of the Old Testament.

It was as though she forgot why we were there and asked me, *"Are you a student of the Old Testament?"*

"Yes," I replied. *"I teach the Scriptures and I especially like the Old Testament."*

"What is your favorite subject to teach?"

"The Tabernacle, although I also like to teach on the priest garments."

Suddenly, she turned and walked over to the manager and pointed her finger in his face and said, "*You better be thankful you had the good sense to hire someone with integrity, because you don't have any! We will purchase two cars.*"

You could have heard a pin drop! She then counted out cash for both brand-new vehicles! Kenny got the commission and I won his respect, which allowed me to share some Biblical truth with him later. I quickly became known as "the preacher." News travels fast and one of the mechanics from the back came up to meet me and asked me to start a prayer group. I asked him why he didn't start one and he replied that he was too chicken to ask the general manager who was also the owner of the dealership. I always viewed it this way: everyone puts their pants on the same way, so no one is better than anyone else. I went to the office door of the General Manager and knocked on it.

"*Come in.*" He looked at me and asked who I was. I told him and he just grunted and asked me to state my business because he was very busy.

"*I would like to start a prayer group around lunch time each day. I promise it will not interfere with anyone's work schedule. I will hold it for around thirty minutes and anyone who is free may participate. If they are called to the showroom floor they will leave immediately.*"

He looked at me as if I had said I wanted to blow up the building, "*Why would I let you do that?*"

I took a deep breath and replied with confidence, "*Because you like money and you like success selling cars. I will make you a deal. Allow me to do this and we will pray for this dealership to sell more cars than ever. As a matter of fact, if you don't sell at least twice the cars as normal for this time of year, I will not only stop the prayer time, but I will quietly leave this employment."*

He must love a challenge or either he was hoping I would fail and he would be rid of me, *"Okay, I will let you do it, but it better not interfere with anyone's work."*

I figured I had already hung myself out to dry. I thought that I may as well go all the way, so I said, *"Thank you. Before I leave may I pray for you?"*

"Why would I let you do that?"

"Well, unless I am really mistaken, you are not a teenager, so the acne on your face is probably from stress and, as I said, you like success so I will pray for that."

"Lady, you are pushing it."

"May I hold your hand while I pray? I promise to keep it brief."

He reluctantly held out his hand and I kept my word and prayed a short prayer for his well-being. That particular season was known in the car selling business as one of the slowest times and car sales were usually down. However, when God is involved, things are subject to change. I knew I had the authority to make a promise of increased sales. That month, sales not only doubled, but almost tripled! God is faithful. I hated working there, but God allowed me to impact some lives and He gave me enormous favor while working there. There is a song that has a line in it, *"If life hands you a lemon, start making lemonade."*

~

Unpleasant Places

"The lines have fallen to me in pleasant places; indeed, my heritage is beautiful to me (Psalm 16:6)."

Maybe you just read the title and the Scripture and you are thinking, *"That sounds like an oxymoron."* If you think about it, you will see that it often takes negative or difficult situations in order for you to get where you really need to be. Let me give an example.

Jesus had to experience a friend's betrayal to get to the cross. Thank God for the kiss of Judas! If you remember the story, Peter, Jesus' other disciple, tried to hold Jesus back from the cross and Jesus called him Satan. Why? Because Peter did not want to see his friend and Savior leave him. In Peter's attempt to hold Jesus back, he was really keeping Jesus from his destiny. Judas, on the other hand, in his betrayal of Jesus, literally propelled Jesus into fulfilling His mandate of reconciling mankind back to the Father. So, you see, an unpleasant kiss gave us the benefit of belonging to a pleasant place in the Kingdom of God!.

Like many of you, I have made many mistakes and wrong choices, and all of them motivated by selfish intentions. The Lord told me once, *"Sandy, you had to go to every place you have been in order to be where you are right now."* Let me make something very clear. God was not saying He approved of my wrongdoing so I could be where I am. God will never condone sin. It is just that simple, but if Romans 8:28 is correct, then all things work out for my good. Only God could take something I made a mess out of and work it out for my good. Of course, it has stipulations; we have a part to play. People are always asking me how I know what to do to be in God's will. This is my reply, *"I don't. I get up each day and just do what is before me. If that means washing dishes, I wash the dishes."* Everything we do takes us somewhere. I have seen the favor of God, but I realize it is not because I do everything correctly. It is because He has a plan for me. He does not want our help. That may come as a surprise to you, but when we try to help God, we usually get in His way. So, what are we supposed to do? It is easier than you might think. We make it hard by trying to be so religious. All He wants us to do is cooperate and trust Him.

> "If you continue in My word, then you are truly disciples of Mine, and you will know the truth, and the truth will make you free (John 8: 31-32)."

We are very good at quoting half of this Scripture. We will say, *"The truth will set you free."* That is a pile of garbage. The truth does not always set you free. You may know something to be true, but just knowing does not bring freedom. In other words, you may know that you are fifty pounds overweight, that may be true, but unless you take action, the truth will not set you free. The Scripture says you must continue in His word, meaning, you must be obedient and live His instructions as a way of life. Leaving home and being on my own put me on a fast-track of learning to live "the truth" in a way I never knew possible. At this point in my life, I had served the Lord for over thirty years. I was about to enter a whole new dimension. I knew how to do church and I knew how to do ministry. I lived it as best as I could, at least I trained myself to believe that. Looking back, I can see what God was doing. He was taking me on a journey to live in Kingdom dynamics. You might ask, "*What is the difference?*" My answer would be, "*Everything.*"

The first year living at my sister's house, I struggled with everything. My life, as I knew it, ceased to be. I spent a lot of time working; I worked a full-time job and two part-time jobs. Still, I never seemed to have enough. My sister was so good to me. She came to visit her new home about every two weeks. Yeah, I know that sounds funny, but she still lived in Virginia. She would pay all the utilities and she always made sure the fridge and cabinets were stocked with food. She really was a blessing to me and still is.

Early in the time I left home, I changed jobs, church, friends, and lifestyle. Everything was different. I was no longer invited to speak or participate in social activities. I was left out due to leaving my husband, but, even in that, God was training me. My sister's house was out in the middle of thirty acres and in the backside of nowhere. When I wasn't working, it became very lonely. It was very quiet in the evenings. I hardly watched TV, but, one night, I turned it on just to have some background noise and I heard the Lord speak to me, "*Turn it off. I am going to teach you how to be single.*" When I heard Him say that, I thought He meant He would teach me how to be alone, but "single" and "alone" are two different things. I would learn the difference in times to come.

I look back now and understand a little bit better what God was doing with me.I worked three jobs and still had little money,. Most of my friends were gone. Ministry as I knew it vanished. It was difficult and confusing. But God was teaching me to rely on Him. First, He had to allow everything I had trusted to burn itself out. There were things I had taught simply because the Bible said so, but I had not experienced them. I said earlier that, although I worked three jobs, I never seemed to have enough money. That is because I looked at money through a world view. I would learn much later how to see the value of money through Kingdom eyes. I first had to learn that God is not only the Creator of the Universe, nor is He only the Supreme Being, but He is my Father. I had taught that principle, I knew that intellectually because I believed the Scriptures, but I did not have a revelation of that in my heart. That was about to change.

~

A Day to Remember

"Call to Me and I will answer you, and I will tell you great and mighty things, which you do not know (Jeremiah 33:3)."

There are many stories I would like to share, but it would take volumes to put into writing all the stories I have. Besides, some of them would not serve the purpose of this book. I really hesitated to share this particular story because it is going to be controversial, at the very least. Had I not heard it for myself, I, too, would have a hard time accepting it. Nevertheless, it is important for someone to hear this or I would not feel the Spirit of God urging me to tell it. I certainly don't need the negative comments it is sure to bring. It will challenge your theology—it did mine. Here it goes.

It was the beginning of July 2006. As previously stated, I left home June 28, 2006. My sister, in whose home I was living, called and told me she wanted to have a cookout in the next few weeks. I certainly had no reason to have a problem with that. It was her home. Her next words were a problem to me, however. Again, it was her home and I had no right to challenge her decision. She wanted to have it on Saturday, July 22, and she wanted to invite the family—the entire family. That meant all my sisters, my children, and even my estranged husband, if he wanted to come. I understood his invitation because Pete had been a part of our family for many years and they loved him. Still, I thought, "*THE FAMILY! Oh, my God! Just what I need—the family!*" All my sisters would be there to tell me how wrong I was. They were not against me; they just didn't understand or agree with leaving Pete. My daughter was very angry and had taken sides with Pete. My son probably would not come, not because he was angry, but he doesn't participate much in family affairs. I knew it was not going to be pleasant for me even if Pete didn't come, and he didn't. I am sure my sister had not thought of the date she picked. It was the date of my wedding anniversary. Oh, help me Jesus!

The week before the barbeque, I tried to get the house ready so that my sister would not have a lot of cleaning to do. I also spent a lot of time crying out to God. I can't say I was really praying, at least not in faith. It was more a crying out in desperation. I bet you know what I'm talking about. It went something like this, "*Oh, God, did I do the right thing? Did I do the right thing?*" Over and over, I cried out that plea for an answer. I guess I wanted to know if leaving Pete was acceptable to God. God does hate divorce, but, as I have learned, He does not hate it because it is sin, although divorce is always a result of sin. He hates it for many reasons. Divorce is a breaking of covenant and God is very serious about covenant. Divorce splinters lives and not just the couple breaking up. It hurts the very fabric of our society. Nevertheless, there is life after divorce. If it is repented and submitted to God, He will bring healing and work out the details.

On this dreadful and fearful day of the barbeque, I had determined to meet the opposition head on. I was standing in the kitchen waiting for the crowd to come. Aunt Barbara and her granddaughter, Carley, were the first to arrive. This was good news to me. She was always there for me. Carley was somewhere between seven or eight years old. She came running into the kitchen with her beautiful red hair flying. She abruptly stopped right in front of me.

She looked up at me and said, *"I had a dream about you."*

"You did? Did I win a million dollars in the dream?"

With a puzzled look on her face she answered, *"No."*

I laughed and asked, *"Will you tell me your dream?"*

She began, *"You were standing in a big field and two really big angels came and picked you up."*

"Oh my!" I exclaimed. *"Did I die?"*

"No, you didn't die. They flew you up to Heaven right into the room where God sits in His big chair."

"You mean the Throne room?"

"Yep, that is what my Maw Maw—Aunt Barbara—called it."

I started to understand this was not just an ordinary dream, so I responded, *"How cool is that?"*

Ignoring my question, she continued, *"Do you know what God did?"*

"No, tell me."

"He picked you up like you were a little, tiny, whiney baby!"

By this time, I knew God had given her a dream with a message for me. Tears were forming in my eyes, *"Wow, how cool is that?"*

Ignoring my question again, she continued, *"When He picked you up, He started rocking you like you were His baby!"*

With tears now flowing down my cheeks, I waited for her to continue.

"Do you want to know what He said to you?"

I did what I always did when I felt uncomfortable. I asked a silly question, *"Carley, you mean you could hear Him?"*

She looked at me like that was the stupidest question ever and replied matter-of-factly, *"Well, it was my dream!"* I apologized for interrupting her and told her to go on and tell me what God said. *"He just kept rocking you and He looked down at you and said, 'You did the right thing!'"*

I was stunned! I could not believe what I was hearing from this small, red haired, beauty. So, I asked her, *"He said, what?"*

"He said you did the right thing."

I totally lost it! I could no longer keep my composure. The strain of the day and the impact of her dream along with God replying to my prayer of desperation several days before became too much. I ran to my room and locked my door. I was totally undone! That was about fourteen years ago at the writing of this book, and even as I am writing it, I am hearing the Spirit of the Lord. He is impressing me with the understanding that, even then, I had no idea what God was teaching me. I understood that He was revealing to me that He is my Father. I always knew that in my intellect. I believed the Bible, but I never had the experience of that truth until Carley shared her dream with me. I believe what the Lord is showing me is that He could not take me down the path that was to follow until He revealed Himself to me as my Father. That was the kickoff to what was to come. You will see that unfold in the stories that follow.

God did not answer my prayer of desperation because I was begging and pleading—God responds to faith. He did not tell me I did the right thing because He loved me more than Pete. He answered me because He had something to teach me in order to serve His Kingdom purpose. He wasn't putting His seal of approval on my divorce. He looks beyond where we are to take us where He needs us to be. All He requires is a repentant heart and a willingness to cooperate. Look at the story of Apostle Paul's conversion in the Book of Acts. God did not go down the list of Paul's wrongdoing. He simply told him what His purpose was for the future.

We try to tell God why we can't do what He wants us to do and He is not interested in excuses. He is interested in obedience and we can trust Him to work out the details. We are His problem. I do want to remind us that all sin has its consequence lest anyone thinks we can just do what we want and God doesn't care. We still have to deal with the fallout and remember that our actions affect other people and God *does* care about that.

~

Now Faith

"Faith is the confidence that what we hope for will actually happen; it gives us assurance about things we cannot see (Hebrews 11:1)."

Buckle your seatbelts—this will be hard for some of you to handle. A few years ago, God said to me, *"Sandy, you had to go every place you have been to be where you are right now."* Whoa, that is heavy! It is funny how you can hear something and you may not understand how all that works, but you also know what God did *not* mean. He was not saying that He approved of all my wrong choices or sin. Every decision we make takes us somewhere, be it good or bad.

Stop for a moment and think about where you are—in your home or the job, friends you have made, situations with which you are dealing—and think about the choices that brought you there. Think about your health. While it is true that some things happen for reasons out of our control, most of us suffer because of wrong choices. By the same token, some of the good things in our lives are due to the right choices we make. Thank God that He is able to deliver us and set our feet on a different course!. He will use anything to change us into the likeness of His Son, Jesus, if we allow Him.

I look back at my life and I can honestly say that I am grateful for my childhood. As hard as it was, it helped me become the person I am today, even though it created some of my brokenness, which, in turn, influenced some of my messed-up choices. I can now have a testimony of God's grace. I am thankful for the neck issues. Through it, God gave me compassion for others who have ongoing illness. In the middle of the crises, we don't see what good could possibly come out of it. God also told me, "*Faith moves My hand, but gratitude moves My heart.*" You will see through the next few stories how gratitude played a great part in promoting faith. Everything God does, and is, promotes faith. Hebrews 11:6 states, "*And it is impossible to please God without faith.*"

If you read the entire eleventh chapter of Hebrews, you find, for example, it was faith that prompted Noah to build a huge boat without seeing rain. The faith of the people listed in Hebrews was not in their faith in themselves, but their faith in God. How do we build our faith to build an ark when we don't see the rain? That, my friend, is a good question. We acquire that kind of faith through trusting Him in the small things one step at a time. That is how I grew in faith. Could I build an ark large enough to hold everything necessary to replenish the whole Earth? Probably not, but maybe I can show you how I grew into a faith strong enough to sustain my life without income for a very long time. You will read how God taught me to trust Him for everything from panties to living without income and still pay my bills on time. Even as I retell these stories, I find myself wondering why in the world would a God who can speak the universe into existence with only His Word care about changing a girl from the wrong side of the tracks into someone who could speak on His behalf. Amazing! Do you know that is exactly what He wants to do with all His creation?

"For the anxious longing of the creation waits eagerly for the revealing of the sons of God (Romans 8: 19)."

I want to help you understand that you did not become a new creature in Christ to be a servant or to stay busy in your church. Christ did not die just to save you from hell and have you believe that your mandate is to just make it to Heaven. He died and rose again to produce in you a son of God. He brought you into the Kingdom of God to be an ambassador of His Kingdom. We are to be an expression of His will, on Earth as it is in Heaven. God never referred to us as "Christians." It is not a bad term. Acts 11:26 says that they were first called Christians at Antioch. That is the term given to Christ's followers, mainly because, after being converted, they no longer acted like the heathens. Folks in Antioch figured it was because they were acting like Christ. But God only refers to us as sons, citizens, ambassadors, to name a few.

While we are physically citizens of the country to which we belong, mine is the United States of America, as Christ-Followers, we are citizens of Heaven as stated in Ephesians 2:19. In reality, we have dual citizenship. A citizen has the privilege of the benefits of the government under which one lives. I not only have the benefits provided by the government of the United States, I also have the benefits of the Kingdom of Heaven. Do you have any idea how that looks? Think about it. In Heaven, there is no sickness, poverty, sorrow, etc., just to name a few. There is no lack. Compare that to how you live and, if you are not experiencing those things, maybe you need to get some revelation from your Father in Heaven. This is not to condemn you, but it is to help you be aware that there is more to your faith-journey than that to which you have tapped. We are also ambassadors for God. Many people want to know what their ministry is and it is really simple.

2 Corinthians 5:20 tells us we are ambassadors for Christ. Verse 18 tells us He has given us the ministry of reconciliation. That is the ministry of every Believer. We are to reconcile others to God through Christ by the power of the Holy Spirit. Wow! An ambassador is one who represents the government of his or her country. They speak as

the King Himself. We are also called "sons of God." Even if you are a woman, you are still a son because it has nothing to do with gender and everything to do with the One living inside you. Because we are sons, we have access to every benefit of Heaven. In God's eyes, we are equal with Jesus because Jesus replaced your life with His.

> "For you are all sons of God through faith in Christ Jesus (Galatians 3:26)."

> "Because you are sons, God has sent forth the Spirit of His Son into our hearts, crying, 'Abba! Father (Galatians 4:6)!'"

> "The Spirit Himself testifies with our spirit that we are children of God, and if children, heirs also, heirs of God and fellow heirs with Christ, if indeed we suffer with Him so that we may also be glorified with Him (Romans 8:16-17)."

You may be wondering why I am teaching instead of sticking to the business of telling my story. That is a fair question. The answer is that the Word of God and coming into more understanding of how it works in everyday life is my story. Besides, teaching the Word is what I do. It is my hope that, through my stories of how God shaped me, it will encourage you to live a life of power and get out of the trap of religion that tells you that just getting to Heaven is the ultimate goal. The ultimate goal of the Spirit is to teach us how to live a life of freedom, peace, and joy right where we are. So, you see, I must back up my stories with the Word of God or they are just stories. The next set of stories is going to be about the real-life experiences of a woman who starts a whole new life. But, more importantly, these stories are about the goodness of God teaching His daughter how to live a life totally dependent on Him.

STORY 53

~

Appointed Places

From one human being He created all races of people and made
them live throughout the whole Earth. He Himself fixed beforehand
the exact times and the limits of the places where they would live.
He did this so that they would look for Him, and perhaps find Him
as they felt around for Him. Yet God is actually not far from any
one of us; as someone has said, "In Him we live and move and exist
(Acts 17:26-28)."

There is nothing outside of the presence of God. In Genesis, the
Bible tells us that the Earth was without form and empty and dark
until God showed up. Our lives are like that. We really are just
going through the motions until we allow Him to call in light. He
is that light.

As I said earlier, I left my home and marriage in June 2006, and
lived in my sister's house for about a year and a half. Shortly after that, she finally retired from the CIA and moved back into her
home. I stayed for a few more months before moving out on my
own. I didn't see how I could ever afford a place, although I had
changed jobs and made a little bit more money. It still wasn't enough,
but God had a plan. A few months before Pat—my sister—retired,

I decided I needed to look for another job. The job at the car dealership had served its purpose. I saw an ad for an assistant manager at a place that hired day-workers. This place hired folks who, for whatever reason, could not get employment through regular means. Due to drugs, severe alcohol use, prison records, and other social dysfunctions, they often wanted to work enough to get the next round of drugs or alcohol. Most of these people lived in the woods in tents or large boxes under bridges or abandoned buildings. Occasionally, several of them would pool their money and rent a hotel room for the night for a shower and to sleep in a real bed. There were some that were truly trying to work to make a better life. This group of people had, in the past, used drugs, lost their driver's license, or had a police record that kept them from getting a regular job. I could write a book on my experiences there. I saw God change lives as a few were open to prayer. It was a true mission field. Just remember, whenever you see folks like these, don't discount their value as human beings. Jesus died for them also.

One day after work I was driving home and the Lord told me to write a children's book. I laughed. I said out loud, *"Please! I don't even like children!"* Certainly, I was just joking. I really do like children, but I had no idea of how to write a children's book. I had taken a course on how to write for publication thinking I would one day write a book about my childhood. I even started it, but, when my mother passed away, I felt it was disrespectful and put it away. The Lord continued as if I had said nothing. He told me how to write it, the characters, the setting, and the title. I started working on it, but it went slowly since I had too many other issues with which to deal. I only tell you this because the writing of this book has significance to other stories. I knew I couldn't live with my sister forever, but I had no idea how to make enough money to pay rent or buy a house. My sister was gracious and would have let me stay indefinitely, but she needed and deserved to have her home to herself.

I was teaching a Bible study at the home of an older man who was a chaplain with a very well-known ministry. One night, I arrived early and noticed a lady's purse on the table. This man, Harold, had been divorced over forty years and was around eighty years old. He was in excellent health and one of the godliest persons I ever knew. After the Bible study that night, Harold made an announcement. He was getting married. It was a shock to us all. We—his friends—did not know he had been seeing anyone. As I said, he had been divorced for at least forty years after his former wife left him. We were happy for him. I went to see him the next day and asked why he had waited so long. He said he felt like he was not free to marry again as long as his ex-wife was alive. He said it was his conviction and he did not necessarily believe that was the case for everyone, just himself. His ex-wife had just died and he was free to pursue marriage with Donna.

His plan was to move into Donna's home and he said he wanted to give me his bedroom suit. I told him that I greatly appreciated his offer, but getting a place of my own was not even on my radar as I could not afford it. This was early summer of 2007. Then he told me something that, I have to admit, I thought was him simply being nice. He told me I would need the bedroom suit because I would have a place of my own before the end of the year. I smiled and thanked him, but I really could not see that happening. But God. I put the bedroom suit in my sister's garage. I had not taken anything from my former home except the few furniture items that had been in my prayer/study room. I also took my personal items, study books, some dishes, and such things I thought, one day, would be given to my grandchildren. Other than those few things, I gave Pete the house and all its furnishings.

Home

"And everyone who has left houses or brothers or sisters or father or mother or children or farms for My name's sake, will receive many times as much, and will inherit eternal life (Matthew 19:29)."

I told you earlier about working at the day labor job. Although I made a little bit more money than I did at the car dealership, it was still not enough to live on my own. My sister, Pat, with I lived, decided to purchase a double-wide mobile home from our sister, Barbara. Pat had the idea of remodeling it and renting it to me. Since Pat does nothing half-way, I knew that, by the time she was through, it would be a showroom home, one I would never be able to afford. Through one of our customers at the day-labor job, I was offered a position making quite a bit more money. It is so funny how God works in just the right timing! The day Jeff offered me a job, Pat called to say she had changed her mind about buying the house, but suggested I call Barbara and try to get it. I called Jeff to make sure the job offer was still good and when I would start. I already knew the money would be enough as long as my sister and brother-in-law would work with me. I called my brother-in-law and talked to him. I was very honest with him and told him I was interested in buying the house, but I had a few requirements I needed him to do the work necessary to make it livable. I also needed him to use his money to do the work, and I needed to keep my payments at a very low amount! I also needed him to finance it for me. I knew it was asking a lot. He was very quiet and then he said, *"I'll do that for you."*

I want to make it clear so there is no misunderstanding. God was not rewarding me for leaving my husband. That is not how He works. He was providing for me for the intent of His purpose—a purpose I could not see, but, nevertheless, He was working out a plan for my life. My brother-in-law and sister worked extremely hard to get the house ready for me. They laid new flooring, put in new bathroom fixtures, replaced doors, painted, and made it look nice. We went to a lawyer and had papers drawn, even though there were no banks involved. They financed it themselves and kept my payment at my requested rate.

In a previous story, I told you that I left nearly everything behind when I left Pete. I had no furniture or household items. It is amazing how God works out the details. Pat had moved into her home during the summer of 2007. She had her home fully furnished while I lived there. She had a small apartment in Virginia, so, when she moved into her home, she had two of everything. Irons, dish sets, toasters, silverware, towels, lamps, TV, and the list goes on. My friends gave me a housewarming party, so I received pots and pans and some of the other items I needed. Now, that might not be a big deal to some of you, but I had everything I needed without any money. That, my friends, is a big deal! Oh, that bedroom suit Harold gave me and told me I would need it before the end of the year, I moved it into my house two weeks before Christmas 2007. Hallmark movies have nothing on me—talk about a Christmas miracle. God knows how to do it big!

There were times, before this house came available, that I would think about having a place of my own, although I could not see it as a real possibility. I've never been one who felt the need to have an extravagant house. What I did envision was a small house with a window over the sink, a large deck on the back of the house, a front porch, and at least one large bedroom with its own bath. Guess what? My little home had it all. Don't tell me God is not a good, good Father!

Life was good and I stayed busy. Christmas that year was difficult because of my family division. Emotions were at an all-time high and none of us had learned to move beyond our hurts and failures. One of the problems with separation is no one has a rule book on how to handle the holidays, deaths, and other life situations. I guess it is different for everyone. That first year I was separated, Pete's grandmother died. Although a couple might split, the relationships you develop do not just go away. I loved her—she was my grandmother too. I wasn't sure what to do. It felt strange to not go and pay my respects, but I wasn't sure if I would be welcome. I had been involved with his family since I was thirteen years old. Pat saved the day, as she did so many times in my life. She called and said she would attend the funeral with me. I could not have done it without her as I didn't know what to expect. Pete seemed genuinely glad to see me there, although I'm sure it was as awkward for him as it was for me. We got through it.

Someone should write a book on divorce etiquette. Of course, everyone's story is different, so what might work in one situation would not work in another. That is why it is important to develop a personal relationship with the Lord. He is the only one diverse enough to work out personal details. In any divorce situation, there are a lot of firsts; this is especially difficult when the marriage has been a long one. I had to learn how to do everything without a husband to help. I cannot tell you how good God was to me to put people in my life to help with the smallest to the most serious things I would have to face.

Father, today I am sure someone reading this is in need of some intervention in a life situation. I ask You, on their behalf, to send a friend, stranger, or anyone who will act on Your behalf to speak a word of life. I pray that they will receive You! Amen

STORY 55

~

A New Beginning

"Now I declare new things...(Isaiah 42:9)."

Life is filled with new beginnings and endings. Life is about seasons and seasons change. Certainly, some things are meant to last forever, like marriage; however, we all know that does not always work. Still, it is painful and you must allow God to heal and reset your future. Like I said in the previous story, I now had a home. I moved in two weeks before Christmas 2007. I had no idea of the changes coming. If I had, I probably would have freaked out! I had started my new job as the office secretary/manager for Jeff. At some point in the first few weeks, the Lord spoke to me and gave me a Scripture. *"Let the peace of Christ rule in your hearts, to which indeed you were called in one body: and be thankful* (Colossians 3:15)." Okay, good verse, but why did God give that to me? I asked Him. It is funny how, if you ask Him, He will answer you. He told me I was to be intentional about allowing peace to rule my heart because my job was going to end in six months.

"*What?*" I thought, "*That couldn't be! God just gave me this job, why would He give me a job that was going to last such a short time?*" I understand life is about seasons, but this made absolutely no sense to me. If I had not known the voice of God, I would have been screaming, *"Get behind me Satan!"* But I knew it was God speaking. Again, I asked Him, *"Why did you let me take this job if You knew it was going to end so soon?"* I need to take a break here and tell you something else that had happened. In the early part of 2008, I had taken my granddaughters to live with me. When I asked God about my job, I was thinking about the house I just bought and having two girls for which to care. It didn't make sense that God would provide me with a house and the care of two girls knowing my job was going to end. I asked about that and this is what He told me.

> *"I wanted you to have the house,"* God stated without further explanation.

> I'm sorry, I needed more than that, so I inquired, *"Why did you let me take the job knowing it was going to end so soon. I could have stayed at my previous job, at least it was going to last."*

> Again, God said, *"I wanted you to have the house."*

I finally understood that, if I had not taken this job, I would have never bought the house and I would not have a place to bring the girls. Still, I had a house payment and all those expenses that come with it and two more mouths to feed. I almost forgot. I also had a word from God—the Scripture from Colossians. I made up my mind to trust Him. I decided to be intentional about letting peace rule my heart. Be thankful. That is a major key in having the favor of God working on your behalf. I did what I knew to do. I printed that Scripture multiple times and hung them all over my office. Several days later, Jeff came into the office and saw the new artwork and asked me about them.

"Why are these hanging here?"

"To remind me to be thankful and not fear when my job ends in six months."

With a look of shock and a bit of anger on his face, he asked, *"Did one of the guys call you and tell you that? I told them not to mention it. Sandy, I am sorry, I'm having some issues with the IRS and you have about six months, so start looking for a job."*

He told me he really felt bad about it because he knew I had just gotten a house and had taken the girls to live with me. I assured him it was okay. God had prepared me. Just as God had said, my job ended exactly six months after I started. I would love to tell you my faith did not waver, but it did! I panicked and went to work in a small office within days of leaving my other job. I was in that job for three hours and knew I was there outside God's will. I have never just quit a job. I was fearful of being without a job. I had two children depending on me. I have had many women tell me how hard it is to be a single mom and I know that the struggle is real, but you should try being a single grandmother! I called my pastor and got his voicemail. This is the message I left,

"Hey Chuck, don't you have a word for me?"

He called me back in about twenty minutes. He has a booming voice, and, when I answered, he was laughing, *"I have never told anyone to just quit a job, but you are not supposed to be there."*

I knew he was telling me the truth. Chuck has a strong work ethic and he has a no-nonsense way of approaching life issues. I knew I could trust him. I went in and told my boss I was sorry to have wasted her time, but I really needed to go home. She was very upset with me, but my agenda was to be obedient to God, not to people-please. I went home. Because I quit my job, I was disqualified from receiving unemployment. I asked the Lord if I should apply for food stamp assistance?

He replied, "*No, it is not wrong for others, but it is wrong for you, I want you to trust Me.*"

I was on my way to learn lessons on how to live by faith. I thought I had, in times past, but I was about to learn about a walk of faith on steroids! I found myself without income. I mean no, nada, absolutely none. I did, however, receive a monthly benevolence, which was a blessing from my church more than covering my main bills. I was very grateful. I was not on staff, but I was accepted as a minister and participated in the ministry, so this was a way of compensation.

I started cleaning two houses, which produced some income. My sister and Chuck both paid me to clean once a week. Seriously, they were doing me a favor as their houses were kept clean. I was appreciative. One day, my sister Pat called to say that she would not be able to pay me to clean due to some unexpected obligations. That was okay. She told me she would help me anyway she could and I knew she meant it. The next day, Chuck called to ask me to lunch. I told him about my sister not needing me anymore, but that I was okay with it even though it was half my income. Chuck got the "Chuck look" on his face.

"*What?*" I asked, "*Why do you have that look on your face?*"

He began slowly as if he was afraid to speak the words. Believe me when I tell you, Chuck wasn't scared of much of anything. *"Well, I hate to tell you this, but you are not going to be cleaning my house anymore either. It has nothing to do with money. Dr. Bruce—a chiropractor in our church—said that, due to your neck difficulties, you shouldn't sweep and mop. I am not going to let you do anything that is going to harm you. We will pray and see what God wants to do about the money."*

I knew there was no need to argue with him. We finished eating lunch and I went home. It was time to get spiritual-minded. After all, this was not a problem I could solve in the natural. I tried to go to work, but God said, *"No."* I did not believe the church was supposed to just give me money. The only place I could turn was to God, which is where I should have initially looked to start with. I began by having a conversation with God.

"Lord, if the brook is drying up as it did with Elijah, just tell me and I will go where you want."

"Do you want to talk about Elijah?" I could sense from the tone of God's voice that He was about to tell me something I might not want to hear.

The Lord continued, *"What happened to Elijah?"* I didn't like where this was going.

I said to the Lord, *"Please don't send me to the widow of Zarephath. I am the poorest woman in town!"* I think God missed my attempt at humor or either He was not in a joking mood.

"What happened when Elijah went to the widow and asked for a cake of bread?"

"Lord, You know what happened. She gave him her last bit of meal and oil."

The Lord said to me, *"If you will trust Me, I will see that you have an abundance of meal, which is your provision and enough oil, which is your anointing. Do not talk to me again concerning finances until you do the two things I already told you to do!"*

Whoa! All I wanted to do, at that point, was run and hide. But hide where? I felt like David when he asked in Psalm 139, *"Where can I go from Your Spirit? Or where can I flee from Your presence?"* There was nothing to do but finish the two tasks He had already laid for me. It is funny how you can forget something and, when it is necessary, you will remember. I knew exactly what He meant, and it had not been recent when God told me, on two separate occasions, to apply for my retirement from Celanese and finish my children's book. He had told me, a few months before, to apply for my retirement and I tried to explain to Him that was not the smartest thing to do. I explained that, if I took it this early, I would only receive a fraction of what I could get if I waited even a couple of years. Either God did not understand how things in our financial system worked, or He didn't care. I think that, because He is God, he gets it; He just isn't concerned about anything that overrides His Word. First, I repented for my disobedience and my lack of faith. I completed the online paperwork and submitted it. Next, I got out my manuscript of *Finley: The Fish with Tales from the Sea of Galilee*. I only had one chapter left to finish and it took me about an hour. Done! I had no idea of what to do with it next, but I felt a sense of relief.

Somewhere, in the next couple hours, I received a phone call. I was being given a donation of five hundred dollars a month. My lost earnings from cleaning houses was four-hundred dollars. In addition, I would be receiving almost four-hundred dollars from my retirement. Obedience to God's instruction always brings blessings. Things were certainly looking up. I didn't have a clue what the next step was concerning my book, but I would soon find out.

Preachers, Preachers, and More Preachers!

"Yet they shall be ministers in My sanctuary, having oversight at the gates of the house and ministering in the house…(Ezekiel 44:11)."

One Sunday morning, during our church fellowship, a young man came up to me and told me he had heard that I had written a children's book. He volunteered to illustrate it. He was a professional artist with a family, and his wife was due to have a baby. He was very busy. Almost a year passed and he still did not have any progress on my illustrations. I noticed he started avoiding me at church. I was not upset about the illustrations, but I guess he felt embarrassed. I finally went to him and asked for my manuscript back. I told him I knew he was too busy to work on it and I was not in the least bit upset, but I did not want it to cause a division between us at church. I think he was relieved. I also had figured out that, perhaps, he was not the one God had appointed to be the illustrator. I had no idea how to find an illustrator and I didn't have any money, so I would wait on God to bring someone into the picture. God already had a plan. Sure He did. He is God and what He starts, He will see to it.

Meanwhile, Chuck called and told me he wanted to invite some ministers over to his house to fellowship and get to know them. He would cook steaks and he really knew how to do that well. His plan was to invite around fifteen people. During this time, we, as a church body, were trying to get a deeper understanding of how to work as a team of ministers as described in the fourth chapter of Ephesians: apostles, prophets, evangelists, pastors, and teachers. Now, many of you reading this may have been taught that some of these do not exist anymore, especially apostles and prophets. We have no problem accepting pastors, evangelists, and teachers. I don't want to take too much time explaining this because that is not the purpose of this book. I will take a moment, though, to challenge your thinking because teaching the Word is what I do. I want this book to build your faith in God and to help you to hunger for His Word and learn things you took for granted because it is what you have been taught. I have two sets of questions for those of you who have believed that apostles and prophets no longer exist. Ephesians 4:11-13 reads, "*And He gave some as apostles, and some as prophets, and some as evangelists, and some as pastors and teachers, for the equipping of the saints for the work of service, to the building up of the body of Christ; until we all attain to the unity of the faith, and of the knowledge of the son of God, to a mature man, to the measure of the stature which belongs to the fullness of Christ.*"

1. Does it, in any way, give a division between the ministries? Is the Scripture broken that would indicate that the Apostle Paul is talking about two groups of people? Apostles and prophets. Evangelist, pastors, and teachers. No, he doesn't. Who are we to change God's Word?

2. Are we still the New Testament Church? Yes! Has Jesus returned and made the Scriptures of the New Testament fulfilled so as to be of no more use to us? No. Therefore, all the Scriptures of the New Testament are needed for our use. I could go on with this challenge, but I think you get the picture. Now, just ask the Holy Spirit to show you truth. That is who He is and that is what He does. Back to the story.

Chuck and I had met some people we recognized as having these gifts of ministry and wanted to see what God was doing. We were going to have the gathering at Chuck's house. At least that was his plan until I mentioned it to my friend, Scott, who lives in Georgia. Scott wanted to come and asked if he could invite some others who fit into this idea of the five-fold ministry—that is how many ministers describe the ministry in Ephesians 4.

I said, "*Sure!*" Before I knew it, our guest-list had grown. I figured I better let Chuck know that we might have a few more than planned, so I called him.

"*Hello.*"

"*Hey Chuck, I need to tell you that I invited a few people and we might need to change where we are going to have it.*"

"*Sandy, what have you done? How many do you think we are going to have?*"

Cringing inside, I replied, "*About fifty.*"

"*What? Oh my! Is there anything else I should know?*"

"Well, yes, Holly—who is in a power chair—wants to come, so we need to have access for her."

"Whew, this changes everything. We will have it at the chiropractor's office as it will handle the crowd and allow Holly access. Instead of me cooking steaks, we will do pot-luck."

"Thanks Chuck."

"Sandy."

"Yeah?"

"Stay off the phone. Don't invite anymore."

Laughing, I said *"Okay, I'll try to behave."*

Many of the people coming were from out of state, so I invited them to hang out at my house; several of them spent the night. I had people in every corner of my small home. I never saw so many ministers in one place. I had apostles, prophets, evangelists, pastors, and teachers everywhere! The next evening, people began to gather at the chiropractic office. There ended up being around fifty or more people. Most of them were ministers in some capacity. We brought covered dishes, so we shared a meal. Chuck had invited my spiritual father, James Shinn, to be our guest speaker. It was a Holy Ghost throw-down! People received ministry.

There was a couple from Georgia named Jerry and Heidi. I had previously met Jerry, but not his wife. Heidi was sitting against the wall. When I looked at her, the Lord spoke to my heart and instructed me to go over to her and tell her that I was going to be her spiritual mother. That is a very unusual thing for me to say. I have many spiritual sons and daughters, but I have never gone to someone to initiate it. I went over to her and told her what the Lord had told me. She just looked at me and said. "*Okay.*" We did not have a clue that would be such a defining moment in both our lives. Three months later, her natural mother passed away. I am still her spiritual mother and we have a close relationship.

I'm uncertain how to describe that night except to say it was extreme. That was also the night Holly told me she was going to illustrate my children's book. I didn't know she could draw. As we talked later, she told me that the Lord had told her she would illustrate a children's book one day. Well, as it turns out, not only did she illustrate both my children's books, but she eventually published them also. Folks, please understand that, when something does not work out the way you thought it would or should have, God knows exactly what He is doing and He always does it well and right on time.

It Cost What?

"For which one of you, when he wants to build a tower, does not first sit down and calculate the cost to see if he has enough to complete it (Luke 14:28)."

I wasn't building a tower, but when I found out how much it cost to publish a book, I was dumbfounded! I knew nothing about publishing. I finished the book and Holly drew the illustrations. The next step was to find a publisher. Holly had used a specific publisher for her book. I sent my manuscript and it was accepted. Then they said it would normally cost four thousand dollars and it would take a year to process. Four thousand dollars? It may as well have been four million! I was truly living by faith. I did what all daughters should do. I talked to my Father—my heavenly Father. He told me to write a letter and send it to my friends. I told them my need and, if they felt led to help me, any gift would be appreciated. You need to understand how much it took for me to do this. I was raised by a man who would never take anything for which he didn't work. He did not believe in charity. I guess the apple doesn't fall far from the tree. Additionally, I had never done ministry expecting money in exchange, but nothing about my life resembled where I had been. The Lord instructed me to put aside every monetary gift that came in for the book without adding it up.

I had a trip planned to a Perry Stone conference in Tennessee. I had been invited by some of the girls from Missouri to stay at a friend's house, so it would not cost much. I went with the intentions of staying about six days. It does not matter where I go, I always seem to find ministry to do. It just comes naturally. Some strange things happened while I was there. Together with four other ladies, we stayed in the basement of a lady's home. This was no ordinary basement. It was a beautiful apartment. One bedroom, living room, kitchen, and a small sitting room, and there I slept. The bathroom was garnished in green Italian marble and an ornate chandelier. It also had a screened in porch and came onto a patio.

One morning, I woke very early, around four o'clock. I decided I would take my shower and get out the way. When I stood up, my right hip and leg felt as though it were missing. I almost fell and had to hold on to the furniture. I thought I had slept on it wrong, so I lay down and dozed for a few minutes. I got up again, this time more slowly; again, I had to catch myself to keep from falling. It was so strange. I just could not stand. I could hear Ellen in the living room quietly praying. She was a prayer warrior and one of the leaders of the ladies prayer team for Perry Stone's ministry. I held on to the furniture and made my way over to her chair. I told her what was going on with my leg. She also had been a nurse. She immediately began to pray. She said she believed it was a demonic attack and instructed me to go back to bed. The next time I got up, it was completely gone. I never understood what happened.

The next day, we were going over to the conference and I had been invited to dedicate a *Wounded Warrior's House* later in the afternoon. All the ladies had walked to the car. Walking to the car, I stopped at a small table on the patio to adjust my sandal. Suddenly, a swarm of wasps covered my face. I was stung twice on one eye, twice on my lips, and once on my cheek. The ladies jumped out the car and immediately began to pray for me while Doris began to apply some essential oils. My first thought was that my face was going to be swollen and I was concerned about my eye. I was stung on the corner of my eye and on my eye lid. It hurt like crazy. The girls said they had not seen any wasps near that table. Within an hour, there was no evidence of a wasp sting. No redness or swelling! There was no phone service where we were staying. I knew I had gotten several phone calls from the publisher, but could never get through. I had about three more days on the trip and the Lord spoke to me and told me to go home. I told the Lord I would leave the next morning, but He insisted I leave right then. It was late in the afternoon and I knew I would be driving through mountains, but the Lord said, "*Go.*" When I told the girls I had to leave, they all shared their objections, but they helped me pack the car and home I went.

Naturally, I wondered if something was wrong at home and if that was why I needed to leave early. As soon as I cleared the mountains, I called home and all was well. It was a four- hour drive. I got home and saw the amount of times my publisher had called, so I called back thinking that I would not get her that late. I was wrong. She answered and said she was glad to hear from me because she had an offer that would not be available the next day. I knew it was a marketing thing, but it was to my advantage. The original cost was dropped a thousand dollars because Holly was a previous client. She told me that, if I could send her the money that night, she would publish my book for a mere twelve-hundred dollars. If I wanted to go the route of quick publishing, it would cost an extra thousand. That meant I would have my book in three months instead of the usual year. I told her I would call her back in a few minutes. Up to this point, I had not counted the money friends had sent. I had simply turned checks over on my desk and put the cash gifts into an envelope. I got it all together and counted. You will never guess how much I had. Oh, my goodness, I had received twenty-two hundred dollars! Exactly the amount I needed! I had to be home that night to get that benefit.

It is true. God is seldom early, but He is never late. In whatever God is involved, it will work out perfectly. I got my book a few months later. It was a small book, but later, Holly and I decided to re-publish it and we expanded it to be a chapter book. It is such an awesome feeling to see your work in print. I decided, along with Holly's prompting, to write another book, also titled, *Finley the Fish With Tales From The Sea of Galilee, A Story of Purpose*. It was based on the story of the fish with the coin in its mouth that paid the taxes for Jesus. I wrote that book in just a few days. Holly did the illustrations and we had so much fun preparing it. She also published it.

Several years later, we, along with five others, wrote a book titled, *Ordinary People Living Extraordinary Lives*. It's an account of how God has taken seven ordinary lives and transformed them into His extraordinary stories of faith. You can find these books on Amazon, but they will be under my former name, Sandy Starnes, since they were published before I married Ray. If that sounds like a plug for the books, you would be correct—it is!

I want to end this story with a word of encouragement. Most of us seem to drift through life. We grow up, go to school, start working, raise a family, and do all the things we do in the middle of living. Sometimes, we get a glimpse of gifts, hopes, and dreams inside us. Many people get too busy with just doing life and, due to lack of time, resources, energy, or knowing how to get started, we leave our dream of doing something sitting in the recesses of our memory banks. I know that, in my own life, I am not good at starting something out of nothing. However, God has always put fire-starters in my path. I am good at stoking the fire once it has gotten started. This published book is the end result of God placing Alexys in my life to push me to write it and He supplied everything I needed to accomplish it. He did the same with Holly in my first publications. You have no idea of what you are capable with God guiding you.

My encouragement to you is this: if God has put something in your heart to do, in His perfect timing, He will make every provision and opportunity for you to cooperate with Him to bring it to fruition. He knows what you need and when you need it to make it happen. You must trust Him and do your part. Now, go and do!

Hijacked!

"For You alone, O LORD, make me to dwell in safety (Psalm 4:8)."

I have several stories of God's provision and glory concerning trips on airplanes, so I thought I would put them together in one place. I'm pretty sure I mentioned this in an earlier story, but I was almost sixty before I traveled to another country. I have been overseas five times as of the close of 2020. I have traveled by plane many times to different states, yet I have never paid for a plane ticket other than flying to Miami, Florida to get on a cruise ship for vacation. All other tickets have been purchased by someone else. I am not particularly fond of flying. I'm not afraid; I simply prefer not to fly. However, it is the fastest way to get somewhere short of time travel! I will say this; I have had some awesome experiences on planes and in airports. These next few stories are recounts of those times. Growing up without a family car makes getting on an airplane seem impossible. I guess I grew up thinking only rich people could afford to fly, at least until my oldest sister got married and moved to Texas.

In some of the early stories, I shared how, even before I was saved, I sensed I wasn't supposed to do something. I didn't really understand it. I thought I was somehow being stubborn, much like the time right after getting married to Pete and we agreed to move into a mobile home. I decided, for no reason at all, not to do it. Later, during a storm, that mobile home was totally demolished. There were a couple of stories like that.

I was sixteen and I had gone to Texas to stay with my sister, Patsy. She was throwing a baby shower and I was there to help. When it came time to leave for home, Patsy made a flight reservation. This was in the time when some flights were being hijacked to Cuba. I would be flying out of Dallas, Texas into Charlotte, North Carolina. This was big-time stuff for a girl who was from Rock Hill, South Carolina and had never been on plane until that trip. I didn't understand all that high-jacking stuff, I was sixteen. I didn't watch the news because I was busy listening to music and talking to my boyfriend back home.

When Patsy gave me the information about the flight, I just knew I wasn't going to get on that plane! I wasn't scared and I wasn't thinking about possibly being hijacked. I just felt stubborn. I told her to change my flight because I was not getting on that plane. She probably thought I was being stubborn as I was known for that. She didn't argue with me. She simply changed my flight. The flight she had originally booked was, in fact, high-jacked to Cuba! I have to assume, knowing what I know now about spiritual things, I was being led by the Holy Spirit and, I assure you, it was before I could even think about being holy. God is good and He knows what He needs to do before we even know Him.

~

Preaching in the Airport

"Your bond-servants may speak Your word with all confidence (Acts 4:29)."

I was waiting in the airport for my connecting flight in Atlanta, Georgia heading to Missouri to speak in a church. I was just sitting, so I used the opportunity to study. The Holy Spirit was giving me some fresh insight concerning John the Baptist. A man waiting for the same flight was sitting beside me and asked me what I was reading. I picked up my Bible for him to see. I figured he would just grunt and look away like most people, but he didn't. He started asking me questions, so I told him a little bit about John the Baptist. He asked me to practice my message on him!

That was weird, but whatever. I started preaching my message, and, before I knew it, people started gathering around. It didn't take long before I forgot where I was and got into what I was saying. When I looked up, I realized I had quite a crowd and they looked interested. The man beside me asked if he could collect an offering. I laughed and said, *"No."* I didn't think the airport officials would appreciate me soliciting. The people started asking questions. They were not challenging my ability or knowledge, but they were actually interested. It amazes me how many people in our country have very little knowledge of the Bible. When I finished, they applauded!

The man who was still sitting beside me shook my hand and thanked me for my boldness. I'm not so sure he was not an angel in disguise. Maybe you are not a preacher, or perhaps you don't feel qualified to give a message like I did. But, if you have Jesus, you have a testimony and that is all you are responsible for. Be ready in and out of every season to share Christ. He shared Himself with you.

STORY 60

~

Speak to the Storm

"For it is not you who speak, but it is the Spirit of your Father who speaks in you (Matthew 10:20)."

I was in flight headed to Missouri to speak at a church. About half-way, we ran into a terrible storm and the plane was rocking and reeling. Almost every flight has some turbulence. No big deal. On this particular flight, it was a big deal. The plane was not full to capacity, so I was sitting alone on my row. The turbulence became almost violent. The flight attendants buckled themselves in. This, alone, was not disturbing, but the atmosphere in the plane changed as the plane was tossed about. I could literally feel fear rising. The people across the aisle had panic on their faces. I was not fearful, but I was concerned. I began to pray to see what the Lord would have me do. In my life, I try to become part of the solution and not feed into the problem.

I can't remember what year this was, but it probably was somewhere between 2009- 2014. I know, I know. I should have been keeping a journal. As I prayed, the storm got stronger and the plane was really being tossed side to side. Fear was almost tangible. You could feel it. People were clutching their loved ones. Before I really thought about what I was doing, I unbuckled my seatbelt, a big no-no when you are in the middle of a storm on a plane. Those people don't play and you will get arrested. I mean, seriously, they don't know if you are some kind of quack or a terrorist!

I jumped to my feet and smacked my hands together and called in a loud voice, "*Listen to me. Stop that right now, stop being afraid. We are going to be alright. You are a blessed people because you are on this plane with me. I have an assignment from the Lord and we will reach our destination safe and sound.*"

No one made a sound. I thought, "*Okay, any minute now, they are going to rush me and take me down.*" So, I did what I was supposed to do. I prayed out loud, "*In the name of Jesus Christ, I command this ship to stop shaking and sail smoothly through the air, right now!*"

Immediately, that plane stopped rocking and rolling and flying became as smooth as butter. You could hear everyone letting out the breath they had been holding. Fear just dissipated into thin air. Please, do not try this unless you have a direct word or strong influence of the Holy Spirit. No one said a word to me. The glory belongs to God alone. I am grateful He will move through us to bring peace to the storm.

The Glory Belongs to the Lord

"Arise, shine; for your light has come, and the glory of the LORD has risen upon you (Isaiah 60:1)."

The airport is not a place to meander unless you have an extremely long layover. This usually only happens on international flights. It explains why you see people running or walking with purpose. They are trying to get to their gate before they have to board. People rarely look at you or anyone else because they are on a mission. I know because I am usually one of those trying to get there. This particular day turned out to be a bit different.

Am I really that weird because I seem to get involved at airports and on airplanes? I don't intentionally draw attention to myself, but it happens to me a lot. Maybe I have an anointing for it. You will see what I mean. Once again, I was going to Missouri. I go there at least once, if not twice, a year. It appears to be more because I am writing stories about it. These stories stretch out over some years. It is sort of like stories in the book of Acts; we read about all those miracles and it seems as if they are happening one after the other, but, in actuality, they are spread out over years.

On this particular day, I am walking at a brisk pace looking for my gate. I am a people-person and take notice of others around me. Coming from the opposite direction, two airline attendants are walking toward me. They were walking rather fast and talking to each other; nothing unusual about that as they are always on the move. Just as they got a few feet in front of me, they suddenly stopped. It was so abrupt that it almost caused the people behind them to collide into them. I realized they were just staring at me.

I stopped and spoke, *"Hi, is everything alright?"*

One of them looked at me as if I had two heads and asked, *"Ma'am, do you know your hair is glowing?"*

"Excuse me?" I really knew what they were talking about. It wasn't the first time that happened to me.

"Do you have something on your hair? It is not just shining, but actually glowing like something is radiating off of it. It is beautiful, but it's glowing."

"No, honey, I don't have anything on my hair. What you are seeing is the glory of God." I knew they had no idea what I was talking about.

Walking away with puzzled looks on their faces, they replied, *"It looks like glory."*

I laughed as I walked to my gate. When I got there, people were boarding. I had an aisle seat. The lady attendant was coming around checking seatbelts getting ready for takeoff. She had a look of elegance about her. I knew she was a Christ-follower. She walked along with her hands by her side. She was friendly to everyone, but touched no one until she got to me. As she walked by, she put her hand lightly on my shoulder. She kept walking doing her job. She finished and started back down the aisle from behind me. As she passed me, once again, she put her hand very lightly on my shoulder and kept going. She did not touch anyone else that I could see. I knew something had caught her attention. I wondered if my hair was still glowing. A few minutes went by and she was coming towards me. Someone stopped her to ask for something. She walked by me and placed her hand on my shoulder and said, "*You are a minister, aren't you?*"

It was more of a statement than a question and I said, "*Yes.*"

"*Your hair is beautiful. I can see God's glory on it. Would you pray for me?*"

"*Of course. What would you like me to pray about?*"

She explained to me that she lived in Florida, but felt like the Lord was going to relocate her to a place called Fort Mill, SC. She asked me if I had ever heard of it. I told her I lived near there. I asked for her name and told her I would be praying for her. She let me know, very quickly, that she wanted me to pray right there. I told her I didn't mind, but I did not want to cause her any problem with her job. She insisted, so I very quietly prayed for her. I know that some of my stories probably challenge most people. I do not take credit for what God does and I'm not sure I always understand why He does what He does. I do know this: God is God and He can do anything He wants with His children. He wants to shine through you. Will you let Him?

STORY 62

The Gray Areas

"So, because you are lukewarm, and neither hot not cold, I will spit you out of My mouth (Revelation 3:16)."

Think about what the Scripture is saying. God will spit you out of His mouth! Have you ever put something in your mouth thinking it was one thing and found out it was the opposite? Maybe you thought it was sweet only to taste it and it was bitter? There is only one of two things you could do: swallow or spit it out. If you swallowed it, you would probably throw up. Either way, you would reject it. That is God's reaction when a person pretends to be one thing, yet all the while behaving the opposite. Remember when Jesus came upon the fig tree and it appeared to have figs but was actually barren. It was deceptive and, therefore, Jesus cursed it and it died.

You get to meet interesting people on an airplane. You have to respect their space and what they are doing. For instance, if someone is sitting next to me and they are reading or have ear buds in their ears, I assume they want to be left alone. This particular flight, I was on my way home from Florida. I was sitting next to a young, black lady, at least younger than me; probably was in her early thirty's. She was reading a book and I felt impressed of the Holy Spirit to start a conversation with her.

"Hi, what are you reading?"

She turned her head to look at me and showed me the title, *"Fifty Shades of Grey,"* and said, *"Have you read it?"*

I recognized it was a very popular read. *"No,"* I replied

"Would you like to read some of it? It is the hottest thing on the market!" She fanned herself to show she wasn't just talking about its number of sales, if you know what I mean.

"No, thank you. My boss would not like me to read it." I knew the Holy Spirit was doing something.

She got a strange look on her face and asked with a bit of sarcasm, *"Your boss tells you what you can read?"*

"Well, He doesn't tell me what I can read but He would not like it."

"Who do you work for?"

Without a word I pointed upward with my forefinger. She looked as if she had gotten caught with her hand in the cookie jar! *"Oh my God!"*

"Is He?" questioning whether God was, indeed, her god.

"Are you a preacher? Did my mama send you?"

"Honey, I am not here to judge you. Yes I am a minister. No, your mother did not send me. Why did you think she did?"

"*Because she is a preacher too! She would not like me reading what she would call trash.*" This woman was distraught! She tried to go back to reading and I got quiet.

She put her book down and said to me, "*I have to tell you something.*"

"*You do not owe me an explanation. I am not your judge, but it is obvious the Lord is dealing with you about something.*"

"*No, I have to tell you. I am the women's ministry leader at my church.*"

"*Where are you leading them? What you put in is what will come out of you. You are responsible for what you live before them. But, I think you already know this. I think the Lord is trying to teach you something.*"

"*I should have known He would put my mama right in my face! Who knew He would use her white counterpart to do it!*"

I laughed. She told me she would do things differently. How about you? What does Jesus see you reading and watching?

~

Missions

"Go therefore and make disciples of all the nations...(Matthew 28:19a)."

I'll bet you have been to a church service where a missionary spon-
sored by that particular ministry came to share their vision, works
of service, and future plans. They probably showed some pictures
or videos of a faraway land where children are in the streets begging
for food, or scenes of tiny grass huts where a family of six lives. This
tugs at your heart. Maybe you get your checkbook out or you sign
up for the next trip. That is what most missionaries do. After all,
they have to raise money to continue the ministries. It takes a lot of
money to feed, clothe, and administer medical supplies.

I, too, have sat through these presentations. Of course, my heart
was moved by the poverty and lack in these places. Watching human beings drawing water from a filth-infested river to drink is
horrific. We, in America, can't comprehend such horror. Even our
poorest of poor in America has at least clean water to drink. I have
been to India twice, Kenya twice, and Honduras once. I have been
asked many times why would I go thousands of miles away and
spend thousands of dollars to go when we have lost and needy

people right here in the USA? Why couldn't we just give that money to a reputable ministry and let them distribute what was needed?

That is a fair and reasonable question. Let me try to bring some clarity on this subject. Definitely, there are serious needs and poverty right here in the United States. I have been to the coal mining towns in the Appalachian Mountains to distribute food and I saw the poverty. I have known many who lived under bridges, in cars, in cardboard boxes, and worse. I grew up in poverty. The difference between us and other countries such as India, Kenya, and some other third-world countries is that we have governmental systems with programs in place to help with food, shelter, and other necessities. I know these systems have flaws and they are not competent to completely eradicate the issues. However, we have other systems in place that help. We have churches that bring relief to those in need. Many are the wealthy in this nation that give huge amounts of money to different needs such as education and job opportunities.

In these countries, the government doesn't care, or either they have belief systems that think they are not responsible for their citizens. Many of the rich do not care for those less fortunate and even go so far as to believe that they deserve their poverty. You might ask, "*Why go and spend the money on an airline ticket when that money could go for supplies?*" I used to ask the same question, until I went. The main reason for doing it is because Jesus said to!

India

On Mother's Day, 2005, I was teaching my Sunday school class. I had two visitors who were missionary friends of the worship leader. When the class was over, they waited until everyone else left. I thanked them for coming and chatted a moment. I could tell the man had something he wanted to say.

"Have you ever been to a foreign country?"

I replied, *"No, I haven't."*

He said, *"Well, you will. I don't know when, but you will. It will probably be India first, but you will go to others countries as well. The reason God is going to take you to other countries is to give you a bigger voice and a broader platform."*

I knew he was speaking a prophetic word. Before God ever allowed me to travel internationally, I was invited to Russia twice for missions, and once to Germany to participate in a prayer-walk. I was also invited to Cuba to lead a women's conference. God would not let me do any! I guess I wasn't as ready as I thought. My first trip to India was in December 2012. We had a team of ten people.

India is an expensive trip. Besides the airline tickets, each person had to give a thousand dollars for the rescuing of a girl in sex slavery or to dig a well for a community. We gave six-hundred dollars per person for the hosting pastor to use for food and travel.

In America, if I go to another state to preach in a church, they pay for my travel and hotel, or they place me in someone's home. They take care of everything I need for that stay and I usually get a ministry offering. In India, you are responsible for your own expenses because they don't have money. While we are there, the pastor under which we sat has five-hundred churches. With those churches, he has the responsibility to care for leper camps, boy's homes, orphanages, homes for the elderly, and the lists goes on. He is not a rich pastor, so he depends on God to send others who can come and bring resources with the anointing to bring his countrymen to the knowledge of Christ. You can't lead someone to Christ when their belly is growling from hunger or a young woman is being forced into sex many times during the course of a day.

My first trip to India was, indeed, a fulfilling of the prophecy given to me by the missionary on Mother's Day 2005. While we were there, we visited a boy's home where each boy had at least one missing limb, some had two. There are different reasons why this is: one, these boys are often taken by people who want to exploit them by begging for money on the streets. If they are missing a limb, it makes them look more pitiful. These particular boys were called "the run-away boys." Two, due to extreme abusive situations in their home life, they jump trains to get away. Sometimes they miss and lose limbs.

We also visited the leper colony. To me, this was the highlight of the trip. To see people afflicted with a disease we only read about in the Bible is unreal. We ministered to people where their fingers, toes, or noses were missing due to leprosy. These people are still looked at as they were in the Bible days: outcasts and untouchables. They are actually some of the most courageous people I have ever met. They did not look like desperately downcast outcasts. On the contrary, they are a people who have a resilient spirit in the face of great adversity.

Two weeks before we arrived, a huge storm hit the area where we were going to be. It wiped out eight of the villages we were scheduled to visit. This storm wreaked havoc on the part of India we were visiting. We would drive down a road and it would just drop because it was washed out. We went to one village to do a medical camp where we gave food and clothes. There were medical personnel to give medical supplies. The storm had wiped out their homes, which were small grass-thatched roof huts. Many were living under a piece of cardboard or tin shoved between two tree branches. We paid for a well to be drilled. Those people were overjoyed! They had nothing, and I mean nothing, so this well was truly living water to them. It forever changed my ability to grumble about what I don't have! Those wells cost a thousand dollars to drill and get them water-ready. They serve two main agendas. One reason, as you may imagine, is giving clean water to a community. Like many in third-world countries, they drink from trash and disease infested rivers. They have no choice. There are others who drill wells in these countries, but the water is only for a select group of people. Another reason is, when we provide wells through the ministry with whom we are associated, we dedicate it to the glory of God for all people. No one group can take ownership of it. This, in turn, gives a Christian pastor access into that community to establish a Christian church. It is a time of great celebration and they express their joy by sharing what little they have with us.

Mainly, were there to hold a women's conference. We arrived in the town where we held the conference. In America, if I attend a conference or speak at one, it is either held at a church or at a conference/banquet room. Tables are set up with tablecloths and centerpieces. It is usually very pretty, if not elegant. In India, some of the women walked as many as twelve miles to attend this conference. There are no McDonalds along the way. We had requested that a stage not be erected, but they built one anyway. We were under an open tent and temperatures were in the upper nineties. It was in December and a three-day conference. We had a morning session, broke for lunch, and then an evening session. Our team had paid for the conference because we also fed the attendees. We had about four-hundred women attending. Those ladies would put us Americans to shame when it came to their Bibles. They actually showed great respect for their Bibles and, boy, they know their Scriptures! If we said turn to a certain Scripture, one of those ladies had it before we got our Bibles turned, and they were up on their feet reading the text out loud!

We were told that one of the local pastors wanted us to be his guest at his home. I thought, *"Oh, goody, we will get to rest in a cooler place and use a bathroom and relax."* I had a lot to learn! We got to his home and his wife asked me if I needed to use the bathroom. She led me around back to a small roughly constructed structure that resembled an outdoor bathroom that was popular in America many years ago. As a child, I had used an outdoor bathroom once, so I thought it wasn't a big deal. When I got in, there was no toilet. It was just a hole in the ground and a bucket of water to wash your hand—they only use the left hand. Toilet paper is not widely available in India as it is customary to use your left hand for wiping. I know that, for the average American, it is almost barbaric, but it is what it is.

A word of advice: anytime you go to a foreign country, always carry small packs of tissue and hand sanitizer, and never try to shake hands or eat with your left hand in India because it is deemed disrespectful. The left hand is the "poopy hand." It is not acceptable to show disrespect to the native people. They do the best they can. So much for a cool, leisurely lunch. They always give you their best, even if it means they do without. It really taught me about gratitude. It was the end of the conference that really tore me. On the last day, the pastor we were with asked some of the Indian ladies to share what the conference had meant to them. Someone who spoke Telugu and English interpreted so that we could understand her.

"One morning, I came to the tent very early to pray. I thought others were here because I could see lights in the tent. When I got closer, I could see it was not the electric lights. I tried to come into the tent, but the Presence of God was so strong, I fell on my face. The lights were the Glory of God shining all over the tent. I laid at the door in worship and crying, for the glory was strong."

We were stunned, to say the least. But, the next woman's testimony totally wrecked me.

"When we heard the storm was going to hit, we were afraid that it might hinder the American team from coming. Many of the women walked as much as twelve miles to be here at four in the morning to pray that the Americans would not be stopped."

I have done women's conferences many times in the USA. To get women together to pray is not an easy task. You have to start around 10 a.m., bring them a biscuit, and let them out before lunch. It will help if you have a drawing for a door prize! Believe me when I tell you this, these women did not come to beg God to protect their homes or families, but they sacrificed their comfort and safety to walk a long way in the dark to pray for us. I will never forget.

STORY 65

~

Honduras

The team that went to India prepared a time of sharing testimonies, and photos for those that had blessed us with the funds and prayers to do what we were honored to do. One of my dear friends Sue was at that meeting. Sue had been to Russia several times and had also gone to Honduras on a regular yearly ministry trip. She has a heart for missions. After the presentation was over, Sue asked me to get a ministry team together and go to Honduras with her in six months. I said, "*Okay.*"

Our team consisted of Diane, Lorrie, Sue, and me. We stayed in the visiting minister's quarters beside the pastor's house. Along with the four of us, there were three other female ministers staying in the bunkhouse as well. Two of them were from Mississippi and the other from North Carolina. We had seven women in one room, which was going to be either extremely good or extremely bad. Thank God we all knew Jesus!

One of our assignments was a women's conference in the mountains. After being in India, I did not expect have accommodations like we have in America, though I had become accustomed to that. I was right not to get my expectations too high. I don't mean that in a negative way. I was learning how blessed we are here in America and yet how ungrateful and spoiled we can be.

Honduras is a very poor country. At that time, the average income was five-hundred dollars a month. We stayed in a facility reminiscent of a bunkhouse. The beds were single beds with worn out mattresses. But, we were not there for vacation; we were there to share the Word of God.

Early one morning, Diane, who was an early riser, decided she would be the first to get in the shower. She let out the most horrible scream! I went to the shower door and asked if she was alright. She said, "*Yes, but the water is freezing.*" I thought, perhaps, she was exaggerating a bit. I didn't expect to have hot water; I had gotten use to that in India. I figured she was reacting to having nothing but cold water. Uncomfortable, yes, but nothing about which to get bent out of shape—well, at least until I got in. Oh my goodness, she was right. It wasn't just cold, it was freezing! The water was piped right off the mountain water. I swear, when I got out, my scalp was frozen. A hair dryer never felt so good!

We arrived at the facility where we would hold the meetings. It had three completed walls and one that was not quite finished. The roof had huge holes in it. I forgot to tell you that it was during the rainy season. During the services, it would start raining, but at least the holes in the roof were mainly on one side. When the rain came pouring down, the people on the rainy side simply moved their chairs to the other side until the rain stopped. It was no big deal to them. Water standing on the floor did not dampen their spirits. They just kept worshiping and we kept preaching! During worship, I was standing with my hands lifted and just worshiping like everyone else. The Holy Spirit spoke to me, "*Turn around and look at who is behind you.*" I turned around and directly behind me was two beautiful Honduran girls. They probably were around mid to late twenties. They had their arms straight up in the air as if in total worship. Their eyes were shut as if they were lost in another realm. I felt almost like I was spying on a private moment and started to turn away. Again, the Holy Spirit spoke to me, "*They are witches!*"

Before I could respond, simultaneously, they both opened their eyes and I just stared at them. They both fell to the floor and slithered like snakes into the center aisle. There were a lot of people already out in the open floor dancing, worshiping, and moving about. These two women began projectile vomiting green pea stuff. It was like watching a B rated movie about possession. The Holy Spirit instructed me to follow them, but do not touch them. They continued to move like snakes swinging their once beautiful hair from side to side through the vomit and water. The minister from North Carolina staying in our bunkhouse was as bold as a lion and came over and started to pull one of them up while rebuking the devil. I told her to let her go. I guess something in my voice convinced her to do so. She dropped that girl like a hot potato!

My friend, Sue, kept asking, *"What are you going to do?"*

"Nothing, unless the Holy Spirit tells me to."

There was so much activity in the room. I guess a lot of people didn't notice the commotion going on with the two slithering around on the floor. These girls were being controlled by a demonic force. They moved in sequence and, suddenly, they both stopped writhing and looked at me. I knew the Holy Spirit was directing me. I looked directly into their eyes and said, *"Stop and shut up in the Name of Jesus!"* It is as though they fell asleep and lay still. After a while, they got up and went out the door. I can guess the question you must be asking is, *"How could witches be in a church worshiping?"* I am sure this story challenges many of you in many ways. Perhaps you have never heard of these types of activities in the church, but all one has to do is read the book of Acts and you see this type of thing going on. It is still happening today.

STORY 66

Prison in Honduras

"Moreover, I will give you a new heart and put a new spirit within you (Ezekiel 36:26)."

While we were in Honduras, we were invited to visit a prison. This was not an ordinary prison. Housed there were girls imprisoned for serious offences. These girls were ages thirteen to eighteen years old and a lot of them had committed murder. Some of them murdered parents, cheating boyfriends, pimps, and the list goes on. Many of them were there because they were drug dealers. It was one of the saddest sights I had ever seen. Some of them were so young looking that you would have thought they were still playing with dolls. Yet, these girls had hardened looks on their little faces. Life for them was difficult and all about survival.

We were ushered into a large room where the girls put on a little play for us. The prison personnel tried to implement a Christian atmosphere, so I knew we would get to minister to the girls individually at the end to the play. I started looking at the opposite side of the room where the prisoners were seated. I asked the Holy Spirit to show me who I was to go to when it was time to minister. Immediately, I spotted a young lady who was, at most, sixteen or seventeen. Her face was hard, and her body language told me she wanted to be left alone. I thought surely there was someone else who was a bit more open to ministry, but I knew that was who I was assigned to.

I do not speak Spanish and we did not have enough translators, so I asked the Holy Spirit how I was supposed to communicate with her. He said. *"You are going to love the devil right out of her!"* I had no idea what He meant, but I was sure I was about to find out! Showtime was over and it was time to minister. Each person in our team went to a girl. I walked over to the young lady and she sat like a stone statue while holding on to the sides of her chair. Her face looked straight ahead. She did not acknowledge my presence. I thought, *"Oh, boy what now?"* I knew I was to hug her. I did not dare let my emotions dictate my actions or else I would have walked away. She did not respond to my embrace. In fact, she was actually resisting my touch. I hugged her tighter and began to softly pray in the Spirit, aka in tongues. She didn't speak English and I didn't speak Spanish, so it really didn't matter. I just kept praying. Something began to change in me. I started sensing the presence of God. I began to feel a supernatural love pouring through me. It was the love of God. Finally, she began to relax a bit, and I was able to pull her up to a standing position. This was good for me as my back was feeling the strain of bending over so long!

I just kept hugging her and praying in the Spirit. The more I prayed, the more relaxed she became. Suddenly, she began to cry, and she hugged me back! The power of God became more real as though God Himself was hugging the both of us! The Holy Spirit instructed me to open my eyes, and when I did, I saw demons actually jumping out of her body! I kid you not, they were fleeing, and the Holy Spirit allowed me to see it. God loved the demons right out of that young girl.

When I finished praying, she was limp in my arms. I looked at her and she was glowing with the love of God in her. She smiled.

The hardness was gone, and she looked like a young girl filled with hope instead of a girl who had hate and murder in her heart. The love of God is the most powerful force in the universe. I wonder why we don't walk in it. After the ministry time, they had refreshments. This was a special treat for the girls. They were allowed to show us their rooms that were actually cells with just a small opening at the top of the wall that served as a window. If you ever saw an old western movie where the jails had thick metal doors with a small slit in the top of the door, this is what their cell doors looked like. This prison had no running water or electricity. It was a hard life. If their sentence was longer than their eighteenth birthday, they were transferred to an adult facility for the remainder of their time. They don't have much of a chance for survival or a different life afterwards. Their only hope is Jesus.

STORY 67

The Bishop

"If we confess our sins, He is faithful and righteous to forgive us our sins and to cleanse us from all unrighteousness (1 John 1:9)."

After the women's conference in Honduras, we returned to the pastor's house. As I said before, all seven of us stayed in one large room. One of the ladies from Mississippi was considered a bishop, so we addressed her by that title. One morning, by the voice of Holy Spirit talking to me, I woke up. It is better than an alarm clock, but it can also be a little uncomfortable when He is instructing you to do something out of your comfort zone. *"I want you to go sit on the bishop's bed and wait for her to wake up,"* He said. That was all I got, and I knew He would not give me more until I did the first thing. The Holy Spirit works through us by faith and we must operate by faith. I got up quietly trying not to wake the others. I had no idea what the Holy Spirit was going to tell me once I got there. I sat on the edge of her bed wondering how she was going to react to someone she hardly knew sitting on her bed staring at her. I know how uncomfortable I would be in that situation.

She must have felt my presence because I was there only a couple of minutes. She opened her eyes and scooted up in her bed at the same time. I must tell you that, in the few days we had been together, we had only exchanged the usual information such as where we were from, what we did for a living, how many children we had, etc. We had only ministered to others, but not to each other. So, when the Holy Spirit told me what to say to the bishop, I was not comfortable. In case you are wondering, let me assure you that definitely is the way He works. He is not concerned with us being comfortable. He is only concerned with our obedience and doing so in a spirit of love. So, as she was trying to figure out a nice way of asking me what I might be doing sitting on her bed so early, I spoke first.

"How long are you going to hate white people?" I asked.

The question startled me! She was a black lady, but had not in any way shown any hostility towards any of us. She had conducted herself with dignity and treated us as co-ministers. But, I knew what the Holy Spirit said, so I just waited. I guess I expected her to deny it. Instead, she started crying. The next statement was revelatory in that I had no way of knowing any of the information I was conveying.

> *"Some white people stole something valuable from your family a long time ago and it has caused you a lot of pain. The Holy Spirit wants to heal something in you."*

She began to tell me how her family owned some land, and on it, oil was discovered. An influential white family for whom her family worked succeeded in stealing the land from her family. Her family lived in need due to the dishonesty of this white family instead of the financial freedom they would have experienced through the discovery of oil. The Holy Spirit was not validating the actions of the thieves, but His heart was to deliver her from bitterness and unforgiveness. She cooperated with the Holy Spirit and I took her through steps of deliverance. She was set free and the weight of hatred was lifted off of her.

God wants all of us to be free from anything keeping us from receiving His blessings. Perhaps you are reading this story and you know you have been harboring ill feelings toward someone. Maybe you wonder why it seems that God is not hearing you or promoting you in that to which you have been called. Ask Him to show you if there is anything you are holding onto from which He wants to free you. Repent and accept His total forgiveness. Ask Him to heal any wounds of your heart that may have been caused by the offense. He will, and you will be in a better position to receive all He has for you.

If you are not familiar with the gifts of the Holy Spirit, this story will leave you with questions. The Holy Spirit was moving through me in a gift of the word of knowledge. He gave me information that I had no way of knowing in the natural. Giving the bishop instruction on forgiving and releasing her anger and bitterness toward white people was the result of a word of wisdom. A word of wisdom is the supernatural ability to apply the answer to the problem. You can read about these gifts in the twelfth chapter of 1st Corinthians.

Backpacks

"Cast your bread on the surface of the waters, for you will find it after many days (Ecclesiastes 11:1)."

I was on the phone with my friend Holly Payne. She lived in North Georgia and I lived in York, South Carolina. I was telling her that I had always wanted to go to a coal mining town in the Appalachian Mountains to help in some way. I had never met anyone who did that type of ministry, so I never had the opportunity. It is so funny how God works sometimes. I don't recall ever actually telling anyone that, we were just talking about things we would like to do someday.

During our time on the phone, I could hear her mother talking to someone, and Holly said one of her cousins was visiting. Then Holly got quiet. I asked her if she was eavesdropping and she told me she was. I laughed. She told me to hold on a minute because she heard them say something about a trip. Her cousin was talking about someone in their family taking a trip to the mountains of West Virginia on a mission's trip. I held on while she went to inquire about it.

When she returned to the phone, she told me that some of her family was going to deliver backpacks to the school children in a coal mining town in West Virginia. No way! I had just gotten out of my mouth my desire to go on one of these trips, and there in her kitchen was someone talking about such a trip. I got the phone number of the one putting the plans together, and, just like that, I was going to a mission's trip to a coal mining town. I was able to take two hundred and fifty of my children's books and give each child a signed copy. We delivered back packs stuffed with food, clothes, and toys. We gave school supplies to the schools. They were some very happy children because God gave me the desire of my heart.

A few years later, I was having my hair cut at my usual salon. One of the stylists asked if I had one of my books, which I did. I went out to the car to get it, and, when I returned, there was a young boy around twelve waiting for his mother to finish getting her hair done. When he saw the book, he asked me if I wrote it.

He said to me with surprise, "*My little cousin has that book.*"

"*Really? Where did she buy it?*" I asked.

"*She lives in West Virginia in a coal mining town and some people came and gave all of the kids in the school one of those books.*" I was so stunned! You never know what God is going to do through you to impact someone's life. He sure has impacted mine and continues to do it in surprising ways.

Tidbits within the Stories

"Behold, I waited for your words...(Job 32:11)."

Going overseas is always a big deal, especially for me. After growing up without a car for transportation, to me, flying is extravagant. Through these trips to the other side of the world, I have learned that while you are going to teach and share things that will change the lives of others, you get changed in the process. Sometimes the real journey is what you learn in getting there and what God wants to do, not only through you, but for you. In this portion, I am going to highlight some of the tidbits that I see as real God-moments.

Along with three others, I decided it was again time to go to India. This would be mine and Lorrie's second trip. By this time, I had resigned my position with my church. My resource pool had greatly diminished. Once you leave a ministry, it is no longer a well you can tap. From where was the money to go to India going to come? As I said, there were four of us going—Scott, Chris, Lorrie, and myself. We had originally planned to go in December of 2015, but, apparently, God had a different date in mind.

This is the way we work as a team. We make our original plan by setting a date. Then, each individual person of the team prays and seeks God on the time, purpose, and how to finance the journey. Next, before we schedule our flight, we come together to hear how we feel the Holy Spirit is directing us. Every single one of us said the same thing: December is not when we are to go. We were all in agreement, so we postponed the trip until February of 2016. As the time got near and we had prayed, we knew it was a go. The problem was as always money. We always depend on God to tell us how to obtain the resources. We do not have yard sales, or bake cakes and cookies. That may not be wrong if you have done it that way, but it is not how God directed us.

I'll be honest, I was a little unsure of how the money would come. I told you earlier that my main resource outlet was no longer available. It is not because some of those in the church I left did not still bless me, but it was not proper to expect them to support me as they once had. The Lord gave me instructions to whom to send a letter of support, and believe me, it was a very short list! India is one of the most expensive mission's trips you can take.

As a team, we never look at the money that comes in as belonging to one certain person. For example, when people sent money for me, it became team money, and that was about to be tested! I don't know how, but money started pouring in for me and Chris. Scott and Lorrie received very limited amounts, and by the time we needed to purchase our tickets, they did not have enough to buy theirs, much less cover the other expenses. We added all the money that came in, and through the money sent to me and Chris, there was enough to cover all the expenses for all four of us!

During this trip, we were going to do a pastor's conference. We had a couple translators to use while we preached. One particular man was very good. Before going to India the first time, I had never worked with a translator. It is a bit tricky, so I watched episodes of Joyce Meyer on TV when she was in other countries to see how she did it, so I want to give a shout out to her. Even though I may never get to meet her personally, I say, "*Thank you, Mrs. Meyer, for giving me instruction through example!*"

The day came for me to preach, and, instinctively, I knew this particular man would translate for me. He had been there for the whole event, but I realized I had not seen him. I got up to preach and the pastor with whom we were staying got up to translate for me. After the service, we had refreshments outside. I saw the translator walking toward me. I told him I was glad to see him, but I really missed him that morning. He told me he had not felt well and how sad he was to not translate for me. As he talked, I became puzzled at his speech. He speaks English fluently when translating. I just assumed he had studied English because people in that area speak little to no English. During this conversation, he was having a hard time getting English words to come out correctly. I told him how amazed I was that he knew the language so well and how impressed I was that he could translate so easily.

Then, in very broken English, he said, "*I am sorry to miss your preaching, I wanted to translate for the prophet. I do not speak English good. I do not really understand the language. Only when I am translating the Holy Spirit gives me the ability to speak and understand it.*"

I was beyond stunned. Although I do have the calling of a prophet, I never use that title in a foreign country and very seldom do I use it in my own country. So, I asked him, "*How did you know I am a prophet? I have never said that nor has the residing pastor conveyed that.*"

He replied, "*The same Holy Spirit that gives me the ability to translate told me you are a prophet.*"

In the USA, we often think of the Holy Spirit as something to give us chill bumps. He is so much more. He is the giver of truth. Maybe we need to learn to depend upon Him for our information.

Jesus Does Hair in India

"Yet not a hair of your head will perish (Luke 21:18)."

We take so much for granted in America. Do not take that as a negative, but rather as a reminder to be grateful. As I am writing this book toward the end of 2020, there is a lot of unrest in our country. Many people think we should give up our way of life because, to a rebellious group, it seems wrong to have such an abundance of goods. I also think that, sometimes, we have more than we need. But, we are a tremendously blessed nation. Instead of apologizing for that, I think we need to make sure we are grateful and share our abundance.

I often read the works of the late Dr. Myles Munroe. I can't quote him, but I read this in one of his books about comments made concerning how beautiful and well-groomed the Embassy of the United States was in a very poor and underdeveloped country. Many thought this to be insulting that such beauty would be situated among the impoverished housing of that country. Then, Mr. Munroe explained that an embassy is a representation of a country. The USA is a very rich and blessed country. By the same token, we as representatives of the Kingdom of God should well represent our King. In having abundance, we can be a blessing. Who do you think is the first to go to the aid of other countries in times of need? If we didn't possess so much, how would we be able to bless others?

Now, back to the hair story. We sometimes get hit with a storm and our power goes out. It always seems to happen at the most inconvenient time. Heck, it is always inconvenient to lose power. We take for granted flipping the light switch and having the lights come on. But in India, at least the area we visited, that is not the case. They have scheduled outages. That means their ability to produce enough power for everyone continuously is limited; therefore, you have access to power so many hours, and then you are without so many hours. It is usually pretty consistent, thus you learn how to adjust your schedule.

Imagine being asleep at four in the morning and you wake up hearing chanting or singing in a language you don't understand. It's over the entire community through loudspeakers on poles. That is your alarm clock. This particular morning, I decided to get ready for the day instead of trying to sleep with the serenading. I plugged my curling iron. For your information, I have thick, straight, bodiless hair. I curl my hair every day. I'm sitting cross legged on my straw-filled mattress waiting for the iron to heat, and guess what? Yep, the power goes out. Being the spiritual powerhouse that I am—that's a joke—I began to whine and complain!

The Holy Spirit began to speak to me, *"Why don't you ask Me how to do your hair without electricity?"*

I felt terrible, so I did what I should do. I repented for complaining. Y'all know complaining is a sin, don't you? *"Okay, Lord, how do I do that?"*

"Spray each layer with hair spray, curl it, and wait for the spray to dry. While it is drying, begin to thank your Heavenly Father for His goodness."

I cried, I worshiped, and I praised God. I learned a valuable lesson. My hair did not look as good as it would have with electricity, but my heart was a lot cleaner, and that, my friend, is better than perfect hair! During the first trip to India, Rhonda, one of the ladies with us, and I would go downstairs for coffee. A man would knock on the door with fresh milk for our coffee. We would open the door and allow him to come in. He only spoke Telegu, but we did not. He would sit with us in the living room and watch as we drank our coffee. He never tried to converse with us; he just would sit and smile. I mentioned to the pastor that we were very appreciative of him to bring us milk for our coffee, but we felt bad that we could not talk to him. We did not want to appear rude.

The pastor replied, *"He does not care that you do not talk to him, he just wants to be in your presence."* I bet that is exactly how God wants us to feel about Him.

~

Rock Climbing in Kenya

"She girds herself with strength and makes her arms strong
(Proverbs 31:17)."

Scott, Lorrie, and I have taken two trips to Kenya, thus far, and plan on more as the Lord allows. Scott has been there many times and has adapted very well to that lifestyle. He is not only accepted, but extremely honored by his ministry friends and the native Kenyans. He aligns the different places to minister and we just flow together as a team. Once, we were going to eat at a place that was way upon a hill, more like a small mountain. At any rate, we had to climb up a small rock wall. There was another way, but Scott likes to do things out of the ordinary. Scott instructed the two Kenyan men with us to help me and Lorrie up the rock wall. Here we were, me and Lorrie in our skirts—it is improper for women ministers to wear pants or shorts in public—climbing up this wall, and Robert, who is my spiritual son, came to help me. I told him to check on Lorrie because I was fine.

"*Oh mum, you are very strong for forty!*" he exclaimed referring to my age. In this area of Africa, the life span is about seventy, if that. Their life is very hard. Forty is considered getting on up there in age.

I laughed and replied, "*Forty? I'm sixty-four years old!*"

He was distressed and said, "*Oh no, Mum, you are not!*"

Then he addressed Scott, "*Mum says she is sixty-four years old!*"

Scott responded, "*Yes, she is the same age as my mother.*"

Robert shook his head in disbelief and said, "*You are very strong for your age Mum.*"

Animals, Insects, and the Gospel

"Let everything that has breath praise the Lord (Psalm 150:6)."

In a foreign country, you never know what to expect. In North America, you go to church and the only animal you might encounter would be a service dog. I am sure there are foreign mission's trips where the buildings are more in line with what we might expect to see in America, but this has not been my experience. I want to state clearly that this is, in no way, an insult to our India or African friends. They always give their best and sacrifice for our comfort. That being said, they don't have the resources we have in America. I was preaching in a church in Kenya, and because of the heat and lack of air conditioning, doors and windows are left open.

Needless to say, it is not unusual for animals to wander in. This particular morning, I was in the pulpit speaking when I looked up and saw a fairly large nest hanging over my head. I am not sure if it was a wasp or hornet's nest, and frankly, who cares? They were swarming all around the nest and just above my head! I looked at Scott who had his *"don't worry about it"* look on his face. He silently mouthed the words at me, "*Just keep preaching!*" I did and it wasn't long before a dog wandered in, and before I finished, a cow looked into the door to check things out. Life with Jesus is an adventure. Life with Jesus in a foreign country is life on steroids!

❦

Stage Fright

"And He has set my feet upon a rock making my footsteps firm (Psalm 40:2)."

I told the story of the women's conference we did in India. This story is a tidbit within that storyline. The conference was held outside under a large, open tent. Scott had requested they not have a stage, but his request was ignored. The stage had the traditional skirt around it to hide what was underneath. We do that here also because it makes it look nice. I was curious because, at times, I could feel that it was a bit shaky. I asked Scott what was holding the stage up and he answered, *"You don't want to know. Do not look. Trust me."*

Well, of course I was going to look. My curiosity to know got the better of me. Sometimes you just need to listen to those who know. Before I reveal to you what I found under the stage skirt, let me tell you about a young Indian woman in the congregation. We had three days to do the conference. I noticed her the first day. One of the most amazing things I noticed was the womens' saris. In case you are not familiar with a sari, it is the dress, but not a dress as we would define it. A sari is made of a very long strip of wide cloth, usually silk or some silky type of material. It is wrapped around the body, which covers from the head to the ankles. There were several hundred women in this tent and not any two saris were alike. They are so beautiful. But my eyes locked in on one particular woman, and every time I looked at her, she was staring at me. When she saw me looking at her, she would pull her sari over to cover her face while lowering her head. I was determined to connect with her. She reminded me of my friend, Shelly, so I call her "*my Indian Shelly*." This went on the whole three days. She always sat in the same place, so I knew exactly where to find her.

On the last day of the conference, we were coming back from the afternoon break and I felt someone tug on my sari. It was my Indian Shelly. I could not find an interpreter, but I could tell she had someone waiting to take our picture together. Bingo, we had connected! She hugged me so hard. I was overjoyed! I was being sternly called to the stage as I was holding up the process. My bad! As I started up the steps to the stage, I could not resist. I stepped back down a step and pulled up the stage skirt. I should have listened to Scott. Holding up this stage was literally hundreds upon hundreds of thin branches that had fallen out of trees! You know, like after a storm and little dead branches are all over our lawns. We pick them up so our yard will be free from all that storm debris. That is what was holding up that stage. Sometimes we had as many as twelve people on that stage. You can't tell me God is not in the miracle business! Scott just laughed, "*I told you not to look!*"

The Indian Ocean Holiday

"He who said to them, 'Here is rest, give rest to the weary (Isaiah 28:12).'"

The first trip to India, the pastor planned to take our ministry team and his ministry team on a holiday. We tried to convince him it was unnecessary, that we would rather that he keep his money for other things, yet he insisted, "*I must take you on holiday. I have squeezed you like a grape!*" He took us to the Indian Ocean. I don't think I have ever seen a more beautiful sunset. We stayed at the Bay Watch Hotel. A few things happened there that you would never expect in America. Like the time I was taking a shower, I had shampoo in my hair and soap all over me and the water ran out. There was a bucket of water sitting there, so I dumped it over my head to rinse as good as possible and got dressed. It is what it is.

The Bay Watch Motel had a rather large swimming pool. It is not proper for women to show their bodies, so we did not wear bathing suits. Men, however, are not restricted to such modesty. Matthew, one of our team members, and I were walking around the pool talking when, right there in front of God and every-body, this young man yanks his swimming shorts off showing his business for all to see! This is not taboo for them. Poor Matthew. It probably would not have bothered him except he was with me. "*Oh Sandy!*" He exclaimed in horror. "*I am so sorry. I did not see that coming!*" I was laughing. It is really hard to embarrass me, but Matthew was horrified. I think he might be scarred for life! If you are planning on going to a foreign country to do missions and you are one that needs your comfort zones to stay intact, do yourself and your team a favor and stay home or be willing to let God stretch you. You will never be sorry.

~

Let's Go Fishing

"And Jesus said to them, 'Follow Me, and I will make you become fishers of men (Mark 1:17).'"

While on this same trip in India, we were privileged to visit a fishing village. It was an awesome experience! We went where the fishing boats were being emptied of the catch of the morning. It was like stepping back in time to what you might see on the Sea of Galilee in Jesus' day. The small fishing boats were painted with bright colors. The fish were as colorful as the boats and laid out in rows on the sand. Bright red fish; some very large and some small, fish of every color and size. The women of the village showed up with large pans to carry home their fish. The women would barter with the boat owners for the fish. As they settled on their price, they would place the fish in the pans. These pans were very large; they would fill them to the brim. Two men would come and pick up the pans. I thought, *"How sweet. They are going to carry that for those ladies."* Oh, they carried them alright. They lifted the pan and placed it on the woman's head. That would never do in America! But, we were not in America. One of the lessons we need to learn when we are in a country with different customs is that we are not there to change their culture. We are there to teach the Gospel of Jesus Christ and allow Him to change what needs to be changed. That is what makes Him God and us not. I had to get over myself, soak in the differences, and pray for the Holy Spirit to invade that culture. Oh, by the way, those women walked back to their village with those pans of fish on their heads and it never fell off. Amazing!

Prison Chains are Shaking

"Hatred stirs up strife, but love covers all transgressions (Proverbs 10:12)."

Lorrie and I were preparing for our first trip to Kenya. The church I was attending hosted a sendoff service. It was an awesome time of fellowship and ministry as different ones prayed over us. One of the plans for ministry in Kenya included going to a couple of women's prisons. A few days before we were to leave, we were informed that a law had been passed that visiting missionaries would not be allowed to go in. Scott, who was already in Kenya, told us we would not be able to go to the prisons. I knew that we were supposed to go, so somehow God was going to make a way. It is important for you to understand that, in America, there are avenues around almost anything, but this is not the case in Kenya. A law is a law. Still, I had a sense that we would go.

During the ministry time at our send off, one of my dear friends, Nicole, who also does prison ministry here in the United States, prayed and gave us a prophetic word that we would go to the prisons. That settled it for me. Scott did not want us to be disappointed, so he continued to warn us that we may not go. I understand that you have to adhere to the natural until you have a supernatural word from the Lord. Once you have that, it is a done deal. On the first night there, we had a visitor, Dennis, the prison chaplain. We sat and talked for a while and, suddenly, he jumped up and said, *"I'll be back."* A short time later, he called Scott and told him we would be going to the prison the next day. That is the power of God at work!

It was reported that eighteen women accepted Christ because of our visit. These prisons are not like the prisons here. They have no running water or electricity inside. Sometimes they spend several years in prison before they are charged or tried with a crime. They grow their food and make dolls and things to provide income. Many of them are allowed to keep their small children with them up to a certain age. Christ is their only hope. These women suffer with a lot of health issues, especially in their stomach and reproductive organs. This is probably due to lack of good nutrition and not healing properly from childbirth. Most of them are in prison due to stealing alcohol, which they sell to feed their children.

One of the women in prison administration stayed as we ministered to the ladies. I was informed she wanted me to pray for her. I led her to a place where we could not be overheard. She spoke English fairly well, so we were able to communicate without a third person to translate. She started to tell me of her situation and, because the Holy Spirit was revealing things to me, I asked her to not tell me anything. By revelation of the Holy Spirit, I knew she was pregnant. She was tall and thin did not physically appear to be pregnant. Because I had asked her not to tell me anything, I was able to reveal things to her I could only know through the Holy Spirit.

I began to share a prophetic word or knowledge, *"The Holy Spirit is telling me your husband has left you and you are trying to get him to come home. The Lord does not want you to do that. He has already beat one baby out of you and he will beat this baby out of you. He will eventually go too far and kill you. The Lord knows you are afraid to be alone, but He will be with you. You must trust God. This man is not good for you or your children. You have a good income and God will give you increase."*

She was crying and had lost her concern about the inmates seeing her so vulnerable. She told me that everything I said was a hundred percent true. She said she knew God was with her now because of the word God revealed to me. That is what the gifts are supposed to do. They are to bear fruit. They build faith in God and that is a fruit of the Spirit. They are also to show the power and the love of God. We left the prison encouraged because we witnessed the goodness of God. We also were invited to Chaplain Dennis's home to minister to some prison guards and a few administration personnel. This turned out to be one of the highlights of our trip. The Holy Spirit moved through us prophetically and it was awesome! The Bible says that a prophet is not accepted in their own house or where they live. Lorrie and I both have that call on our life, and when we get to exercise that gift and see the hand of God move through it, there is nothing so sweet.

This should be a no brainer if you know us and the ministry we serve, but it needs to be plainly said so that no one accuses us of being prideful. It is always God's glory when lives are changed through us and it is never about us. That, in itself, is very humbling that God would move through such imperfect vessels to bring about His perfect work.

STORY 77

∾

Q and A's

*"A man has joy in an answer, and how delightful is a
timely word (Proverbs 15:23)!"*

When attending church here in North America, you know what
is going to take place and when—at least in most churches. The
events might be shifted a bit, but usually you take your seat, announcements are made, there's singing and worship, offerings and
preaching, sometimes alter calls, and prayer are offered. I don't
mean to demean church in that bland lineup; it's simply an outline
of events. In the middle of it, God can and will do what only He
can do in the hearts of people.

In a foreign land, it is very similar. You do all the same things.
However, in Kenya, because of the varying conditions, things can
change quickly. Such was the service on this day. In the area where
we were ministering, they love the Gospel of Jesus Christ. They
must go to great lengths to get to church. Sadly, in America, many
will stay home on Sunday morning if the weather is bad. Travel in
Kenya can be very challenging as very few own cars; they come by
walking, motorcycles, and bicycles. It was the rainy season and,
seriously, when it rains it rains!

This particular day was going to be a full day with breaks to eat and fellowship. Due to the amount of travel some Kenyans endure to get there, they plan to stay all day. Scott was going to minister, and then Lorrie and I would take a turn. Scott was not feeling well and he wasn't improving, so he went back to the hotel and Lorrie and I planned to fill in. This did not throw us for a loop as we are used to having to improvise. We both preached and then they served us a mid-day meal. We probably would have called it a day, but at that time, the bottom dropped out of the sky. It rained so hard you could not see outside the door. It was coming down in sheets and showed no signs of letting up. No one was going anywhere in that weather.

After the meal, the pastor came and told us the women would like to have a time of questions and answers; this was mainly a women's conference. We told him we would be glad to. I was a bit apprehensive because, in their culture, things are very different. But, we consented and they wrote their list of questions. Most of them speak fairly good English, but some don't, so we still used a translator. Lorrie took the list of questions and said she would go first. She looked at the first question and answered it with ease. After the first question, she stopped and looked at the other questions and handed me the list. She said she didn't think she was qualified to answer them, and I should take it from there. Lorrie is not as old as I and she had not been in ministry as long as I. However, she is a very capable minister. I read the list quickly and saw her concern and rightly so.

In that area of Kenya, some practices are still in existence, even in Christian circles. They are very tribal-minded and confuse some of their tribal beliefs with Christianity. It was no different in Apostle Paul's day. The husband still has the right to beat his wife with a cane. Most believers do not allow this, but it still happens. The husband also has a right to bring other women into the home as wives and the first wife has to train her in the ways of the household responsibilities with no say so in the matter. This is what most of the questions were about. I went to the pastor who is a great teacher of the Word and full of wisdom. I showed him the list and told him of my concerns. While I was going to only use the Gospel as my guide, we have such different cultural practices that I knew I would have to be cautious.

He looked at me and said, "*I trust you.*"

I thanked him and told him that, at any time he felt the need to intervene, or if I crossed any boundaries, I would gladly step back. Again, he said, "*I trust you.*"

I walked to the back of the stage and prayed, "*Dear Lord, I need your wisdom to answer these concerns without confusion. Amina.*"

I felt something like warm honey pour through my entire being. I suddenly felt empowered and I understood it was the Holy Spirit giving me what I needed. I answered hard questions for hours. Every now and again, I would look at the pastor and he would give me the thumbs up until I finally answered the last question. Lorrie talked a bit more and then we ministered to those ladies. God was so gracious!

When we were finished, the pastor came to me and blessed me immensely saying, "*Pastor Sandy, I have never heard anyone answer with as much wisdom and knowledge as you did today. You are free to minister in my church anytime. I trust you.*" I assure you I know it was the wisdom of God moving through me that day; I am just not that smart!

~

A New Name

"The nations will see your righteousness, and all kings your glory; and you will be called by a new name which the mouth of the Lord will designate (Isaiah 62:6)."

This is truly a short story. In Kenya, the natives are very in tune to the tribe whence they hail. When they first met Lorrie, immediately they were confused. First, they wanted to know if she had been a slave in America. When she answered, *"No,"* they wanted to know if her parents were slaves. Again, she told them, *"No."* This was very confusing to them. Because Lorrie is black, they assumed that she had to be a slave. They have been led to believe that all black people are slaves in America. Then they wanted to know from what tribe she originated. Of course, she doesn't know, and this became a game for them to figure out her tribe. It was really funny. They took her skin color, her cheekbones, as well as her other facial features, and tried to guess. They never agreed. It did raise her curiosity to try to trace her heritage.

One night at church, a few days before we were to leave Kenya, they gave us a celebration. There was dancing and the ladies wrapped us in cloths with African prints and gave us gifts. It was

very honoring and a lot of fun. The Kenyans are fun-loving people. They gave us something else—a gift neither of us has ever received—a new name! Lorrie was given the name Akiru. It means
"*the rains bring*" because we visited during the rainy season. My
new name was Makena which comes from the Meru tribe meaning "*joy.*" When we go to Kenya, they refer to us as Pastor Akiru
and Pastor Makena. What an honor! We have grown to love them
so much. They are like family to us.

Walking in Divine Health

"Bless the Lord O my soul and forget none of His benefits; who pardons all your iniquities, who heals all your diseases (Psalm 103:2-3)."

One of the hardest topics to understand for people, especially believers, is physical healing. We have so many questions, certainly more questions than answers. All you have to do is watch one of those ads where some organization is raising money for children with serious diseases such as cancer. Nothing is quite as heart wrenching. What is God thinking? Why would He let this happen? Why doesn't He stop it? These are some of the questions that plaque our minds. Even for the strongest believer, this picture of such suffering in our most vulnerable is too hard to comprehend how a God of love allows this to go on. There are no pat answers to these heartrending questions. Of course, the Bible gives answers and many within the Body of Christ are discovering the secrets of how to understand the provision of healing. Still, there are sicknesses that seem to escape the truth that God heals.

In these next few stories, I will share with you healings and revelations that I have witnessed and experienced in my own faith journey. I will share what the Holy Spirit has taught me and how I have put them into practice. I am sure many others in the Body of Christ have learned and received revelation on this subject.

Other questions can be answered, but like most answers, they will lead to more questions. We must do what we know until we get further revelation. Some of the questions are raised out of our experiences, out of past teaching, out of wrong belief systems, and some questions are raised out of our refusal to believe the Bible simply because it doesn't fit our narrative. Does God want everyone healed? Does God make us sick to teach us? We all are going to die, so some of us have to endure sickness, right? Again, I may not answer all these questions. After all, if I could, I would be an extremely wealthy woman because I would be writing a book on that and I promise it would be in every home. In these accounts, I will share with you what I learned and how that is based on the Bible, and never on the premise that I am more worthy than you to be healed. I am just like you in that I don't have clear understanding why some are healed, and some are not. I do believe we are getting more and more revelation on God's Word, which has to be our standard.

Brenda

"The case that is too hard for you, you shall bring to me, and I will hear it (Deuteronomy 1:17)."

I have read many accounts of miraculous healings. Like you, I have listened to accounts of God restoring body organs. I personally met a man from New Zealand who was dying from cancer and had almost all his digestive system removed. He had been in every prayer line and had the most well-known ministers lay hands on him, and still the cancer raged in his body. In the last hours of his life, a group of regular, quiet men and women gathered around him and prayed. He later said it felt like a freight train ran through his body. His friend, thinking he was delirious, took him to the hospital. The doctor looked at his scars from extensive surgery as well as his medical file with the information of how his entire digestive system had been removed. The doctor was in total confusion because, in the test he ran, he saw a complete healthy digestive system fully functioning! That was quite a number of years before the writing of this book and he is still living with his wife in New Zealand.

That is not just a miracle, but it is a documented, creative, and restorative miracle. The doctors cannot explain that away. Religion cannot annul it. Only God could bring that into being. This story, while not every healing is that dramatic, is every bit miraculous and I was blessed to be a part of it. If you have read the previous stories in this book, then you have been introduced to Robyn. She is my friend from Missouri. One day, she called and told me about her friend, Brenda. Brenda had been diagnosed with an inoperable brain tumor. The doctors told her to go home, get her things in order, and make her funeral arrangements. She did just that. Robyn helped put on an event to raise money due to her lack of insurance. She called asking if I would get a team of my people together to pray over Brenda if she brought her to South Carolina. I was surprised and asked her why she would drive this sick woman nearly a thousand miles for someone to pray for her. Surely she knew people who could pray there. Her reply was that she did not know anyone who had the ability to believe God the way she knew us to believe for the miraculous. I told her to bring her. I immediately called my pastor, Chuck. We set a date for the prayer time.

We were to meet at my house the day after their arrival. Chuck and our two worship leaders came along with a couple of others for prayer support. Of course, I was there and my granddaughter Clairey who was around fourteen at the time, so this had to have been around 2010. Greg, our worship leader, brought his guitar and we spent quite a bit of time in worship and seeking the Lord for direction. We began to pray. I had requested for Robyn and Brenda not to divulge any information concerning the location of the tumor other than it was in the brain. Chuck asked me to bring out my tallit and do a short explanation of what it is. You may be curious as well. A tallit is a Jewish prayer shawl. Jesus, being a Jewish rabbi—teacher—would have worn one. It has four corners with tassels with a blue thread running through it. These corners are called wings and the tassels are highly symbolic of the names of God. When the woman with the issue of blood pressed through the crowd to touch the hem of His garment and was healed, this is what she was after. She understood the meaning of the corners.

I am not implying that this garment can heal anyone as it is not a magic cloth. The story in the Bible says that Jesus felt power leave His body. He is the healer. After I explained about the tallit, Pastor Chuck told Clairey to pray and ask God to show her where the tumor was. She took the tallit and placed the corner on Brenda's head in the spot she felt the tumor was located. Brenda began to cry. Brenda told us where Clairey placed the tallit was the exact location of the tumor. We began to give God praise for healing her tumor and that she would live. We spent about eight hours in worship and prayer that day. I do not say that to take any glory on how spiritual we were, but to say that, sometimes, we want fast results. God wants us to spend time with Him, and not just to treat Him as if He is our genie in a lamp.

Earlier in this story, I mentioned that this took place around 2010 and I am writing this in 2020. Each time I go to Missouri, I get to see Brenda. When she was diagnosed with a brain tumor, she had gotten to the place where she could not function in day to day activities such as driving, reading, or working. She was making plans for her funeral. Today she is doing life and giving God all the glory.

Shaley

"Behold, the former things have come to pass, now I declare new things (Isaiah 42:9)."

I want to say right up front, I am not an animal lover. I can appreciate those who are. If you treat your little dog or cat like part of your family, I have no problem with that. I am just not one of those people. That is why this story is so funny. God has a unique sense of humor!

This story took place during one of my many trips to Missouri. I always stay with Robyn, a dog lover. At this time, she had three dogs. They were what I call mop-dogs. You know what I mean. They look like little mop-heads walking around. Their hair touches the floor and it helps keep the floors clean! Their names were Chloe, Shaley, and Tinka; Chloe was the oldest and largest while Shaley was somewhat smaller. Tinka could easily fit into a teacup. I liked them just fine, especially when they stayed on the floor where they belonged. Shaley thought she was Robyn's favorite because she had nothing to do with anyone else.

On this particular trip, Robyn had taken Shaley to the vet the day before I arrived. Tinka had been jumping on Shaley while playing and her nail went into Shaley's eye scratching it badly. The poor dog would not open her eye and had stopped eating. She was very lethargic. The vet had put her on some medication, but Shaley was not responding well. When I entered the house, I sat down in the kitchen and the strangest thing happened. Shaley jumped onto my lap. Robyn was shocked because Shaley never jumped on anyone's lap other than Robyn's, and she had not done that since she had been injured.

My first instinct, when an animal does jump on me, is to push it off. I didn't push off this animal. At first, I thought it was because I knew she was hurting. I really am not as hard as I seem. Then the Holy Spirit spoke to me and told me to place my hand over her eye and pray for healing. What? I don't pray for animals. Nevertheless, I did as I was instructed. I prayed and asked God to heal her, and then I thanked Him for His healing power. Immediately, Shaley jumped down and opened her eye. It was totally clear. She went over to his bowl and ate. God healed that dog!

The next morning, I was still in my red polka dot pjs, lying on the couch, and all three dogs were all on top of me. Robyn took a picture and put it on Facebook. My reputation for being a hard case where animals are concerned was forever lost. Then, after she told the story of Shaley's miracle, I became known as having an animal anointing. My phone started ringing with people wanting me to pray for their animals. Geez!

Building Bridges

"O Lord my God, I cried to You for help, and You healed me (Psalm 30:2)."

I gave an account of how the discs in my neck ruptured and in the middle of that trauma I had a stroke. That initially took place in 1999, between then and 2005 I had three neck surgeries with a bar and eight screws placed in the front of my neck. That was just a refresher so this story will make sense. The doctors will tell you that fusions and bars that are put into your neck will last about ten years. I have one natural disc in my neck left and that is the very top one which my head sits on. The doctor told me that all the other discs that are fused will wear out the strength of the good disc.

That being said, fast forward several years. I don't know exactly how many years because I am lousy at journaling! Somewhere around 2010 give or take a year, we were having a ministry meeting. This meeting was at Pastor Chuck's house. There were about eight people present. When I got there, I did not tell anyone how much pain I was in. It was severe! I could hardly focus, and my eyes felt as if they were continually rolling back into my head. I can't explain this any better but to tell you I knew my neck was crumbling, literally deteriorating. I had just got through praying before I arrived at the meeting and this is exactly what I prayed, *"Dear God, if You don't touch me tonight, I will have to leave and go to the hospital."* The doctor had warned me that when it came necessary to do surgery again, it would require totally re-doing all the work in my neck and it would not leave me with much quality of life as it would put great restrictions of movement on me.

We discussed a few ministry issues and then we went into prayer. I was sitting on a sofa which was sitting in the middle of the room. One of our worship leaders, Justine, came over quietly behind me and put her hands so gently around my neck and she prayed silently. It wasn't but a few seconds into her prayer time that I began to feel a strange sensation in my entire neck. I knew in my spirit that God was doing something. The only thing that came to my mind was God was building a bridge in my neck. I could feel as if my neck were being lifted almost like jacking up a car. I did not say a word. I opened my eyes, Justine kept praying. Then Chuck looked at me and pointed and this is what he said, *"Sandy, God is building a bridge in your neck!"*

That is exactly what God did! After that, the only time I have any neck pain is if I just do something stupid like sit with my head turned to the side a long time or when I know that there is spiritual warfare going on around me, I will feel pressure. Other than that, my neck never bothers me.

That is the goodness of our Father.

Faith or Fear, You Have to Choose

*"And Jesus said to him, 'Go; your faith has made
you well (Mark 10:52).'"*

Five long years of CT Scans, Myelograms, brain scans, MRIs, steroid injections, three neck surgeries, and blood patches— not counting the endless doctor visits and recovery time from a stroke—my doctor decided I was able to do all the normal things a forty-plus year old female should be doing. Seriously, during that time, I did not have to do the regular pap smears and breast exams. It was all I could handle to just do the "neck thing," as I like to refer to it. My doctor said it was time to get back to normal, so I joined the rest of the female world and had a mammogram.

I was at work when I got the call from the doctor's office where I had my mammogram test. The nurse stated that I should come in for another mammogram. I asked her why, and of course, she was evasive in her answer. I just assumed they saw a shadow or some problem with the film. I know that happens often, so I wasn't overly concerned. I told her I would make an appointment. She quickly informed me that I was to come in immediately and bring my husband with me. She said the doctor was waiting for me. His office was in Charlotte, North Carolina, about forty-five minutes away. Now I was a bit concerned, not so much for me, but my then-husband, Pete. He had lost several family members to cancer and I knew that was going to scare the daylights out of him. I would have to wake him because he worked the third shift and slept in the daytime.

I hung up the phone and simply prayed, *"Father, what do you want me to do about this?"*

He answered, *"Call three people that you trust to pray in faith and not fear. Tell them only what is necessary for them to have the information to pray effectively. Do not have a discussion about it."*

Immediately, I knew who to call: Mrs. Oree, Steve, and Melissa. These were the three friends I trusted. They never asked me details, but said they would pray as soon as I hung up.

I called Pete and told him I would pick him up and to be ready. We got to the doctor's office and he was waiting for me. I had to have a mammogram that was a bit different. I promise you, some man who was angry with women had to develop that test. It is excruciatingly painful! Bless his heart. I waited a few minutes while the doctor looked at the images. He simply told me I could go home, all was well. I told him I was not going home and I asked him if what he saw was just a shadow or what?

"Mrs. Starnes, I do not call patients up in the middle of the day and tell them to come immediately and bring their husbands for a shadow. I have been doing this a long time and I know the difference. You had a large mass in your right breast. I would have to do other tests, or even a biopsy to be sure, but my educated guess of what I saw, I believe it was more than likely malignant. It simply is not there now. It is

gone and I have no explanation for that. I guess the technician cured you."

"If your technician cured me then you should give her a raise!"

"Hallelujah, I know that is right!" the technician laughed.

"If anyone cured me it was God Almighty." I pointed upward as I made my declaration of faith.

"Well, I don't know what happened, you had a large mass and it simply is not there now."

I believed I had breast cancer, or at least a tumor of some kind, and God healed me. Perhaps you are going through something. Determine to believe the goodness of God rather than the dark report. It could save your life. Fear or faith, your choice.

Raindrops Falling on My Head

"The Lord sustains all who fall and raises up all who are bowed down (Psalm 145:14)."

Holly and I were in Georgia when my friend, Jerry, called. At that time, he and his wife lived in Sanford, Florida, Holly lived in North Carolina, and I lived in South Carolina. Holly is from Georgia and I had taken her there to take care of some business. It was in the early evening, around five or six o'clock. We were about four hours away from Holly's home in North Carolina. Heidi and Jerry are more than friends, they are my God-appointed spiritual children. I already had a plane ticket to go visit them in a couple weeks until I received Jerry's call. Heidi had been having some issues that seemed to be heart related. They had not told anyone. Jerry said Heidi did not know he was calling me, but he knew that she would want me to be there.

Of course I was going to be there. Her heart catheterization was scheduled two days away early in the morning, which meant I needed to be there the next day. While I was driving, Holly was on the phone getting me a plane ticket. The only time I could fly was early the next morning, which meant I would have to be at the airport by six a.m. and that was about an hour's drive from my home.

I drove almost four hours to take Holly home, and then I had another hour and a half to my house. I got home just before one a.m. I showered, packed, and took a nap and got up at four am. Not bad for an old girl. I was around sixty at the time. Actually, this was my normal lifestyle; I was always on the go. I had no idea I was not the only whirlwind blowing into Florida; a hurricane was on its way! The day I arrived, the winds were already blowing and power to their apartment was out. Heidi decided she did not want to try to recover from a heart catheterization without air conditioning, so they rented a small house for a couple of days. Meanwhile, Heidi and I went out late that afternoon to find gas. The service station where we stopped was out of gas, so we thought we would go inside to get something to drink.

By this time, we were seeing the hurricane preview; it was raining cats and dogs. It was raining so hard you could hardly hear yourself talk in the car. It did not look as if it was going to slow down, so we thought we would make a run for the door to the store. I had on flip flops and the water was already standing several inches on the curb. I stepped up and my foot was covered with water. Before I could get my balance, my feet slid forward and I hit the pavement. I fell flat on my back, and, even with the water to cushion it, my head slammed against the pavement. The sound my head made hitting that concrete was so loud that the man parked next to us heard it through the noise of the pouring rain. He jumped out to help. I could have saved Heidi the trouble of having a heart catheterization because the horror on her face was enough to send her into a heart attack if that had really been an issue! She looked terrified. She knew the problems I had with my neck and that I had a bar and screws in it.

"What do you want me to do, Sandy?"

I was surprisingly calm. The rain had let up a bit, but I needed to stay still and evaluate my condition for a moment. *"Just let me lie here for a moment."* The man was still there and looking to see if there was a river of blood. There was no evidence that I was bleeding. I slowly got up. We went into the store and the manager was already on her way out to see about me. She said she saw my head hit the cement. She wanted to call an ambulance, but I refused. I asked her to get me some ice as my head was swelling. She asked me if I was cold because the air condition was running, and I should have been soaked. Heidi was soaked.

I told her, *"No, I'm fine."* She gave me some ice and they were all trying to get me to go to the hospital. I told them to let me have a minute to pray. I walked around the corner and prayed.

"Lord, what do you want me to do in this situation?"

"Trust Me."

That is all I heard, then I realized that I was not wet. My clothes and my hair should have been soaked! I had lain in a puddle of water and it rained on my face. I was totally dry! Except for my flip flops, they were wet. Go figure. I did, however, have a tremendous lump on the top of my head. Have you ever seen those cartoons where the character get a goose egg on top of their head and it rises up like a pointed mountain? That is exactly what my head looked like. I have very thick hair and it was sticking out through it. It was visible to everyone. The store manager was genuinely concerned. Of course, she probably thought I might sue the store. I had no intention of doing that. They did not cause the rain. She had already called the insurance company.

We went home, or at least to the apartment, to get some clothes. My head hurt terribly and now my elbow felt as though it was cracked. I could not touch it without pain. Sleeping was difficult, I was sore all over. It would have been sensible to have gone to the hospital to be checked, but I had a word from the Lord. Trust Me. I chose to do just that. I called a friend who is a nurse and she told me how to apply ice and what to take to rest.

The next morning, the insurance representative from the store called to see how I was doing. She asked me the normal questions while we were being recorded. She assured me that I would be covered if I wanted to go to the hospital.

I told her, "*No, that isn't necessary.*"

Then she asked if she could ask me something off the record and I agreed, "*Ms. Starnes, the store manager was extremely concerned. She said your head was truly injured. Most people would see this as an opportunity to get some money. Why didn't you? You certainly have a legitimate claim.*"

I replied, "*I have something better than insurance money. I have a Word from the Lord of healing and His provision. That is more important to me. I know it may seem that I am suffering injury and pain, and I am, but that will pass. I choose to trust Him. It will be alright.*"

She was flabbergasted. She had never heard of anyone passing an opportunity to get a large settlement by trusting God. I knew that I could have won a lawsuit. I believe I actually had a concussion and a cracked elbow. But, I knew God was doing something in me that was far greater than a settlement of money, but it would take my trusting Him more than money. Healing does not always come quickly and that is where our faith has to override the circumstances. I did not understand all of it then, and, truth be told, I still don't have the fullness of how it all works. My head had soft squishy places for six months and my elbow hurt for months. I still knew I had heard from God and that He was teaching me something greater than the momentary pain. I would see that clearer in the coming years.

By the way, my sweet spiritual daughter, Heidi, came through the heart catheterization just fine. It also gave me time with her precious daughter who, at that time, was seeking the Lord. She found Him!

These Feet Were Made for Walking

"But he must ask in faith without any doubting…(James 1:6)."

Have you ever had bone spurs in your feet? If you have, then you will understand what I am talking about. My feet hurt for two years, both of them. It felt like I was walking on broken glass. Pain would shoot up from my heels all the way up my legs. I received prayer continually from my church friends. I did foot exercises and I only wore good walking shoes. Nothing worked. I had experienced healing before, as you have read in previous stories, so when people tell you that you just have to have enough faith, that alone is not the whole truth. I don't have time here to unfold that teaching, but the Bible says that, if you have faith as a mustard seed, you can have a mountain move. A mustard seed is such a small seed, and yet it can produce a huge tree. It is not referring to the size of faith. I believe it is talking about the integrity of the seed itself. If that seed is compromised in any way, it will not produce a healthy tree. If our seed of faith is compromised, it will not produce the results we should see. Many things will compromise the seed of faith, but whatever was going on at that time, it was not producing good health in my feet.

I knew it was time to go to the doctor. I did not have a word from God concerning the situation like I did when I fell in Florida. Long story short, the doctor told me I had huge bone spurs in both heels. He said they looked like large hooks. We tried shots twice, and it gave me some relief, but it would come back with a vengeance. Finally, he decided it was time to do surgery on both feet. He put me on an anti-inflammatory medication for thirty days to get as much inflammation out as possible. By the fifteenth day of taking this medication, my feet were feeling much better. At least I could walk across the floor without crying.

I need to take a break here and tell you a couple of things about me. One, I have a high pain tolerance, and that can be good and bad. Good, because it has kept me from taking a lot of medication and I hate taking meds. Bad, because I will press through until I cause myself serious consequences. The second thing you might find interesting is I have discovered the pattern of how God talks to me. I bet you have a pattern too. I have figured out that, if God wants to tell me something about what is going on in the heavenlies, aka atmosphere, He does that when I am washing dishes. It took me quite a while to figure that out and I will tell a story later as an example. My friend and ministry partner was at my house while I was washing dishes one night. I looked over and saw that he had been watching me. He acknowledged that he could see I got lost when washing dishes. I laughed because I actually like washing dishes. But, it occurred to me that God often talks to me when I am washing dishes. When God wants to speak to me concerning our personal relationship, He does that when I am in the shower. When He is going to give me revelation on something concerning the Word, He does it as soon as my eyes open in the morning. I think those are the times I am quiet and still.

What a rabbit trail! Back to the feet.

Halfway through the cycle of thirty days of medication, I woke up. Before I could get my feet off the bed, the Lord spoke, "*I am going to teach you to walk in divine health.*"

I felt like Sarah in the Bible when she heard the angel tell Abraham that she would have a baby in her old age. She laughed and so did I. "*If I am going to walk in anything, You need to heal my feet!*"

The Lord did not reply to me, and I knew He had said all He was going to for the time being. I told Him that I was going off the medication and trust Him to teach me. I went off the meds and I knew it would take about three days for the medication to get out of my system. I assumed that, after the meds were out of my system, I would experience no pain. That is reasonable thinking. Right? The third day after I got off the meds, I eagerly jumped out of bed and pain shot up my leg! I got upset. I pointed at my feet and the other hand I pointed toward heaven.

"*NO, that is not what You said! You said I would walk in divine health. This is not divine health.*"

Do you know what God's response to me was? Nothing! Nada! Not a word! I decided I was going to take Him at His promise regardless of how I felt. I did not go back on the medication. I called and canceled my doctor's appointment. That night, as I got ready for bed, I realized all the pain was gone.

I thanked Him and He said, "*I want you to walk in divine health.*"

That was good enough for me. That was about twelve years ago and I have not been to a doctor since. I am not saying I will never go to a doctor; I would pray and be led by the Holy Spirit.

Now please hear me. I am not against doctors or medication, and, until you get this revelation for yourself, don't go on my word, but only on God's Word and your level of faith. Walking in divine health does not mean you will never experience illness or problems. Each case requires you to be led by the Holy Spirit. There are many reasons we suffer things. We live in a human body of flesh and bones and it is subject to injury. We live in a fallen world and have the elements of things in the air that affect us. There are many reasons we suffer sickness. I still wear glasses. There are promises in the Bible, but there are no formulas or pat answers. We are to live by faith and be led by the Spirit of God. I do believe I will receive more revelation or hear more from another member of the Body of Christ as time goes on.

~

Only the Strong Survive

"Glory in His holy name; let the heart of those who seek the Lord be glad (I Chronicles 16:10)."

Several months passed after the feet episode and I continued to pray to understand how divine health looked. God is so gracious. He gave the Body of Christ gifts. Through the Holy Spirit, we have gifts of healing and the wonderful promises in the Word of God. As I sought the Lord on this revelation of divine health, by the Spirit, I came to understand that God does not want us to always have to run to those we consider as having a gift. The Holy Spirit is the gift, and, if you are a born-again believer, the Holy Spirit lives in you. Divine health is a characteristic of the Holy Spirit. He is never sick. I still don't have all the answers, but if I did, I would be writing a different kind of book and making millions!

Do you know how some things just seem to creep up on you, and, one day, you realize you have been having some pain or discomfort? I went to bed one night and my chest felt a little tight and my breathing seemed to be labored. I realized it had been going on for a while, although I couldn't pinpoint when it started. I prayed and fell asleep. Over the next few weeks, I realized the discomfort had not only persisted, but had increased. My arm felt heavy and my breathing was more labored. I know how the signs of heart trouble look. Heart trouble is an issue that runs through my family. Both my parents had heart attacks at an early age. I did not tell anyone and, actually, only lately even talked about it. The pain began to increase, and I was getting concerned.

Considering what the Lord had told me about walking in divine health, I asked Him, "*Lord, I do not want to be negligent in my health. I know what these symptoms mean. Do you want me to go to the doctor?*"

He replied and simply asked me a question, "*Are you going to believe their report, because their report will not be good?*"

I got nothing else. I have learned a few things about God in the many years I have communicated with Him. He gives instruction through asking questions and always gives us a choice. I knew He was telling me to do what I wanted, and He would not be angry about it. However, I also knew He was indicating that I could choose to believe what He had told me earlier about walking in divine health. I could go to the doctor and medical route, but, once I saw the report that was not going to be a good report, it would take more faith to overcome the issue. I knew the consequences if I missed God. I made a decision that moment to trust Him as never before.

"*Okay, God, I choose to trust You and walk this divine health agenda by faith. If I die, then I die.*"

I know you are wondering if the pain and breathing difficulty left immediately. The answer is, "*No*" It persisted and, while it did not get any worse, neither did it get any better. This went on for at least another six weeks. Then, one night, I was getting ready for bed and realized that the problem was not present. The tightness and heavy breathing had stopped. I could not remember if it had been there the night before, but it certainly was completely gone. The heaviness in my arm had vanished! I raised both my arms and began to praise Him for His goodness and faithfulness.

After a few minutes, He spoke, "*This is where you usually give up. When the symptoms persist, you think I did not heal you. You must learn to trust Me more than you trust your pain.*"

I never again experienced any more of those symptoms! At times, I still have issues, like allergies and minor things, but I can honestly say I am very healthy and rarely feel ill.

One day, the Lord told me to pick up my Bible. I did and this is what He said, "*Sandy, when you learn to believe My Word over everything you feel, think, or experience, then you will walk in peace and good health.*"

I try to remember and practice it every day in every situation. He is God and there is none like Him.

Angels and Demons

"Beloved, do not believe every spirit, but test the spirits to see whether they are from God...(I John 4:1)."

Alright, here we go! I am going to talk about something quite controversial. The spirit realm is more real than this physical plane we live in because it is eternal, and this life on Earth is so temporary. I know that, in previous stories, I talked about both angels and demons, and how they can interject themselves in our lives. We certainly know they have influence in our activities and even our thoughts. All one has to do is read the Bible and understand that these entities are real and active. That has not changed. I am sure that some of these stories will challenge a lot of you. I will make this clear. I do not worship angels, nor do I try to tell them what to do. That is God's right and no one else's. I do not talk to or foolishly challenge demons, nor do I call demons derogatory names, and you shouldn't either. I am not afraid of demons and I don't show them honor, but I do respect the position God has allowed them to have, for now at least.

I am going to share some of my interactions with both, and, even if you have trouble wrapping your mind around what I am saying, at least look for the lesson in it. I am not telling these stories so you will oooohhh and aaahhh over me, but rather that you may see how God guides and provides for us. The weird stuff has its place, and we can learn a lot about how to view the unseen world when we get a glimpse into the other side.

Angels in the Choir

"Praise Him, all His angels; praise Him all His hosts (Psalm 148:2)!"

In one of the earlier stories, I told you how I saw demons. Yeah, I know, it was weird, but I want to tell you about the first time I actually saw an angel. To be exact, it was three angels. I assure you, I am not one to see angels all the time. A lot of years went by without me seeing an angel, though I have felt their presence. I will say this, seeing demons do not scare me. Now, let me clarify that statement. I do not say that with pride. When I am allowed to see demons, I suppose the Holy Spirit has a reason for allowing it and He gives me the ability not to fear. Seeing angels is a whole different ballgame as they put the fear of God in me! I will tell you why in the process of these stories because I asked God why they scared me. If you look at the Scriptures, every time a person came into contact with an angel, the angel had to tell them to not be afraid. So, I am in right alignment with the Scriptures on that.

I was in a United Methodist Church and it was fairly small. The building itself was old; one of those little white chapels with a high steeple. In the moonlight, it could have been a perfect picture for a postcard. I am sorry to say, it was not a healthy church. Many of its parishioners were not as interested in learning about the true nature of God as they were interested in honoring their ancestral heritage. This was not the pastor's fault. He was a friend of mine and I knew him to be serious about bringing his congregation into a deeper relationship with the Lord. Most of them were satisfied with church as they understood it.

This particular Sunday morning turned out to be quite different, at least for me. We were in worship and the choir was singing. This sounds bad, but the truth is the truth. There were only about six people in the choir and most of them were the most problematic in the church. It is sad to admit that such discord goes on in some churches. Anyway, as they were singing, I glanced up to the choir loft and I could not believe my eyes. I saw what I thought at first to be three strange looking men in the choir. They were tall and dressed in white robes with a gold sash around their waists. They stood with their hands straight up in the air in total worship. It was as though they had no idea where they were. I was almost afraid to look, but, at the same time, I could not take my eyes off them. Their sleeves fell down towards their shoulders as they kept their hands lifted in adoration. I would not say they were body builders, yet they had muscular arms and something about their physic gave an air of being physically powerful. Then it dawned on me that they were angels!

I could tell no one other than me seemed to be aware of the angels' presence. That is when I noticed something strange, yes, stranger than it already was. Their robes did not go all the way to the floor, but stopped just before they reached their ankles. There was something sticking out from the edge of their robes. Wings—I saw their wings, which seemed to be hidden in the folds of their robes. I had heard angels have wings, but I wasn't sure how true that was. This only lasted about ten minutes or so and then they simply vanished. I could not speak. I sat like a stone for the rest of the service. After the pastor finished preaching, he came running to me trying to tell me something while I was trying to tell him what I saw. He held out his hand and in it was a pure white feather. He told me he could sense a presence there and then he saw the feather floating in the air. He caught it. It took me a few minutes of stumbling over the words, but I finally managed to tell him I saw from where the feather came. We were dumb struck. I don't know how to end this story except to say that there are so many things we may never understand until we get into His Presence when we leave planet Earth.

STORY 89

~

Mighty Warrior

"Bless the Lord, you His angels, mighty in strength, who perform His word, obeying the voice of His word (Psalm 103:20)!"

This story would probably qualify as the most powerful angel story I have. I know you probably have heard many accounts of those who talk about seeing angels all over the place. I can't say they are not true, but I am skeptical when I hear people say they see little angels flying around as if they are sweet little mythical creatures just floating around in the air. I am highly suspicious of those type of accounts after reading the Bible. Angels in the Bible are not what fairy tales are made of. There are many accounts in the Bible where humans encounter angels that look like mortal men, such as Abraham encountered. We see the angelic beings in Heaven worshipping around God's throne, and they are not what we would consider normal in appearance. In the book of Daniel, it depicts angels fighting other beings in order to deliver a message to Daniel. In 2 Kings 19:35, we are told that the angel of the Lord put to death 185,000 men by himself. I assure you, angels in the Bible do not represent the versions of fairy tales. They are God's agents sent to men to accomplish His purpose.

With that as my opening, I will tell you what I witnessed during a ministry meeting at Pastor Chuck's house. I guess, after reading a few accounts of things happening at his house during ministry meetings, you begin to see that we did not hold meetings to discuss the next fund raiser. We may not have always done it perfectly, but we sought the heart of God with the express intention of moving with Him in order to promote His power for the change of others and ourselves. I believe this is why we had powerful God-encounters.

About seven or eight of us were sitting in Chuck's living room and talking about ministry. I had not been a part of this ministry for a long time. We were trying to learn how to move as a team that consisted of apostles, prophets, evangelists, pastors, and teachers. Ephesians talks about that. We knew we had those callings within our ministry circle. During that time, I had introduced them to things I had experienced concerning the influence demons had on individuals and the ministry of deliverance. They already knew some of that, but had not witnessed seeing demons and were limited in their ability to deal with them. They knew that, on occasion, I saw demons.

As I said, we were sitting around the living room. Suddenly, I saw something out of my peripheral vision. I turned my head and froze. Standing just a few feet from me was a being, an angel. Up to this point, it was only my second encounter with an angel. This angel was very different than the ones I saw in the church choir. He was massive! I don't mean in his size, although he was large. It was his sheer presence. He seemed to fill the room. Chuck's house had high ceilings, about ten feet high in the room. This being almost reached the ceiling with his arm raised. He was dressed similarly to what you saw in the movies with Roman soldiers. His arms looked as if he could kill you with his bare hands. He stood with feet slightly apart, had a huge sword in his raised hand, and his eyes were fixed looking upward. It seemed to me as though he were almost unaware of being in the room. I felt like, while he was in the room, he was actually caught in a different dimension. I don't know why I thought that, but that is the only way I know to describe it. In other words, he wasn't impressed at being in our presence, but was intently looking toward heaven.

I was torn. I wanted to look away because of his fierce appearance and, yet, I was frozen, unable to look away. I must have looked terrified because Rhonda, Chuck's wife, looked at me and said, *"Please tell me you don't see a demon in my house!"*

All I could respond with was, *"Worse than that!"*

"Worse than a demon? I'm not sure I want to know what you see!"

I did not speak again, but silently asked the Lord, *"What is he doing here?*

"Tell them that I have sent him to go before you in the thing I am showing you. He will fight your battles."

That was the end of the angel's presence, at least visually. I finally was able to find my voice and explain what I saw. Our words fail in the ability to describe such supernatural beings. This is when I asked the Lord why angels look so fearsome.

He said, *"Because, they come out of my Presence and you see My glory on them. Your human eyes and mind have trouble comprehending that."* Angels do God's will and do not respond to man trying to give them orders. They will respond to the Word of God spoken by direction of the Holy Spirit. Angels are to be honored, never worshipped.

~

Holy Spirit the Teacher

"But the Helper, the Holy Spirit, whom the Father will send in My name, He will teach you all things…(John 14:26)."

As a church, we treat the Holy Spirit with such extremes. We have a camp where the Holy Spirit is called it. These people will never say the Holy Spirit is not real because they are not silly enough to deny the Scripture references of the Holy Spirit. But, due to their lack of understanding, they think the Holy Spirit is mystical or spooky. Then we have the other camp where they treat the Holy Spirit like a lamp with a magic genie inside. They treat Him like a fairy godmother where they get all their wishes granted. He is neither.

First, look at His name, *"Holy."* Need I say more? Second, He is God. He is not a part of the triune God head. He is wholly God, God the Father is not part of the triune God head, and neither is Jesus a part. They are all three, totally complete, totally holy, totally in perfect unity with each other. I once had a conversation with a young man named Kenny who asked me some questions.

He asked, *"Sandy, have you ever baptized anyone?"*

"Yes, I have."

"What did you baptize them in?"

"Water."

Now I knew where he was going. This was not my first rodeo! *"That is not what I meant. Do you baptize in the name of Jesus only?"*

As I said earlier, I have been in ministry a long time and I am familiar with a lot of different teaching. I knew immediately where this man had gotten his teaching on baptism. He believed you should only baptize in the name of Jesus. Several decades ago, there was a prominent minister that taught that. It was built on the premise that, if you baptized in anything other than the name of Jesus only, you were taking the focus off of Him.

I explained to him that I had no problem baptizing in the name of Jesus only, however, in the Gospel of Matthew, Jesus Himself said to be baptized in the name of the Father, and the Son, and the Holy Spirit. I even showed him the passage.

He shook his head no and said, *"If you baptize in any name other than Jesus only, you are taking away from His importance."*

"Kenny, you are deceived in believing that, because there are no divisions in the Godhead. They are not in competition with one another! They would cease to be holy if that is how they thought! That is how man thinks and they are not like us. They are holy and completely in unity. They have order, but never competing to get above the other."

He could not see that. That is how deception works. It blinds us to the truth. That is why you should never limit yourself to only one man's or woman's teaching. God has called many teachers among the Body of Christ and it should always be in alignment with the Word of God as the standard. I just wanted to take a break and teach a bit. Now back to the story.

I was sitting in my bedroom at my desk around nine o'clock. I was working at my computer, which had my back to the room. Behind me, to my left, was the entrance to the bathroom. I caught some movement behind me and turned my head to look. Standing in the doorway was a tall, dark figure. It had the shape of a man with no real facial features. He was just staring at me. I recognized, right away, that he was a principality. In case you aren't familiar with that terminology, it means a demon with a higher rank. In the Bible, we see the spirit realm such as angels and demons having different ranks of power or position. Some examples are Michael the archangel, or Satan as the leader of the fallen angels. I was not scared when I saw him, although you can't be at total ease with a demon in your room. At the same time, I heard the Holy Spirit laugh. Seriously, He laughed. Not like a belly roaring laugh; just a chuckle really, and He said, "*Act as if he is not here!*"

I felt a peace. I knew the Holy Spirit had empowered me to act as if there was not a high-ranking demon in my bedroom. Otherwise, I don't know how I would have handled it. I have said this before: I am not afraid of demons, but I am not used to them dropping by to visit either! I turned back to my computer and began typing again. A few minutes passed, and the being was at my side. He picked up my left arm and swung it into the air. The Holy Spirit spoke again, "*Act as if he is not here!*" I could still hear the humor in His voice. I started typing again. Although I did not see the demon leave, I did not see him again. I worked for another hour or so, and turned off my computer. I did not see anything, and I got ready for bed. I laid down and turned off my lamp. I had perfect peace and a sense of safety. The Holy Spirit spoke again, this time there wasn't any humor in His voice. It was a solemn command, *"Sit up and tell him to get out of your home!"*

I did exactly what the Holy Spirit told me to do. I did not feel or see anything, but I sensed something took place. What did I learn through this experience? For one, I learned that we should never move in the spiritual realm without the guidance of the Holy Spirit. The other thing I learned is that no demon is more powerful than the Holy Spirit. Believe me, the demons know it too. He is our teacher and He will only instruct us in righteousness. Many want to know how the demon spirit got in. I do not know or really care. Demons are not my focus. God, in any form He chooses, is my focus. He is my protector and my provider. I will not fear.

~

Praying Angels

"Are they not all ministering spirits, sent out to render service for the sake of those who will inherit salvation (Hebrews 1:14)?"

I told you before that I really have not seen angels often. I am always amazed at the sight of them. You have to be very careful not to elevate them to a place that becomes unhealthy. The truth is, if it is an angel sent from God, he will not allow you to worship him. But there are other things we can get out of order concerning angels. We can desire to see them so that we can appear more spiritual than others. I have seen people who actually think they can command angels to do their bidding. Be very careful when interacting with the spirit realm. Angels are sent by God for His purpose, and they only carry out His agendas. They respond only to the Word of God out of a clear heart.

There was a small group of people at my house to pray. We did this on a regular basis, most of the time it was as few as two or three. We were not concerned with the number, we just tried to be consistent and pray as led by the Holy Spirit. On this night, we had about six or seven people. We were not being loud, most of us were praying silently, or in very low voices. We have learned that

God is not deaf, but He is not nervous either. It doesn't matter how loud as long as it is in faith and passion, and not just to be heard over everyone else.

We were about half-way through the prayer time, and I opened my eyes. I was surprised and I instantly remembered the story in 2 Kings 6 where the prophet Elisha prayed for the servant's eyes to be opened to see the angels stationed all over the mountain to help them in the battle. There, in my small living room with just us ordinary people, were eleven angels standing in different places, and they were all in a position of prayer. They were silent, but I could tell they were in prayer along with us. I waited until we were finished praying before I said anything. One of the girls let out her breath and said how she could feel the presence of the Lord. I told all of them about the angels. The response was not about the angels, although we were grateful that our prayer time was rewarded by their presence. It showed us that God was aware of us and our willingness to gather to seek Him. He sent us reinforcements. My daughter, when she was small, would say, "*How's better than that?*"

STORY 92

~

Angels on Assignment

*"And it will be said, 'Build up, build up, prepare the way, remove
every obstacle out of the way of My people (Isaiah 57: 14).'"*

All one has to do is read the Bible and see how many times the
Lord used His angels to promote His assignments on the Earth. In
both the Old and New Testaments, we see angels in many forms.
They bring answers to prayers, make announcements, perform
miracles, give instructions, and pronounce judgments, and many
other acts as they are assigned by the Father. I don't know why
we have such a hard time receiving their ministries without a lot
of strife and controversy. Why would God not still use them and
allow us to see them occasionally? I have already addressed appropriate behavior concerning their interaction with us.

If you have read previous stories, you will remember I told you
how I have learned the different ways God gives me insight. One
of those ways is when He reveals to me things concerning the atmosphere or spiritual actions in the atmosphere. It is usually when
I am washing dishes. Maybe that is when I don't have my mind
busy with other things; I'm not sure why He chose that to be the
time, it just is. Washing dishes was not my favorite thing when I

was growing up, but I have learned to appreciate the quiet time. No one bothers you while you are doing it because they are afraid you might want help! We all think how spiritual we want to be, and we want God to talk to us the way we hear about others getting a down-load from the Spirit. Perhaps you have been avoiding the real spiritual places such as washing dishes.

I had a window above my sink and I really enjoyed looking out while washing dishes. Suddenly, I heard a whoosh sound. It seemed to go by my face just outside the window. I looked and didn't see anything. Again, whoosh, it happened very fast, but I knew I had not imagined it.

I have learned that, if something strange happens, I try to find a natural reason for it. You don't have to invent spiritual phenomena; they are all around us, we just can't always see with our natural eyes. After checking every possible natural explanation, I did what I knew to do.

I asked God, "*Lord, what was that whoosh sound?*"

"*The enemy just released a hoard of demons, but I released a host of holy angels.*" What is so hard about that? Why don't we just ask and trust Him to convey the information we need to know? He is waiting to converse with you.

"Call to Me and I will answer you and I will tell you great and mighty things, which you do not know (Jeremiah 33:3)."

STORY 93

Provision

*"Avraham called the place Adonai Yir'eh [Adonai will see (to it),
Adonai provides]...(Genesis 22:14 CJB)."*

I used this Scripture reference out of the *Complete Jewish Bible*, so
I know it may look a little weird to you if you have not used that
version. Sometimes our English name for God loses its impact after reading the Jewish way of saying it. In the twelfth chapter of
Genesis, God tells Abraham that he will be blessed to be a blessing. It is awesome to receive something when you know you did
nothing to earn it. But, a blessing from God is not just about us. It
is always to serve His purpose and to show His goodness; we simply reap the benefits. We are just a participant in His plan.

Perhaps you have felt the call, or maybe God has put something
in your heart to do and you want to, but you feel like you don't
have whatever it takes to get the job done. Maybe you think there
will be a better time, or you don't have the money, or you don't
think you are smart enough. The list can go on and on of the whys
and why nots! All these stories show how an extraordinary God
can take an ordinary life and move miraculously. He can put people into places and situations that would be impossible for them

to do on their own. These next few stories are going to be brief accounts of how God provided everything I needed to live. Most of these stories took place while I was unemployed and without any income! God was building my faith in Him and showing how He will provide to do what He has called us to do.

We will often say, based on a Scripture, in the tenth chapter of Acts that God is no respecter of persons. We take that out of context and think that what He does for one He will repeat the process exactly the same way for anyone or everyone. I want to give you an example of how this works. God had gotten me to a point where I had to trust Him for everything, and I mean everything. He was faithful and patient with me. I was beginning to find a place within the staff of a church, but not in a paid position—that would come later. This group of people was always a blessing to me, but they knew how to follow the leading of the Holy Spirit and did only what He told them as far as giving to me. They had a heart to help me, but also to help me put my trust in God and not them.

We had a man in our church who found himself unemployed. He had just bought a truck and had a nice small house. Pastor Chuck helped him make right decisions about his situation and finally told him to prepare to sell it before the situation got to a place where he might have to give it back to the bank. He chose to ignore that advice. He came over to visit me at my home and we were just chatting, and the subject came up. I asked him why he wasn't taking Chuck's advice.

"I have decided to do what you are doing. I'm going to trust God."

"Of course, you should trust God, but that doesn't mean you should not do what you should do. Are you saying you are not going to put your house on the market?"

285

"*Well, God pays your bills. I figure He is no respecter of persons, what He does for you He will do for me.*"

"*Okay, let's examine that a minute. Are you behind in your house payments?*"

He was quiet for a moment, "*Yes, two months.*"

"*I have never been late on any payment since going into full-time ministry. I have never had to receive government help with groceries or my power bill. God has worked through others to provide for my needs.*"

I could see he was having a hard time with what I was saying. I simply asked him another question, "*Are you called to do what I do?*"

"*No, I don't have a clue about any of that.*"

"*If that Scripture meant what you and others say it means, no one who is a Christian would have to work. The problem with that is God works through people. He does not rain money from Heaven. Actually, God does not have any money. He doesn't need it. He works through His Body of Believers. We all have our place in the plan of God. That requires us to pray, listen, and obey.*"

I worked a secular job for most my life and still did ministry, but where God was taking me required more of my time and my willingness to trust Him for my provision. Oh, one more thing. God did not put a month's worth of money in my account, so I did not have to think about it. At first, I had to trust Him each day, one day at a time for my needs. As I grew in faith, the provision came, and it was enough for several days. It did come to a point where the money was enough to take care of finances for a month. It was a process of faith. It still is. One of the hardest things to learn is not to put your trust in the people who support you continually. Thank God for their faithfulness, but, at any given moment, their situation or guidance from the Holy Spirit can change. Our trust has to remain in God.

I am sad to report that he didn't give any attention to what I said. He ended up losing his home and, therefore, had nothing with which to start over. God works through us in different ways to accomplish His plan. He is faithful to His Word and that is always His standard. Even if you are called to full-time ministry, do not assume God will work your situation out the way you see it working in others who are called. He has a designer plan just for you, no matter what you are called to do. Maybe God placed a desire in your heart to be a nurse, mechanic, or a politician. Be faithful and exhibit Christ wherever you are. That is ministry.

STORY 94

❧

First Things First

"But seek first His kingdom and His righteousness, and all these things will be added to you (Matthew 6:33)."

Just after I left my first husband, I started going to a church called *Christ Fellowship*, actually the name was something else and was changed to this name shortly after I started attending. During these years, I learned how to walk by faith. God was very gracious to place me with this group. If you have to learn a whole new way of living, I pray you get to do it with people who love God and want what He wants. It made the journey so much easier. I stayed there eight years. You have already read a lot of stories, many of which took place through the time I was with *Christ Fellowship*. Some of the next few stories happened while I was still there, but there came a time where God was calling me to another place. That, my friend, was one of the hardest moves I have ever made.

This story took place at the end of the eight years with *Christ Fellowship*. When you are called from one ministry to another, it is never easy. I had not only worked alongside this group; they had become my family. It wasn't that I suddenly got word from the Lord about leaving *Christ Fellowship*; I had a knowing. That is actually how the Holy Spirit leads us from the inside. At any rate, I knew the Lord was speaking to me about leaving. Leaving to what, I wasn't sure. God usually does not give us the whole picture. That is why it is called walking by faith.

As I said, these people had become family to me. They were always there for me and my granddaughters. It also was my income. After a few years there, I was put on staff and they paid me well. I wasn't going to get rich, but I lacked nothing. My friend, Scott, defines true prosperity this way: no lack.

When the Lord first let me know I would be leaving, I knew He did not mean immediately, although I wasn't sure why. He knew it would take me some time to get used to the idea of leaving. I had strong relationships with Pastor Chuck and the others. Not only that, God would have to get me to the place where I could trust Him to leave my paycheck behind. It took six months for the right time to make itself known. I went to Pastor Chuck a couple months before and told him what I sensed the Lord leading me to do as far as leaving, but I did not have a definite date. He knew I was only there for a season, we just didn't know how long of a season. He said he would be in prayer for me to know the right time and the ability to trust God in the next season.

The Lord gave me a date and I really did not give it a lot of thought. I went to Chuck and told him the date. He said that date would mark the eighth year, to the day, that I started coming. I had not even thought of that. The number eight in the Bible means "new beginnings." I asked Chuck if I could take my paycheck with me. He laughed. I was just joking; however, I had no idea how I was going to pay my next month's bills. But God knew. The day after I said my goodbyes, two things happened. My well went out! I called someone who worked on them as a side job. You might have known, he was also a pastor. God is so funny. This pastor had been praying for some extra money—I don't know why it had to be my money! I managed to scrape the money together, but while he was working on my well, my water heater went out! Thank God my well could be fixed. Together, the bill was eighteen-hundred dollars. I don't know how I had that much, but I counted out the cash and then the Lord told me to pray over it and bless it for this pastor.

Later that day, I received a phone call. It was from a friend who lived in another state. She told me the Lord had spoken to her and her husband to give me seven-hundred dollars a month. Wow, it would not cover all my expenses, but it certainly would be a good start as I kept my expenses at a minimum. The next day, I received another call from her.

She asked, "*Sandy, how much did I tell you we were supposed to give you?*"

My first thought was, "*Uh oh, here it comes, a change of mind.*" That was not godly thinking; that was fleshly fear. I guess I had not yet learned to trust solely on God instead of man.

"*You said seven-hundred, but you do whatever you are supposed to do. I will be okay.*"

I was trying to have the right attitude. "*I was wrong. That is not what we are supposed to give. We are going to give you a thousand dollars a month. I will send you the check for two months this week.*"

God did not have me bless that well money for the pastor. He blessed the money for me. That was many years ago and they still support me faithfully. Even if they didn't, they are awesome people of God and I am blessed to have them as friends. That was the beginning of a new phase of this awesome faith journey and there is more to come.

Coats for Jews

"He also warms himself and says, 'Aha! I am warm, I have seen the fire (Isaiah 44:16).'"

After the well and God supplying my finances, I still had to watch my money, as most people do. I tried to be faithful as a giver. Being a giver is part of faith, you cannot be just a receiver. I was in my bedroom folding clothes while watching a Christian talk show. The speaker was asking for donations of thirty dollars. He had negotiated with a coat maker to make a warm coat and hat to give to the Jewish people in Russia that were returning back to their rightful country of Israel.

The Lord spoke to me, *"I want you to purchase a coat and a hat for a Jew. I will see that you will not be cold this winter."* I instantly thought about my checkbook. I knew I had only fifty dollars, and unless more came in, that was all I had for the rest of the month. Besides, my furnace was old, but worked fine.

"Lord, I only have fifty dollars."

"I only asked for thirty."

I knew that was the end of the conversation. I had a choice, trust and obey, or not. I immediately wrote the check and put it in the mail. A few months later, winter arrived. We hardly ever get any snow, at least not a significant amount. This time a real snow showed up and stayed for three days. The temperature never got above the teens. I bet you can't guess what happened. My furnace went out! I have a friend who has a brother that works on furnaces, so he came right over and told me he could fix it, but it would take two weeks to get the part because it was such an old furnace. He suggested I find a place for me and Clairey to stay. It was cold.

I remembered what the Lord had promised and decided to trust and take Him at His word. You might find this hard to believe, but it is the truth. My mobile home never got below sixty degrees, without heat, in the snow, and eighteen degrees outside. We were chilly, but never cold. That was about ten years ago and that furnace is still working, although two experts have said they can't understand how. God's goodness is immeasurable!

~

Gratitude

"He who offers a sacrifice of thanksgiving
honors Me…(Psalm 50:23)."

In the beginning of learning to walk by faith, I understood that gratitude is vital. What parent wants to give a gift to their child just to have that child act as if it is nothing? It would be years later, though, before I would get a word of revelation from God concerning gratitude. This is what the Lord said to me, *"Faith moves My hand, but gratitude moves My heart!"* I have never forgotten that. During those early years of my real faith-journey, I had just taken my two granddaughters to live with me. As I've said, Clairey was twelve and Elizabeth was not quite five. God kept us. He supplied all our needs, but it required an everyday faith. I literally prayed, *"Give us this day our daily bread."* There always seemed to be just enough to do what we needed to do. If you want or need increase, you must be thankful for what you have and be a good manager of what you get. I went through that season by showing my gratitude to the Lord. When I went to the grocery store, I always had enough to get everything I needed. When the cashier handed me the receipt, I would wave it in the air and say out loud,

"*Lord, I thank you for the groceries You have provided.*" When I put gas in my car, I was always able to fill it up—and that was when gas was near five dollars a gallon! I would wave my receipt in the air and verbally give God thanks.

Elizabeth would stand quietly by and watch me. One day she asked, "*Meme, do you have to wave that paper and say that out loud?*"

"Yes, *Elizabeth, I do.*" She would just sigh and shake her head. Several years later, we went through another level of growth that required a new level of faith for provision.

Elizabeth heard me talking about it. One day, we were at the store, and, as we were leaving, she said, "*Meme, you remember how you used to wave the receipts in the air?*"

I shook my head yes. She went on to say, "*I think we should start doing it again.*" We did and, of course, God was faithful. That is what He is!

Panties, Power Bills, and Haircuts

"And my God will supply all your needs according to His riches in glory in Christ Jesus (Philippians 4:19)."

What possible connection could panties, power bills, and haircuts have in common? Absolutely nothing—unless you have need of all three! I did, but on different days. This was during the time I was learning to trust God for my needs day by day when I didn't have income; when I had no on-going supporters outside the church I was attending.

I was cleaning my dresser drawers and realized my undies had more holes in them than necessary. I really could not afford to buy more, so I did what I had been learning to do: ask God and expect a response. He didn't answer me right away and, when he did, it came in an unexpected way. The day after I had the panty revelation, one of my church friends called and asked if I could take her and her husband to the airport the next day. I told her it would be no problem; I was glad to do it. She said they would buy me gas, but I told her I had just filled my tank at God's expense, and she could not give me money for gas.

The next day, I picked them up, and, on the way to the airport, they tried to give me money for gas. Again, I refused. She then handed me something and explained, *"This is Kohl's cash, and it has to be used tomorrow or it will not be any good. There is not a Kohl's store where we are going. It is not a lot, just thirty dollars. Maybe you could buy some panties with it."* I declare before God that I had not said anything about panties to anyone. Do you know how awesome it is to know that God cares about your panties when He has a whole universe to run?

Power Bills

It was that time of the month; time to pay the utilities. I did not have the money, although it was not very high. It was around ninety-eight dollars and some odd cents. Well, when you don't have any money and no income, it may as well be a million. I stood in the middle of my living room and held the bill up in the air and said, *"Lord, this is a power bill. It is due tomorrow. If you don't pay it by such and such date, You will have a late charge. If it is not paid by this date, they will cut my power off and I will be in the dark. That is how it works down here. Thank You for paying the power bill. Amen."* I didn't hear a thing.

The next day was Sunday morning and I held a fellowship in my home. Everyone would bring a covered dish and share a meal. It was inevitable; someone always left something. Once, someone left their shoes. Elizabeth came into the kitchen holding the shoes in one hand with her other hand on her hip, and, in her usual sassy self, she asked, *"Meme, how can a grown person leave their shoes at church?"* It was no surprise to me. As I cleaned the kitchen, I noticed potholders on top of the refrigerator. When I reached up to pull them down, something hit the floor. When I picked it up, it was folded money. I unfolded it expecting to see a note. It was a hundred-dollar bill! The Lord spoke, *"You can pay My power bill now."* How cool is that? God has a great sense of humor!

Hair Cuts

When you have silvery gray hair and you are not old, but not as young as you used to be, it is not attractive to let your hair just do its thing. It requires a good hair cut to wear it short and cute. All I needed was fifteen dollars. So, I asked my Father. The next Sunday we had fellowship. I started to bed that night, and as I pulled my cover down, there was something pinned to my pillow. It was a note and twenty-five dollars. The note said, "*He never slumbers, so you can.*" I cried. But, the next day, my hair was looking good again. Thank You, Father, for Your provision.

Love Thy Neighbor

"All the trees of the field will know that I am the Lord...(Ezekiel 17:24)."

My mobile home was surrounded by trees, lots, and lots of extremely tall trees! When the wind blew hard, those trees could be a real threat. If you read some of the earlier stories, you know that, as the Lord instructed, I had to pray that those trees stayed in their place when the strong winds blew. One day, I was getting ready to have lunch with Pastor Chuck to discuss ministry needs. My lights started flickering off and on. I knew that was not good, so I went outside to see if I could tell where the problem was. It didn't take long to see the problem because a tall tree at the back of the mobile home had split in half. One half had fallen onto the full length of the driveway and had pulled the power line from the pole to the house to the ground.

I immediately called the county. They wasted no time getting there and put the power line where it belonged. The tree, however, was my problem to deal with. I called Chuck and he got some guys from our church to come over and cut the fallen tree into small portions to clear the driveway. I knew that grace had lifted off those trees. I simply told God I needed some help. It cost a lot of money to bring down trees and there were several that needed to come down. God is seldom early, but He is never late. Now, you might think, yes, God was late because the tree fell before help arrived, but everything has its purpose.

I had a neighbor I did not really know. I would occasionally see him walking his little dog. I was sitting on the swing on my front porch the day after my friends cut the tree. My neighbor, Mr. Rogers, walked down my driveway and said he was curious about what was going on the day before. I told him about the tree, and he wanted to know what I was going to do with the wood. I told him I had no plans and, if he wanted it and was willing to haul it, he was welcome to it. He thanked me and started looking at some of the other trees. He pointed to several and said they needed to come down.

"Yes'r, they do." I replied.

"I got a man I use a lot to do that and I am going to call him to come and take a look and see what he says."

He didn't ask me as he seemed to be talking to himself. He told me he would get the wood and he walked off. The next day, I heard some voices in the front yard. I went out and found Mr. Rogers and another man talking. Mr. Rogers introduced me to the tree guy and I actually knew him from high school. His name was Mike. They walked around and Mike told me the tree that had split and fallen needed to come down in a controlled way so it would not later fall on my house. Then he showed me several other trees that would eventually cause me a problem. Mr. Rogers asked him how much it would cost. Initially, he said thirteen-hundred dollars and I asked him about two more trees. He said he would do those for two-hundred more for a total of fifteen-hundred dollars. It was really a very reasonable price, but for me, it may as well have been a billion. Mr. Rogers never looked at me for a response. He told Mike to put it on his schedule. I was really shocked.

"Wait a minute, I appreciate all this, but I need time to pray about the money and where it might come from because I don't have it right now."

"We will worry about that later. Go ahead Mike and put it on your schedule."

Mike got into his truck and Mr. Rogers walked toward his house. I went after him and told him I appreciated his help, but I didn't have the money. He told me he knew I was a preacher, so if my church would give him a tax receipt, he would donate the money to the church in my name. Then he said for me to come over in a while and he would give me a check. I went over and Mr. Rogers gave me the check.

"Mr. Rogers, I greatly appreciate what you are doing, but I want to know why you are doing this?"

"When I saw those trees could possibly fall on your house and hurt you and your little granddaughters, it became my problem. I have the means to do something about it and I would have to live with that on my conscience if something happened and I had not done anything to stop it."

I left with the check in my hand. The Lord spoke to me, *"He just loved his neighbor as himself."* I was totally undone. How can we ever doubt that kind of love?

~

Tax Time, Again?

*"So do not worry about tomorrow; for tomorrow will care for itself.
Each day has enough trouble of its own (Matthew 6:34)."*

Have you ever felt like you barely get your taxes paid and it's time
to do it all over again? Getting my own home was nothing short
of a miracle. I had never been on my own. I lived with my parents
until I got married, and, when I left Pete, I lived with my sister
until my own home became available. Living on your own is very
challenging. You are responsible for everything, including house
taxes. In my home state, if you have two homes, you get a special tax rate for the home that is considered the primary home.
That would be the one I left where Pete resided. The one I moved
into was considered the secondary property. That left me with the
higher tax rate because we were not divorced.

That first tax bill was twice what it would have been if I had
been divorced. This created a bit of apprehension for me, but,
thankfully, taxes don't rock God off His throne! As with many other financial needs, they seem to be bigger than normal when you
are trying to live by faith. I was truly trying to do it with a correct
mindset and not be fearful. I began to pray. That is what you do

when you are faced with something you can't handle. Actually, we should not limit our prayer to that standard. God wants us to trust him in all circumstances.

I had three days left until the taxes were due, and then the penalties would start adding. I told no one because I was determined to trust God. That afternoon, I got a check for a few hundred dollars. Things were looking promising. The next day, I got a check from a friend who I had not heard from in quite a while. She said she had been praying and felt like she was supposed to send me money. Yes, God! The next day, the taxes were due. More money came in and I had enough to pay the taxes. Actually, I got four-hundred dollars over what I needed! I was able to buy Clairey some things and extra groceries, and we splurged on a special meal in our favorite restaurant. Hallelujah, glory to God—and I don't mean that flippantly!

The next year rolled around and, yes, it was tax time again. I remembered how God had taken care of it the previous year. It was all good, until I opened the envelope. What? It was four-hundred dollars higher than last year. This had to be a mistake, so I called the tax office, and it was accurate. The taxes went up. I felt like I needed some reinforcement of faith. I called Pastor Chuck and told him about the taxes. I also told him I was not telling him so he would pay it out of his pocket or the church's unless God told him too. I really meant that. He has a big heart and gives out of his heart, but he agreed with me that we needed to seek God. I made him promise me not to tell anyone. I knew he wouldn't since he has a lot of integrity. I went into some serious prayer. The Lord began to speak to me.

Maybe He doesn't speak to you this way, but this is what I heard, "*I can see where you would think that four-hundred extra dollars would throw Me into a panic. But how much did I send you last year?*"

"*You paid the taxes.*"

"*How much did I send you?*"

"*You sent me thirteen-hundred dollars.*"

"*I did that, not so you would have extra money, I already knew this day would come. I sent you the extra amount last year that would be the increase of your taxes this year.*"

I felt like maybe I had used the money from last year when I should have saved it for this time. "*Should I have saved the four-hundred dollars last year for the taxes this year?*"

"*I only sent you that so you could have faith in Me that I would provide, and the amount does not scare Me as it does you.*"

That was the end of the conversation. Three days before the taxes were due, Chuck called asking, "*Do you have your tax money yet?*"

"*No, but I have three more days.*"

"*You don't have to wait any longer.*"

"*Chuck, I don't want you or the church to pay it.*"

"*We are not going to pay it. Someone came by the office this morning and gave me a check for twelve-hundred and fifty dollars for you. They asked me not to reveal who they are. The man said he woke up in the middle of the night and the Lord told him to write you a check for that amount, then his*" *wife woke up and said, "We have to write Sandy Starnes a check for twelve-hundred and fifty dollars today."*

My tax bill was twelve hundred and forty-eight dollars and some odd cents. I asked Chuck if he was sure he had not mentioned my need to anyone; he assured me he had not and I believed him. If I live to be a hundred years old, I will never get over the goodness and the faithfulness of our Father. It does not puff me up, but rather humbles me to think He sees me. Out of this entire universe, He sees me. He sees you too.

There are so many ways God has supplied my needs and a lot of my wants. I have opened my purse and money would be waiting for me to find. I have opened my Bible and found envelopes with hundreds of dollars in it. I walked into a chiropractor office once and was handed an envelope with a thousand dollars in it. None of the people left their name or any hint of their identity. I was handed two one-dollar bills once, and, because I knew it was a sacrifice for that lady, it was as meaningful to me as the thousand dollars. We cannot measure His love for us or His desire to bless us.

~

Odds and Ends

"Your eyes will see strange things…(Proverbs 23:33)."

This is the last section of this book. The stories in this last portion are not really any stranger than some of the others. I just happened to think about them after the fact. I really could have written many more stories. Some of them may have fit the profile of this book, but I will save those for another time. After all, my story is still developing! I wanted to tell stories of faith and of struggles while learning to believe God for the impossible. I pray this book has challenged you to get out of your comfort-zone and dare to live as though we serve a God who is beyond what we consider normal.

I am sure that, for some of you reading this book, you will find yourself shaking your head and thinking, *"I'm not sure I believe that."* That is okay. I find myself shaking my head too! Whatever you believe, I assure you, these stories are true, and I did my best to tell them as accurately as possible.

After forty-plus years, I still find it hard to understand why God chose me to do these crazy things. I am not a famous TV preacher, nor do I want to be. I am not wealthy, although I am blessed beyond measure. I am not well known, but I never lack in ministry. I have people who love me and people who hate me. I have been the object of gossip and the recipient of jealousy. At times, I have been lousy at handling those moments with grace. Please forgive me.

At the writing of this book, I am four years away from becoming seventy years old. When I say that, it feels impossible. You might wonder if I have any regrets. Of course, I do. I wish I had done a lot of things differently. I wish I had loved my family more perfectly. I wish I had served Christ better. I wish I had treated every person I met with the love of Jesus. I wish a lot of things. We cannot go back, so, while I have regrets, I do not live in them. I forgive and I receive forgiveness and try to do with excellence what the Lord has placed before me today. I have learned to stop and enjoy the moment because it will never come again. I try to not get angry with people for being imperfect and responding imperfectly. I hope they can remember that I too am imperfect.

While my life has been a wild adventure, I don't see these last years, however long that might be, as the end. We have a new beginning each day. I have a fresh opportunity each day to show Christ to someone. You do too. Let's see how well we can run the rest of this race set before us.

I want this book to be a legacy of faith for the generations to come. I hope this book will inspire my grandchildren and great grandchildren to build a life of faith in Christ as they read how God did great and mighty things through their Meme. I hope something in this book brings inner healing to my family as well as yours. I hope they can see a woman's journey of becoming imperfectly perfect and that God has a plan for their lives no matter what mistakes they have made in their past. I want them to see how God loves each one and He has the power and desire to redeem them from the enemy of their soul and even from themselves. We are often our own worst enemy.

I always encourage people not to ask themselves, "*What if?*" You know the "*should've, would've, could've*" questions. Instead of asking those defeating questions, ask yourself this, "*What if God truly would like to give me an extraordinary life of faith, hope, and love causing me to be one of those who walks on water, or raises the dead, or lays hands on the sick and watch them get radically healed?*" It can happen. Maybe today, God could move in you to just be a blessing. Go ahead, give it a try. What do you have to lose? Really, all you have to lose is going through this life without an encounter with the One who created you! That, my friend, would be a shame.

Perhaps you are reading this book and you haven't heard of such things. Maybe you have been in church all your life and never seen any of these things take place. It is possible you have never been to church; maybe you have heard of Christ or maybe not. You might be living totally for yourself—what you want, or what you need, is the ruling force of your life. Let me assure you, God is not far from you. You could be wondering if you have done too many bad things and God could not possibly forgive you. I can tell you this, He already has forgiven you. He did that through the death, burial, and resurrection of His Son, Jesus Christ. All you need to do is receive that by faith. Just believe it in your heart and, with your words say, "*I choose to live for you, Lord.*" Then, allow the Holy Spirit to do what only He can do. He will change you and you will be better for it. It is that simple.

He made from one man every nation of mankind to live on all the face of the earth, having determined their appointed times and the boundaries of their habitation, that they would seek God, if perhaps they might grope for Him and find Him, though He is not far from each of us; for in Him we live and move and exist, as even some of your own poets have said, 'For we also are His children.' Being then the children of God, we ought not think that the Divine Nature is like gold or silver or stone, an image formed by the art and thought of man. Therefore, having overlooked the times of ignorance, God is now declaring to men that all people everywhere should repent...(Acts 17:26-30)

~

A Funny Story

"A joyful heart is good medicine...(Proverbs 17:22)."

My Aunt Barbara, my friends, Heidi and Lorrie, and myself went to a Perry Stone conference for several days. We did not want to spend a lot of money, so we decided to stay in one room. It was a nice hotel and the room had two queen beds. We would be in the conference services most of the day and would only need the room to bathe and sleep. We even managed to wrap our heads around four women in one bathroom. That is how you know you are becoming mature, godly women, when four women can use one bathroom and not kill each other!

While waiting for check-in time, we sat in the hotel café. The room was full of others who were also going to the conference. We were drinking our coffee and discussing who would bunk with whom. I spoke up, *"It doesn't matter to me who I sleep with. I have been sleeping with Barbara for years, and Lorrie and I have slept with each other all over the world, and I slept with Heidi that time in Georgia."*

Just as I was finishing that sentence, I noticed the look on the other ladies faces and realized how quiet the room had gotten.

Every eye was staring at us. This was a Christian event. It dawned on me what my conversation sounded like to those who didn't understand what we were talking about. All they heard was I had slept with all of these women. It was hysterically funny, at least to me! Oh, lighten up, it was funny!

STORY 102

~

Praying Nuns

"...And he said to him, "Your prayers and alms have ascended as a memorial before God (Acts 10:4)."

It was that time of life for me that comes to most of us women as we get older. I was fifty-two and needed a hysterectomy. I was scheduled to have surgery at a hospital in Charlotte, North Carolina. At one time many years ago, the hospital had been a Catholic hospital where most of the nurses, if not all, were nuns. The surgery was supposed to take about an hour and a half. Nothing ever seems to go that way for me. It took over four hours because my uterus had stretched six times its normal size and was quite difficult to remove. My body felt it too.

The day after surgery, I had to get up and walk. This was very difficult as I was cut more than they had planned due to the difficulty of the removal. My steps were slow and very small. Pete stayed with me and was beside me holding onto my arm. I had a pretty good gait going on when I abruptly stopped in the middle of the hallway.

"*What is wrong? Do you need to sit down?*" Pete thought I was going to faint or something.

"*Do you feel that?*" I asked.

"*Feel what?*"

"*That! You don't feel that strange sense in the air?*"

He looked at me as if I had too much anesthesia, "*I don't feel anything.*"

I just quietly prayed while standing still, "*Lord, what am I feeling?*" It was so strong; I was not imagining it.

"*You are sensing the prayers of the nuns. They walked these halls and prayed consistently. Their prayers still influence the atmosphere!*" The Lord further explained, "*Don't ever think your prayers of faith dissipate into thin air.*"

God in a Shampoo Bottle

"Where can I go from Your Spirit? Or where can I flee from Your presence (Psalm 139:7)?"

A group of us were sitting around my living room. Clairey was around five years old and I guess she spent more time with adults than with children, so she was able to sit with us older folks and listen. There was a young married couple in college studying theology and ministry and all that jazz. They were working on their thesis and the subject was the Trinity. They had been working on it for months and discussing with us the different views and deep theological theories.

Clairey had been listening very intently for a five-year-old. She spoke up, *"I can splain it real good. It is like that shampoo my Meme buys me. It has shampoo in it to clean my hair, then it has conditioner in it, but I don't know what it does, and it has tangle stuff to get the tangles out of my hair. They all do different stuff, but, because they work so good together, they can be together in the same bottle."* We just stared at her. This little girl explaining this deep subject with such child-like simplicity left us almost speechless. The two college students were dumbfounded. Of course, they could not use that analogy; their professors would have had a stroke!

My friend, Sue, was there, and, to this day, when she speaks on the subject of the Trinity or the Holy Spirit, she will use Clairey's example. It seems to make simple sense. We make it too hard sometimes and we need to let a child lead us.

Answered Prayers

"Now, O my God, I pray, let Your eyes be open and Your ears attentive to the prayer offered in this place (2 Chronicles 6:40)."

You never know where opportunity will knock. The Bible says to be ready in season and out of season. When you least expect it, a knock comes at the door. Such was the case one Sunday morning. My Missouri friend, Robyn, wanted me to come visit. I always enjoy going there, but this time was special because they paid for my granddaughter Clairey to come with me. It was her first time flying. It was fun watching her as we took off and she was able to have a window seat. As much fun as that was, a greater adventure would unfold during that trip.

It was Saturday night, and we were going to church the next morning. Robyn was trying to decide where we were going because she wanted me to experience a couple places. Finally, she decided we would gather her family together and let me show them how we do home fellowship where I live. Robyn lived in a home that was around a hundred years old and she is phenomenal when it comes to decorating. Her home looked like an old English inn.

While we were getting started with Sunday morning fellowship, we heard someone knocking on the back door. Robyn went to answer it as we all waited. An older man, probably in his eighties, was standing there explaining to Robyn that his grandfather had helped build her house. He asked if she had found a small piece of wood with a date burned into it. She said she had and still had it. He went on to say that he lived about four hours away and was passing through, and wanted to see the house one more time before he passed away. He told Robyn that he was suffering some serious illnesses and did not expect to be around much longer.

I was sitting and listening, but felt the Holy Spirit prompting me to go talk to this man. As I was getting up, Clairey spoke, *"Uh oh, Meme has the look!"* It had become a joke among those who know me that, when the Holy Spirit is messing with me, I get a certain look on my face. I just laughed and headed to the back door. I said hello and Robyn introduced me as her friend from South Carolina.

> I asked him, *"Sir, I heard you say you don't think you have very long to live. If that is the case, what will happen to you then?"* His answer totally gave away his spiritual stance.

> *"Well, little lady, I will be cremated, and they probably will scatter my a** all-over Jefferson County!"*

> I gave a little laugh and replied, *"That may happen, but that will be your body. What is going to happen to your soul?"*

> He hung his head as he answered. *"I'll probably go to hell."*

> *"Do you want to go to hell?"*

"Not especially, but I lived pretty rough, so I guess I don't have any choice this late in the game."

I explained to him, very simply, the plan of salvation and how the Lord had made provision for us. I asked, *"Is that something you would like to accept?"*

"Yeah, if you will show me how."

I lead him into prayer and explained what he needed to do in following his new life and I went to the bathroom. I was very emotional at what occurred. I talked to the Lord about it, *"Lord, I thank You for saving him, but I don't like leading someone to salvation and not have any way to follow through with discipleship."*

I was shocked at the Lord's response, *"It is okay, he will only be here for a few more days. I had to answer the prayers of the people who have faithfully prayed for him."*

I knew the Lord meant the man would only be on the earth a short while longer. But, what really got me was the Lord saying He had to answer the prayers of the people who had prayed in faith for him. That tells me we should never give up praying for someone unless the Holy Spirit tells you too.

I told someone how the Lord took me a thousand miles away to lead someone to Jesus. Their question was valid, *"Couldn't Robyn have led him to Jesus?"* Of course she could have; however, they would not have been home. They would have been at church! God will never force us to salvation, but He will do everything He needs to do so we have that opportunity, even if someone has to travel a thousand miles.

〰

Friend or Foe?

"For consider Him who has endured such hostility by sinners against Himself, so that you will not grow weary and lose heart (Hebrews 12:3)."

If you stay in ministry for any length of time, you will run into difficult places with people. I once had a friend who often went with me as I ministered in different places.

This is what she said to me, *"I never see you having spiritual battles. Do you ever struggle?"*

"Where have you been? Yes, I struggle. Every person who is in ministry is going to struggle with at least two things. Jealousy and pride. You will deal with pride when you are the flavor of the month. That is what I call it when everyone seems to want you to speak at their event. When you are not the flavor of the month, jealousy will rear its ugly green head! It also presents itself when someone seems to get a better report or do something better than you."

She listened and replied, *"I have never seen you act that way!"*

"Trust me, I have been there many times. I have learned to get rid of the pride by humbling myself before God. I have disarmed jealousy through understanding I have strengths others don't and they have gifts that I don't have. The key to not having jealousy is to realize we are all called to something different and it takes all those gifts working to form the Body of Christ. The reason you have not seen it is because I have learned to deal with it before God. I still have to kill those ungodly emotions on a regular basis. I have seen how ugly those things are working in other ministers and realized they don't look any better in me. Besides that, pride and jealousy will stop the anointing of God from flowing through you. You might seem to get away with it for a while because God is gracious and slow to anger. He will bring it to your attention and give you every opportunity to allow Him to deal with it. When you don't, it will cost you."

Through the years, I have been hurt by people. Hurt people only hurt people. I have had many ministry leaders say horrible things about me. I have had them stand before congregations and call me names. I have had them privately accuse me of saying things that I didn't say. I have been talked about unmercifully. I once had a Sunday school teacher use his entire Sunday school time to talk about me and it wasn't nice. I witnessed a man get up before hundreds of people and call me a false prophet and a false teacher. The list goes on. You might ask, *"Why?"*

Pride and jealousy. Whether it is real or just their perception, they viewed me through their own insecurities or brokenness. It is hurtful and destructive for me and for them. The only good that can possibly come from a scene like that is to forgive, allow the Holy Spirit to heal the wounds inside, and let Him teach you how not to be defensive. That is a hard thing to learn. It took me many years to learn that He is my shield and defender. I have learned that, each time I have been attacked by someone, it takes me further into God's purpose if I allow Him to handle it and heal me. It still is not fun, and I pray no one ever has to suffer that pain due to my insecurities. If you are reading this story and a memory of a time I may have caused you pain comes up, I ask you to please forgive me, and let God heal your heart. I may not even be aware of it. If you know that you have hurt someone and it keeps coming to your mind, you should ask God how to handle it and then just do it. That violation may still be coming to their mind as well. This is a story about one of those instances. I share it, not to point my finger at anyone, but to show you how out-of-reality it can get when an accusation is built on false information twisted by the enemy. Remember, he is the one who kills, steals, and destroys.

If the person in this story reads this, she may know it is her about whom I am speaking. If that happens, please know that I have no hard feelings; I choose to remember all the wonderful things I experienced through your friendship. But, if it bothers you, please do what you need to do for your peace of mind. You will only receive a blessing from me and the Lord. At the time, I was terribly hurt, but it began the process of God teaching me how to properly handle adversity. The crazy thing about emotional pain is that it can be as real today as it was twenty years ago. That old saying, *"time heals all wounds,"* is a lie. Only God can heal soul-wounds—let Him.

I will call her "May" so as to protect her identity. May and her family loved me. I was invited to their house all the time. If they did anything, I was included. They gave me gifts, and I knew she prayed for me. There are specific things, really awesome things, she and her family did for me. I would like to mention them, but that would be too revealing and I don't have a need to show her wrong to the world.

When at church, I began to notice she started avoiding me. At first, I thought it was just my imagination. I tried to remember if I had done anything to hurt her feelings, but I honestly could not think of anything. One morning, I thought I would test the waters, so I asked her what they were doing for lunch after church. Her answer was vague, and she would not look at me. I asked her if I had done anything to upset her. She said, "*No.*" I let it go for a while. It became more and more obvious that something was out of order. I went to her again and asked if something was wrong pointing out that she had been avoiding me. She denied it. I also noticed her daughter would not speak to me and she had me involved with some ministry that stopped suddenly. I asked her if I had done something to offend her and I got the same evasive answers.

It didn't take long after that to find out the problem. I got a call from her sister and she asked if she and May could come over after work hours to talk to me. I told her that would be fine. I asked my boss if I could use the office for a while to have a meeting and he complied.

They came and, for four solid hours, May let me have it. She felt like every problem the church was experiencing—from really serious matters to very silly things—was my fault. I won't go into details because that would involve others who will probably read this book. Trust me when I tell you, none of it made any sense. She was brutal to me and I was deeply hurt. Nothing I said made any difference. She was offended. Proverbs 18:19 says, "*A brother offended is harder to be won than a strong city, and contentions are like the bars of a citadel.*" There was no reasoning with her or working it out—that is how offense works. My heart was shattered. I had been attacked before, but not in that way. It was the only time I wanted to give up ministry. I knew her accusations were not true, but they were painful nonetheless. This is how David describes such a betrayal in Psalm 55:12-14, *"For it is not an enemy who reproaches me, then I could bear it, nor is it one who hates me who has exalted himself against me, then I could hide myself from him. But it is you, a man my equal, my companion and my familiar friend; we who had sweet fellowship together and walked in the house of God in the throng."*

I went home after feeling like I had been torn to shreds. I walked into my house and told my husband, *"I quit. I don't quit God, I just quit ministry and people!"*

The phone started ringing. I told Pete that, unless it was Jesus, do not call me to the phone. He held out the receiver and said, *"It is not Jesus, but it is James."* As a reminder, James Shinn is my spiritual father. He lives about an hour and a half away from me, so I had not seen or talked to him in about six months. I took the receiver from Pete.

He immediately began to talk to me strongly, *"Don't quit!"*

"What?"

"Don't quit. I was walking down my stairs and I heard the Lord tell me to call you and tell you not to quit. Whatever has happened at that church, you will not quit until the Lord tells you to."

It is amazing to me how God can speak to someone who knows how to hear and discern things you need to hear. The relationship with May never got back to its original state. We would speak in passing at church, but the issue was never resolved. I did not understand until much later what that was about. It really was not people-centered and it certainly was not God-centered. It was demon-centered. No, May is not evil or demonic, but something that was out of order in her, some brokenness that God needed to heal, was influenced by the enemy of our soul. It happens to us all who seek to follow Christ. This is where we learn to be powerful or pitiful. Powerful is when we allow God to heal and remove our hurts and broken places we encounter in our lives. Pitiful is when we make pets out of those places. We protect them because we identify with them. Those broken emotions will keep you from being all that Christ has died to give you.

> "It was for freedom that Christ set us free; therefore, keep standing firm and do not be subject again to a yoke of slavery (Galatians 5:1)."

STORY 106

House Cleaning, Oh What Fun!

"When the unclean spirit goes out of a man, it passes through waterless places seeking rest and not finding any, it says, 'I will return to my house from which I came (Luke 11:24).'"

I understand this subject will challenge many of you. Many churches or denominations will never touch the subject of demons inhabiting people or places. Either they do not think it important to a believer's faith-journey, or they are unskilled at handling the matter. Either way, you cannot deny the existence of evil influences in man's life. We see all through the New Testament where Jesus cast spirits out of people. I know most of your responses would be that Jesus did away with that on the cross. How do you explain the Apostle Paul also cast spirits out of people after Jesus was gone? At any rate, I am not writing this book to convince you about the existence or the activity in demons. I am simply telling my stories. I hope that you will see there is a world that we cannot explain within ourselves and we must trust the Scriptures on these subjects. Search it for yourself.

I have had many experiences with the demonic world, not because I am fascinated with them, but I have a ministry where they present themselves through people and circumstances. God has given me the gift of being able to deal with them. I once was listening to a minister who moves in the deliverance of demons and I remember what he said, "*I am not a deliverance minister. I am a minister of Jesus Christ and, while I am ministering Jesus and a demon gets in the way of that, whether through a person or otherwise, I simply deal with it and continue ministering Jesus.*"

I was going to church with a lady I will call "Mindy." She and her husband had purchased a house as an investment. They used their own money to remodel it. It was a cute little two-bedroom home. It would have made a perfect starter home. It was in a decent location and neighborhood, but it would not sell. She called me and shared how they had put it on the market months before. She said many people looked at it and seemed very interested, but, at the last minute, they all backed out without explanation. She told me they were financially to the place where they needed to recoup their investment. She asked me if I would go to the house with her and pray through it. She wanted me to bless the house and ask God's favor in selling it quickly. I told her I would, so she picked me up and we drove about thirty minutes away to the house.

I asked her to wait in the living room. When I pray through houses, I often like to do it quietly and I always start in the back of the house. I went down the short hall where two bedrooms were across from each other. I felt compelled to go into the room on the right. I instantly felt like the air in the room was thick, heavy. I passed it off because the house had been shut and you could still smell the fresh paint. However, my spiritual senses were very alert, and I knew it was not just because the house had been closed. I still try to eliminate the natural before I look at it as a supernatural situation. I really am not into freaky, although it does seem to be that way. As I began to pray, I felt an intense sadness come over me. I walked to the small closet and, as I put my hand on the doorknob, I heard a child crying. I opened the door and half-way expected to see a real child in the closet. I did see a child, but it was only a vision for lack of a better way to explain it. I could see her plainly. She was about five years old wearing a plaid dress, white socks, and sitting with her knees pulled to her chest with her arms around her legs. I knew the Lord was going to tell me something and it did not take long. I stood looking at this crying child knowing she had been hurt. Then the Lord told me, *"There have been many children violated in this house."*

That was the end of the vision and the child was gone. On the way into the room, I noticed an odd closet or cabinet at the end of the hall. I called for Mindy to ask her about it. She said it had been a very shallow closet, not really deep enough to hang clothes. They converted it to make a small cabinet with shelves. I had this intense sense they had found something in the closet and I knew it had to do with child pornography. As I asked her, I could tell it upset her. She told me they had found several magazines with disgusting pictures of questionable activity and burned them.

I knew how to pray after that. I prayed for a cleansing from all the unrighteous acts of the violations of children. I prayed a denouncement of any legal rights for demons to stay attached to that property. I prayed for the children who had been violated and asked God to send people into their lives to bring healing, restoration and forgiveness. The very next day, the house sold! I can only do what God has given me the understanding to do. It is the work of the Holy Spirit that deserves the glory for His love for us as human beings.

STORY 107

Redeemed!

*"Now when Jesus was in Bethany, at the home of Simon the
leper, a woman came to Him with an alabaster vial of
very costly perfume, and she poured it on His head as
He reclined at the table (Matthew 26:7)."*

There is a line to a song which says, *"You don't know the cost of the
oil in my alabaster box."* The young lady this story is about sang
that song in church one Sunday. I have heard the song many times
and by more gifted singers. But never have I heard it sung with
more emotional pain and gratitude.

I was attending a fairly large Southern Baptist Church during
this time. I only tell you that because the ministry I do isn't one
you normally find in that particular denomination. I had made
some really awesome friends there and one, in particular, named
Sue. This story started around the year 2000 or so. It was Sunday
morning after the worship service when a lady approached me
as I was gathering my Bible and purse. She introduced herself as
Irene—not her real name—and said Sue had told her that I had
an unusual ministry. She went on to say she had a daughter who
had been in the hospital for a long time from eating disorders.

327

This daughter, we'll call her "Mary," was at the end of every known treatment and had been force-fed through tubes. That was no longer an option. The hospital was going to release her for a day or so and then, unless something else took place, this young girl would probably die.

Irene asked if I would come to her home on Monday and talk to her daughter. She said she did not understand what a deliverance ministry was, but she had nothing to lose at this point and was willing to try almost anything. She trusted Sue; therefore, she chose to trust me. I told her I would come and meet her. She gave me her address and left. Monday morning, I drove out to their house. I had no idea what to do. I had never ministered to anyone with eating disorders and I also knew this girl had to be in serious medical peril. I would have to be careful as I am not a professional counselor. I simply follow the leading of the Holy Spirit and He is an expert on everything.

I went into the house; Irene took me into the living room, and introduced me to Mary. This tiny wisp of a girl sat on a pillow with a blanket around her. She looked like a skeleton with skin draped over her. I had never seen anyone so thin. She had absolutely no body fat, thus the blanket and pillow. That wasn't the worst of her problem—she had a nasty attitude! Her mother left the room to give us time to get acquainted.

Mary spoke first, *"Well, did you come to pray for me?"* with sarcasm dripping from her mouth.

"No," I replied with matched sarcasm. *"I came because I have never seen a human skeleton that could talk! Pray for you? So far, I don't even like you!"* I sat down beside her on the sofa. It would have been easier for me to sit across from her because, at that time, I was having neck issues and turning my head was not the best thing to do. But, I was not going

to give her the pleasure of distance. I continued, *"Okay, I'm here now, so let's pretend we are having some conversation. Tell me a little about yourself besides your situation."*

We managed to talk a little bit about normal things such as school and the sarcasm seemed to dissipate as we talked. I could tell she did not like or trust me. That was fair enough. This young girl had been through a lot of trauma. She was about sixteen years old at the time. I was not going to stay long, but, before I left, the Holy Spirit revealed to me another facet of her issues. He told me she had been cutting herself and she somehow had been able to hide it.

I leaned over and, in a whisper, I asked her, *"Do they know you are cutting yourself?"* She did not answer, but I could see the anger and fear of being exposed on her face.

"Don't worry, I am not going to tell on you, at least not now. I am going home, but, before I leave, at least let me pray for you so I can say I tried." She told me to do it and get it over with. I may have broken a record for the shortest prayer I have ever prayed. *"Father, show Yourself to this girl. She is going to need You. Amen."*

I said my goodbyes and, frankly, I was glad to be leaving. I thought that was the end of that. I was sad for this young girl since she was probably going to die. I felt terrible for her parents. They had fought a long and difficult battle. I didn't have any idea that meeting was only the beginning of a long journey with Mary. God had a plan, and I am glad He didn't ask my permission, because I would have said, *"NO!"* A few hours later, I received a call from Irene. I started apologizing for not being able to help the situation.

She was excited and said, *"You don't understand. Yes, Mary was really angry when you left. She came to the kitchen and watched you through the window leave the driveway. She wanted to know if I really thought it would work calling someone to pray."*

I replied, *"I am sorry Irene. I don't think I helped any at all. I will continue to pray for all of you."*

"Sandy, you don't understand. As she watched you drive out of the yard, she was eating small bites of a chocolate cake that was sitting on the table. She has not put solid food in her mouth in a long, long time!"

Perhaps, someday, Mary will write a book about her journey; it was long and difficult. I don't have time here nor could I do it justice, but I do want to share a few things about my interaction with her through the years. I learned a lot from her. I had never dealt with someone with her disorders, or a person who cuts themselves, but it was a real education—one I would need in the years to come. I since have ministered to quite a few young people who cut. It happens a lot more than you would believe.

As the next few years went by, I had many opportunities to work with Mary. Sue often was a part of that ministry. This one particular Saturday, I got a call from the pastor of the church. He told me I needed to meet Sue and Mary at his office. Mary was in a desperate place of depression. Truth be told, she should have been taken to the hospital; however, they would not have been able to address her real issue. Her real problem was on a spiritual level. Mary had been inhabited by demons. Like it or not, understand it or not, that was true. This was not the first time I had to deal with it concerning Mary, but this was different, and I was about to run into something I had never encountered. Sue and I were praying, I was calling out

demons, and something occurred that scared me. Demons don't scare me, but their affect on people can be devastating for those who don't know how to overcome them. Mary started slumping down into the chair as if she couldn't hold herself upright. Her eyes rolled back into her head and her breathing almost stopped. I had never seen this before and I had been doing deliverance for a long time. I called my spiritual father, James. I had not told him where I would be or what I would be doing. He answered the phone and, the minute I said his name, he started almost yelling, "*You tell that devil of death to get off that girl right now! He has no power over her, tell him now! Little girl, don't you ever cower down to a demon in fear again, you hear me?*" He hung up.

My faith was renewed, and my resolve became clear. I did exactly what James told me to do. Immediately, I commanded the spirit of death to take his claim off her, that she was a child of God and he had no rights to her. Her color returned, her breathing became even and strong, she sat up, and began to cry. God had rescued her from the clutches of death once again. It was a great victory, and the glory is the Lord's.

I wish I could say that was the end of the nightmare; however, there would be more attacks and hurdles of life for this young lady. I had to intervene for her several times after that spiritual death threat, but she grew up and went to nursing school, despite her inner conflicts. Several years passed and I lost track of her. Occasionally, I would run into her mother and she would tell me that Mary was doing well.

One night, out of the blue, I heard the Lord tell me to call Mary. I had changed my phones and numbers, but, through a little searching and calling a mutual friend, I found an old number for her. I didn't have a clue she would still have that number, but I called anyway. A voicemail answered and I couldn't be sure it was her voice, so I simply said, "*Mary, if this is your phone. This is Sandy. Call me.*"

Five minutes later, my phone rang, and her voice was the same Mary I remembered, she said, *"Sandy Starnes, I cannot believe this is you! This has been one of worse weeks of my life and I just finished saying, if only I could talk to Sandy!"* We talked for a while. She told me she was going to come to town to visit her parents in a few weeks and I made her promise to call me so we could meet for dinner. She kept her promise and we agreed on the place to meet. I got to the restaurant before her, and, when I saw her get out of her car, tears filled my eyes. She was so beautiful. It is an awesome blessing to be a part of God's plan and fulfill your assignment. She had left nursing and entered a career with the FBI. She now works in bringing international pedophiles to justice. God has done great and mighty things through what the world would have considered a hopeless, broken little girl and created in her a heart of faith, hope, and love. I am honored to call her a friend.

STORY 108

~

Without a Word

"…Until He pleads my case and executes justice for me.
He will bring me out to the light, and I will see
His righteousness (Micah 7:9)."

This is a difficult story to write because I have no desire to paint anyone in a bad light, least of all, members of my own family whom I love. But, the story needs to be told to show how God can bring about justice for those who need it. Every victory requires a battle. I once heard a minister say, *"The size of your victory will be determined by the size of the giant you face."*

After leaving my husband and home where my daughter and two granddaughters lived, life for me was difficult. I was working three jobs for a while and most of my friends had abandoned me. I didn't understand all the things God was working out of me and the changes He was bringing in the background. He required things of me that were hard to deal with. There are many details of these stories concerning my times of separation and divorce that I will leave untold. I have no reason to bring scorn or humiliation by sharing the wrong choices of others. We all sin and come short of God's glory and I am no different.

After I left, life for my granddaughters became more difficult. I am sure Pete was dealing with a lot of pain and anger at my leaving. My daughter was making choices that were not in the best interest of herself, and certainly not for her daughters. I was getting calls nearly every day from people who expressed concern for their safety. This was around the time I procured my own home as circumstances were becoming more unstable at my former home. The environment was not a healthy one. One weekend, I found it necessary to get the girls and bring them home with me. Elizabeth was only four at the time and Clairey was about to turn twelve. I had no intention of taking them back home nor did Clairey want to return.

I was determined to find a way to keep them, and the Lord spoke to me, *"Take them back, it is not time."* I was horrified—take them back! I could not understand how God would require me to do such a thing. He knew better than anyone what dangers were waiting them.

> *"Why would you want me to take them back? Do you understand what You are asking me to do? It is not safe for them!"* I was distraught, to say the least.

> Again, He stated, not asking, *"Take them back, it is not time."*

I was utterly confused and terrified. What was Clairey going to think? She felt safe with me; she trusted me to keep my word. How was I going to explain to her that God told me to take her back to chaos? What was that going to show her about God? All these questions ran through my mind. I got a suitcase out of my closet and started packing my clothes.

> The Lord asked, *"What are you doing?"*

I said, "*I will take them back, but I will return with them. At least if I am there, all the things that are going on will cease and all those people hanging around will leave.*"

Then the Lord spoke to me in a tone I seldom heard and one I don't want to hear again, "*So, you trust Me with you, but you don't trust Me with them?*"

How was I supposed to answer that? I figured He is God and He already knew what was in my heart. "*I guess I don't. I just know that if I am there, all the mess that is taking place will stop because I will be there to stop it and watch over them.*"

Then the Lord said something that chilled my blood, and I will never forget the finality of His words, "*Then go.*" He didn't say it loudly, but rather quietly.

I knew He was not resigning His position, nor was He giving me His permission. I knew what He was actually suggesting was, "You may go, but not with Me." I knew in my heart that would not be beneficial to me or the girls in the long run. When I tell you it was the hardest thing I have ever done, that would be an understatement. I knew this was a test of my faith like none I have ever faced. I can't explain how I knew this, but I knew that, if I did not trust God in this situation, it would determine the course of our lives and I would never get where God was ultimately taking me.

I went into the living room where my little trusting eleven-year old granddaughter was standing and told her that I was going to have to take her back home. I will never forget the look of hurt and fear on her little face. She cried out, "*You promised me, Meme! Why would you do that? Why would God tell you to do that?*" I don't think I will ever have that kind of pain in my heart again as long as I live. If ever I thought of leaving God out of my life, it was then! How could I subject her and Elizabeth to that kind of abandonment? Yet, I knew that our very existence depended on me trusting Him as I have never trusted before.

"I don't know why Clairey. I don't understand why God is telling me to do this. I hate this more than you can possibly understand, but I do know He has a better plan than I can see, and not just for me, but for you and Elizabeth as well. You will have to trust me and Him."

Without a word, we got into the car and I drove them home. I was totally drained. I felt as if I had lost my most valuable treasures. I can't even begin to imagine how Clairey must have felt. Elizabeth was so young that all she wanted was to see her mom. She didn't understand the seriousness of what was taking place, nor did she see the dark side of her home-life. But, Clairey knew and I am sure God had to preserve her love for Him or else she would have lost all trust and hope.

This took place in January 2008. Clairey's birthday was February 18 and she had asked me if we could have her birthday party at my house because of the chaos going on at hers. I made the necessary plans, ordered her cake, and bought party favors. When I tried to get in touch with my daughter to make plans to pick up the girls, she was nowhere to be found. She wouldn't answer her phone. I called Pete and he said he didn't know where they were. I didn't believe him, but who knows if he was being honest or not? Finally, I called Chris, a friend of Amy's, and I could tell she wasn't going to help me. She was rude and told me straight out that she wouldn't help me or tell me anything. That let me know Amy was being intentional about keeping her whereabouts secret. I was fuming.

I called her back and gave her an ultimatum, *"Chris, I am going to find my grandchildren tonight and I don't care who's butt I have to plow up to do it! I am going to give you five minutes to reconsider, and then I am calling the police, and they will be on your doorstep. You know I have friends in the police department."*

I know Jesus had taken me out of the ghetto, but I'm not sure you can ever get the entire ghetto out of a person. After I finished my threat, which was not a threat, I would do what I said I would do. I hung up.

A minute did not pass before my cell phone rang, *"Sandy, I will take you to where they are. Meet me at my house and you can follow me."*

I was at my son's house during this conversation, and, when I got ready to leave, my son said he was going with me. I was glad because I didn't know what I might be walking into. Chris showed me which apartment and we knocked on the door.

Amy let us in and immediately began to get defensive, *"My phone wouldn't work, and my car won't crank, I wasn't trying to hide."* I assume her dad had gotten to her since she didn't seem surprised to see me.

"I'm here to pick up the girls. If you want to go back to your dad's, I will take you, but the girls are going home with me."

It is really hard for a parent to be in such conflict with their children. They may be grown, but you remember when they were your babies and your whole life was consumed with what they needed and wanted. You don't always know how to keep that in your heart and still deal with them as adults, especially when they turn into people you don't know or like. I loved my daughter then and I always will, but her choices—and I am sure my choices—caused a deep rift in our relationship. There was a driving force that I need to mention. The Lord had told me to take them home before, but just before I made that call to Amy's friend Chris, the Lord spoke to me, and I will never forget His words, *"Go get them and you will never take them back again."*

I want to make it clear that God was not angry, nor was He being vindictive against Amy. He loves her every bit as much as He loves me. He has a plan and only God knows how to work a plan that will work out for all our good if we will submit to Him. He was giving Amy a chance to do things differently. I dropped Amy at my former home and the girls went home with me. A few days later, I asked my sister, Pat, if she would go over to Pete's with me to keep Elizabeth busy while I talked with Amy and Pete. I didn't want to go by myself. Clairey was in school. Pat agreed and we went over. I told them I would not be bringing the girls back unless things drastically changed. I would not keep them from seeing the girls, but this is the way it was going to be. Needless to say, that did not go very well. They made threats and I told them to do whatever they wanted, but the girls were staying with me. We left.

I found out that Clairey had missed a lot of days at school. I talked to her counselor and she told me she knew Clairey's home life was not healthy. Clairey often came to school tired with dark circles under her eyes, and, while her grades were good, she was sullen and withdrawn. Clairey finished the year at that school, even though it meant I had to drive about fifteen miles one way to get her there and home again. I went to enroll her in the school near my home, and, due to the fact that I did not have custody, that was going to be an issue. I made an appointment with the school district superintendent. He informed me that many children were in the predicament in which we found ourselves. Many grandparents had to step in and raise grandchildren. I asked him how to enroll her since the state says these children must be in school, but it has to be in the district of the one who has custody. He said the fill-in parents lie about it because the children have to be in school. He went further to say the school district officials have to turn their head until a better solution is found. I told him I did not know how I would work it out, but I was not going to lie about it. Later, I contacted legal aid. They told me they would write a document to get her into school and they would start the procedure for me to get child support and custody. They would get me the affidavit for school immediately, but the other would take months. However, God had another plan. I told you, He likes to develop a plan that takes care of multiple issues.

Clairey's dad, Jackie, knew she was staying with me, but he did not know the extent of it. He and I never had a great relationship, and I was not about to borrow trouble, so I just kept quiet. One day, he said he knew that Clairey was living with me and he did not want to cause trouble, but he wanted me to write an affidavit for court to state that Clairey was living with me. According to him, this was so the court would direct his court-ordered child support to come to me instead of Amy. Seriously, I was not about to trust that he was concerned for her support. He was already extremely behind in his child support, so I did not think for one minute I was going to get any money. I did not really care because God was our provider. To minimize controversy, I wrote a short two paragraph document stating that, due to some extenuating circumstances in Clairey's home, she was staying with me and had been for six months. That was pretty much the gist of my statement.

The court date arrived. We had a ten-minute time slot. I have worked in the family court system as guardian ad litem, and I know the only thing the judge wants to hear are the facts as they are related to the issue at hand. We were there for a child support reversal order. The only reason I was there was because I was party to the action. Amy was there also. The judge got right to the point. He asked Amy if she had any objections to the procedure, and he asked Jackie a question. He never looked at me or addressed my presence. He gave his approval for the action and picked up his pen to sign the court document. That is when something in the atmosphere changed. The air literally became charged with a presence. I noticed the officer standing guard began to look around as if he were looking for something. The judge put down his pen, looked up, and said, *"I am going to sign the reversal order, but I am going to do one more thing. I am going to give complete physical and legal custody of this child to her grandmother, Sandra Starnes."*

The lady recording the procedure almost dropped her steno mask. I was overwhelmed! I never opened my mouth to speak, the judge never acknowledged me, nor did he ask me if I wanted custody. That was not even on the table. This was not normal for a family judge. That presence in the room was God. He had said I would never have to take her back. I had no idea how He would secure that, but He is always true to His word.

Later, I was asked by an attorney how I came to have custody of Clairey, and, when I told him, he just looked at me with unbelief. He said he had practiced family law for twenty years and never saw anything like it. My daughter-in-law was a social worker at the time, and, when I told her what happened in court, she had a hard time believing it. She had worked in family court and seen judges do some strange things, but never had she seen a judge give custody to someone when that was not the agenda, or without a case being built. But, God is the final judge.

You are probably wondering about my younger granddaughter, Elizabeth. She stayed with me for six months and her dad went to court to get full custody. He was not trying to take her from us; he just wanted the best for her. He always allowed me to have her as much as possible. He and I had a rocky start as he had been told a lot of things about me that simply were not true. We managed to work out those things and built a great relationship. Elizabeth had a lot of difficulties along the way. She was taken from her mom at age four. Six months later, she was taken from me and her sister to live with her dad in another city and started school. That is a lot of change for such a small child. Her heart was broken, and she did not have the maturity to understand what was going on. She will be eighteen about the time this book is published. It has been a long journey, but she is a beautiful and intelligent, caring young lady. I am very blessed to have her in my life. She will remember who her God is, and she will be a mighty woman of God no matter what pitfalls she might encounter.

Marching Orders

"...Behold, I have put My words in your mouth...(Jeremiah 1:9)."

My dear friend, Harold, went to be with the Lord. You might remember him in an earlier story. I taught a Bible study at his home
and he was the guy that gave me his bedroom suit because he said
the Lord was going to give me a home before the end of that year.
He got married at age eighty. I did, indeed, get that home before
the end of that year. He was a man of great integrity. They gave him
a memorial service at Fort Jackson, Columbia, South Carolina. My
friend, Holly, and I attended that funeral. It was a short military
service. Two ladies dressed in their pristine white navy uniforms
stood at attention throughout the service. One of the women was
tall, while the other was short. The Lord began to speak to me
concerning the tall lady, *"I have a word for her, and you will give it."*

He and I had a silent exchange while I tried to tell Him why
that would not be possible. I explained to Him there would be
no appropriate time to speak to these ladies. They were there to
do the military honors, and, at the end, they would disappear
into the sunset. It would be over, and Holly and I would get into
her van and drive away. I reminded the Lord that we were on a

military base and things did not work that way. I wasn't interested in getting shot or arrested for approaching an officer of the United States Navy. I mean, what would I say, *"Excuse me, could we stop the service for a moment because I have a 'word from God' for one of these officers?"* I don't think the Lord was amused at my attempt of humor. He simply said, *"You will give her the word."*

The service came to a close; the officers did their usual folding and presenting the flag to Harold's widow. They saluted and, just as I thought, they marched off across the field. Under my breath, I said to the Lord, *"I told You so."* He replied, *"You will give her the word."* I gave up. How was I supposed to give her a word? She was gone. I would never see her again, I was sure of that! Holly and I spoke to the family and prepared to leave. We were driving down the winding roads toward the main highway. Just before making the final right turn off the base, I spotted a stopped car on the side of the road. Right in front of my eyes were the two women who had, moments before, stood at attention in honor of my friend. They were standing outside the car talking. The Lord spoke, *"You may give her the word now."* I pulled over and stopped the van. I was very aware that I was still on a military base and I wasn't sure if it was proper to approach them. I got out slowly and walked toward them. They both stopped and turned around to look at me. I knew I was going to have to say something to open conversation.

> *"Hi, we were just at the service and I wanted to thank you both for honoring my friend and for your service to our country."*

They both thanked me and said some kind words about Harold. I continued, *"I know you may think this a bit odd, but would you mind if I prayed for you?"*

I pointed at the tall one. She said she would like that very much. I started to pray, but quickly told her that was not what God had instructed me to do. At the risk of them thinking I was some kind of lunatic, I told her that the Lord had impressed me that she was concerned about her next assignment. I told her that the Lord knew she was afraid, but she had nothing to fear. She would return safely, He had a plan for her life, and she already knew that what was in her heart was put there by Him. He would make a way for her to do what she was born to do. I went on to say a few more things, and, by this time, both of them were crying. The shorter lady told me that the other lady was leaving for one of the Middle Eastern countries the next day, and she had been fearful of not returning. She said everything I said was true. I prayed for them both and left. I have done this type ministry for forty-plus years, and I will never get used to how God works. Why do we doubt Him? Nothing is too hard for Him. If He says it, that should be enough for us to believe!

~

The Dating Game

"Do not call to mind the former things, or ponder things of the past. Behold, I will do something new...(Isaiah 43:18-19)."

Just after I left my first husband, Pete, the news of that day was filled with the divorce of two well-known ministers. Considering my own failed marriage, I was filled with sadness. It didn't seem that the church had any better grip on marriage and divorce than the people who do not profess Christ. This should be of a great concern for all of us. As I see it, the strength of any nation depends on two things: 1. its commitment to God, and 2. the very fabric of the family. As a nation, we stink at both. This became the main topic of my prayers. I needed to look at my own failure and figure out where I had made a mess. It was easy to point fingers and think how Pete could have done better, but I was part of the problem. I had to face me every morning.

I was talking to the Lord one day and this was my summation of the issue, *"Lord, we have a divorce problem in this country!"*

The Lord startled me with His reply, *"You don't have a divorce problem. You have a marriage problem."*

I had never thought of it that way, so I asked more questions. This is what He revealed to me, *"First, you get married without knowing Me. If you do know Me, you don't really consider what I want or think. You will say you have prayed about it, but you don't actually wait for Me to answer. You go ahead with your agenda. Once a marriage has failed, most of you do not wait until you are healed of the past, nor do you stop to clean out the dirty baggage before you pack a fresh one. Therefore, you have a marriage problem."*

I did not leave Pete because of looking for another relationship, though many do. They think they will find happiness with someone new, yet they end up carrying their emotional baggage from the previous marriage into the next. Most couples who separate are in a new relationship, usually before the divorce is final. Thus, generally speaking, they are doomed to fail. I had my own issues, so I am not trying to make my situation look any more holy than the next one. Having seen how too many get caught in a relationship with someone else before they hardly get their suitcases unpacked, I was determined to look at me and let God change me. I did not leave for someone else; I did not even think about dating. I wanted to see what kind of life God wanted for me. Seriously, I did not think about getting married. It would be another six years before I would file for divorce. I wasn't just thinking about me, I wanted to give Pete time to unpack his baggage as well as get used to the idea of divorce. It was hard on him and I take no pleasure in that.

While divorce is usually due to one of the 'big' sins—adultery, alcohol, drugs, partying, money issues, and so forth—this was not our problem. We simply went our separate ways in life. We drifted.

We did not wake up one morning with this problem, it came on slowly and we both were at fault. I could only allow God to fix me. My hope was that Pete would do the same, whether we divorced or not. I caught a lot of flak from some friends because I stayed separated so long without divorcing him. I would not have hindered him if he had wanted to divorce me, but I was not taking that huge step until I had let God clean my heart. Another marriage was not part of my thought process. The first years without Pete were hard; I had never been on my own. Being estranged from my family was lonely; my friends were bewildered by my decisions. My ministry took a nosedive because the church, as a whole, does not know how to properly handle divorce within its own community. We become judgmental and take sides leaving someone out to fend for themselves. We leave them widely open to the enemy. Sorry, I had to do a little preaching there.

On with my story. Six years after our separation, I filed for divorce. Life got busy, ministry started picking up, I had my granddaughters to raise. I honestly did not think about dating, much less marriage. I was not disillusioned about marriage. If done correctly, it is a great gift from God. I loved my life! Many changes came about through those years as you have read some of the awesome things God did in those times. Let's fast forward to the years of 2015-2017. Clairey did something like most kids her age; she grew up and decided to move out on her own. At the same time, my friend Holly needed to relocate from North Carolina. I did not particularly care about living alone and Holly did not need to live alone being she was in a power chair. We already did a lot of things together, so it seemed reasonable and natural for her to move in with me. We had a great life! We traveled and worked on ministry projects—it was fun. Did I say I loved my life? Well, I did. Holly and I were very aware of change in the air and we both know God works with us in seasons. We knew a new season was approaching, we just did not know how that looked. I had become her caregiver out of necessity. I honestly did not have a problem with it, but we both knew it would not be forever. She couldn't afford a full-time caregiver, so we just kept seeking God and doing life in the meantime.

One night, we were watching a Christian TV show. It was a talk show where a female Christian comedian was being interviewed. Her husband had died a few years prior and her friends had signed her up for a Christian dating service. She was so funny! She said it was either the stupidest thing she would ever do, or it would give her the best material. Holly and I were laughing when she had a brainstorm like she often had. When she did, you had to be ready for battle. Once she gets an idea, she is like a pitbull that will not turn it loose!

She turned her chair so she could face me and said, *"Let's do it!"*

It did not register what she meant, so I asked, *"Do what?"*

She wasted no time with her answer, *"Let's join a dating site."*

The very thought made me cringe, *"Uh, no, that is creepy! I realize your age group meet people through those avenues, but I am old school and that is just creepy to me. No thank you. Besides, I love my life. I come and go as I please, I travel, I have a full-time ministry, and I have no interest in getting married, so why would I date? To me, dating is nothing more than running interviews for marriage. No!"*

She was not about to take that for an answer—the pit bull effect was in full swing! She started her reasoning, *"Oh, come on, just for one month. I will write your profile and we will do it for just one month!"* The argument continued and I knew I was losing the battle. She will not relent once she has it in her mind.

I said, *"I don't even know what a profile is, but do whatever you like. One month and I am done with this ridiculous idea."*

I had no idea what I was doing. She wrote my profile and I proofread it to make sure it was accurate. I told her she had to state that I was a minister and that it was my top priority. I figured that would scare off any prospects. I did not understand the process, but I started getting winks, blinks, and nods. I did not even understand the lingo of online dating. She, however, did. She had done it before, so she knew all the pitfalls and of what to be wary. She also teaches computer science, so she knows how to scope someone to make sure they are who they say they are.

Every day, I would flip through just to make her happy, but that was not acceptable to her, *"You have to speak to someone."*

I thought to myself, *"No, I don't."* I said to her, *"I told you, I would look and that is what I am doing for one month. Besides, this is goofy. The pictures of the men my age either try to look twenty standing in front of their sports cars, which they can't get into due to their arthritis, or they are sitting on their motorcycles with their shirts open so I can see their gray chest hair. Oh, help me Jesus! Then you have the ones lying on their beds with no shirt on with an oxygen tube in their nose! No, thank you!"*

Okay, I want to clear the air. I love old men. I love motorcycles. I love sport cars and I don't have a problem with older fellas or women enjoying their vehicles, it is just the persona some try to create as if they are not on Medicare. Give me a break!

"Just say 'hi' to someone," Holly urged.

I thought out loud, *"Yeah, yeah, yeah!"*

I kept turning the pages. Bingo! Finally, I saw a guy with some real appeal. He was dressed as a professional cyclist standing next to his bike. Yes, he was handsome, but whether you believe me or not, that is not why he appealed to me, not at first. He was very fit, and my first thought was, *"He does not look like he leans on his grocery cart!"* I get really irritated when I see older people lean on their carts. Stand up guys, we are not finished yet. That is what first attracted me to Ray—his energy. I mean, you must have energy to be a cyclist.

I read Ray's profile and it said he was an event coordinator for the Governor's Cup Race of South Carolina. That should be easy enough to check to see if he was legit. He also said he was Christian, of course that would take a little conversation to determine. Being a "Christian" can mean a lot of things to a lot of people. He was tall, I liked that.

I thought this might get Holly off my back, so I took the plunge and said, *"Hi."*

It wasn't long before he replied back with a *"Hi."* That was it. I told Holly this was stupid.

The next day, she said to reach out one more time. I said something very generic like, *"Hi, I hope your day is going well."*

He responded with an affirmative answer and said pretty much the same to me. I told Holly, *"I am done with this. It is so sixteen-year-old, I feel as if I am in the first grade and writing a boy a note, 'Do you like me? Check yes or no.'"*

I had decided I would not be the first to reach out again. If he didn't, then I had served my time and commitment to Holly, and I would be through with this foolishness. I had too many irons in the fire as it was; I really did not need the distractions of a romantic relationship. The next day, my little dating alarm dinged. I checked and it was Ray. Over the next few days, we went back and forth until I decided I was either going to develop a real relationship as a potential interest or cut it off. I told Ray I was not interested in doing the typical line dating scenario. I suggested he take the info from my profile and do what he naturally does: plan a mock ministry event. Likewise, I would write a motivational speech of how older Americans should take care of their physical bodies using him as an example. He agreed saying that the idea was out of the box. I told him he had no idea how "out of the box" I could be! He needed my email address because we could not do that on the dating site due to the volume of information. I knew that was true, but I was a little nervous. However, I knew it was going to get more personal. We exchanged email addresses and it took both of us a few days to complete our assignments.

When I received my event plan, I was impressed, and, believe me, I am not easy to impress. This guy really knew what he was doing. He had planned a fund raiser event for my ministry and he seemed to appreciate the speech I had prepared. We had broken the barrier from the mundane cycle of on-line relationships. We had to actually look at our profiles and form a persona of what we thought the other person was like. It dawned on me that he had more information than what was in my profile. It wasn't long before we started talking on the phone and I asked him about it. He admitted that he had Googled my name and found my website.

Of course, he came back at me, *"Don't tell me you didn't check me out as well!"*

I laughed, *"That was the first thing Holly did! We found you on the staff page of the Governor's Cup website. At least I knew you were who you said you were. There are some real freaks out there!"*

We began to have regular phone conversations. He would say things like, *"I'll call tomorrow night at 7:42."* At exactly that time, the phone would ring. Weird! I had not told anyone about this relationship other than Holly and my two granddaughters. We talked for several weeks, he asked a lot of questions, and I listened to what he was saying as well as what he avoided saying. He was forming an idea of who I was through the questions, and I was figuring him out by listening to his way of communicating. I have a lot of ministry experience listening to what people say. We were trying to decide a time to meet in person. We both had busy schedules and there was geographical distance between us; we lived an hour and a half away. Meeting was not proving to be easy. He knew I had a lot of upcoming trips.

He asked, *"Do you have a Google calendar?"*

I am computer illiterate! I responded with, *"A Google who?"*

Holly could hear some of our conversation and she was laughing and mouthed at me, *"You do have one. I created it for you. I just didn't tell you because I knew you would not know what I was talking about or care!"*

Holly gave me an on-the-spot education about Google calendars and exchanged it with his for me. In the next conversation we had, he asked with a bit of shock, *"You have seven trips planned over the next five months? One of them overseas! Do you travel like that all the time?"*

Laughing I replied, *"No, I can't afford to travel like that all the time; just about once a year. It comes in spurts."*

He saw where I was going to be in Florida at the end of summer and asked where. I told him I would be on the gulf coast near Clearwater. He said he was going to be near there at the same time, that maybe he could come over and meet my friends, and we could hang out at the beach.

Finally, we decided on a meeting date. He would go to downtown Rock Hill on St. Patty's Day. I knew the area very well and a lot of people would be around. I wasn't going to let him come to my home yet. The night before I was to meet him in person, I prayed, *"Lord, if You are not in this, I don't want to be either. I will cut this thing off first thing in the morning, but You must make it clear. I don't want to guess. Make it clear. Amen"*

I went to sleep and woke up at 6 the next morning and my phone was beeping. I had a text message from a friend who is very prophetic. I had not seen or talked with her in months. The message was this. *"The Lord woke me up with this message for you. 'Divine favor has come to your house, a new relationship. I am with you says the Lord, go ahead. The way is clear."*

I guess I was sort of hoping the Lord would tell me to break it off, but it was just the opposite. The very words I had prayed were in the message from the Lord, and she knew nothing about Ray! The day of reckoning was upon me. I was telling Holly bye and she said, *"I'll see you in six hours!"* I laughed and said, *"That's crazy, I'll be home in two."* Six hours later, I walked in my front door. We had a great time walking around downtown and looking at all the old town buildings. We talked and had fun. I figured it was time to tell folks, just in case this developed further. I decided that, on the same day, I would tell everyone who needed to know. When you have been in ministry a long time as I, telling everyone at the same time about a major change is called damage control. I had been separated almost fourteen years and, by choice, I had not dated. I know I am not the cutest and youngest chic on the scene, but I certainly am not the worst choice either. I just left dating out of my life.

I called my two children first, my four sisters next, and then my immediate ministry partners. Then, I worked my way to the outer circles of friends. I was shocked that everyone was so happy for me. A couple weeks later, one of my close ministry friends, Maxie, called wanting to get together. She and her husband have a ministry where they travel around America calling people back to God. She has an awesome testimony. I had not seen her in months due to her travels, and I had not told her anything about Ray. We met in a nearby town. I listened as she talked about the things God was showing her. After about an hour or so, she was getting ready to call her husband to pick her up. I figured now was a good time to break the news of my new relationship to her. I told her I had something to tell her before her husband got there.

She is a prophet and, immediately, she held up her hand in a stop position, *"Are you seeing someone?"*

"Why would you ask me that?" She had known me several years and never seen me with a man or heard of it. None of my friends had either, other than the ones who knew me when I was married.

She went on to explain, *"I had a dream and dismissed it, but I couldn't get away from it. I dreamed I came into an old church, which I thought was one of the older mainline denominations. I saw you sitting near the front and there was a man sitting with you. He was tall and his hair matched yours. Then, the scene changed, and I saw you two walking down a beach holding hands. It was not the South Carolina sand, I believe it was the gulf coast because the sand looked like it. Are you seeing someone?"*

I was shocked as I listened to the details. She had no way of knowing. It is awesome to have friends who can hear from God so clearly. I told her about Ray. His hair is exactly the color of mine, he is tall, and he was Presbyterian most of his life, which explains the older church deal. I asked her if she felt anything negative in her spirit concerning this relationship, to which she said, "No." In fact, just the opposite. She felt very good about it. She asked me about the beach scene. That actually happened later while we were both in Florida at the same time; he was there for a wedding and I was visiting my friends—I actually told that part earlier in the story. We really did walk down the beach holding hands just as Maxie dreamed. I felt pretty sure God had put His seal of approval on it.

We did not date a long time. Let's face it, we were not exactly kids as we both were into our sixties. We certainly know how to do marriage wrong, but now we had a chance to do it right. We planned our wedding for November 3, 2018 and I was planning a wedding on a shoestring budget. My sister, Pat, hosted our wedding at her beautiful home, which saved a lot of money. I should have known God would take care of His daughter's wedding. My sweet friend, Holly, paid for the products needed for the reception because she wanted it to be nice. She knew I would only throw on some cheap paper plates. I am too practical sometimes. My friend, Rita, called and said her husband, Denny, wanted to volunteer his services as a disc jockey. Wow, what a gift. I thought that, since it was going to be outside and it was fall, I would have a soup, salad, and sandwich bar for the reception. All my wonderful girlfriends put that together and donated the items. Ray took care of the tents and chairs. I had just made some new friends, which I will tell about in the next chapter. Brenda called and said her husband, Doug, wanted to donate his photography services. Sarah Jane called and asked about a wedding cake and told me she and her husband, Jay, wanted to purchase that as a wedding gift. My Father God took care of my wedding expenses through His other children. What a wonderful family of which to be a part!

One big problem though; it rained that entire week prior to our wedding day. The wedding was to be outside and it was already potentially going to be cool. It rained a lot. Everyone kept telling me to make a backup plan, but I did not have one. Pat had worked very hard and cleaned her garage and dressed it up for the dance floor. I decided to trust my Father to be in charge of the weather. After all, if He can calm the storm, He can stop the rain. I knew He would not let me down. It rained all night! I still held firm. Our wedding was at eleven the next morning and we were expecting at least a hundred people. I woke up early that morning, and, by the time it was light, the sun was streaming in the windows. Yes, I knew it! The ground was still a bit wet, but not sloppy. It was a bit cool, but the sun was shining beautifully. We had a beautiful wedding filled with friends and family. My oldest granddaughter, Clairey, and my oldest grandson, TJ, walked me down the steps where we were joined by my other two grandchildren, Gabriel and Elizabeth. All four of my grandchildren gave me to Ray. It was precious.

During the planning stage of my wedding, the big question was, *"Who was going to reside over my ceremony?"* I know a lot of ministers, all of which I would have been honored to officiate, so I had to make a decision. I chose a man whom I consider a great friend and a man filled with wisdom: Joe Dillard from North Carolina, and a long-time friend of Ray's, Dan Cunningham of Lexington, South Carolina.

We had friends and family present from Missouri, Florida, Georgia, South Carolina, and North Carolina. I am overwhelmed with the goodness of God and His people. At the publishing of this book November 2020, we will be celebrating our two-year anniversary. We are constantly adjusting as we change, and new challenges are put before us, but it has been a fun journey. It is exciting to see what God will do as we grow in Him and learn how to do marriage well.

STORY 111

~

Moving On!

"...Go forth from your country, and from your relatives and from your father's house to the land I will show you (Genesis 12:1)."

I was born and raised in upstate, Lancaster, South Carolina, and moved to Rock Hill about twenty miles away when I was around five. I lived in Rock Hill all my life until I moved to York about twelve miles away. So, pretty much, I lived in the same area all my life and never considered living anywhere else. All my family, friends, and ministry were in that area.

In the previous story, I told the story of Ray, and, before that, how Holly came to live with me. I also mentioned that I had seven trips planned in a five-month timeframe as I was just getting serious in my relationship with Ray. I went to Kenya and was gone for sixteen days. I had two days before leaving on another trip to Virginia, and, after that, I would be leaving for Missouri. I would have about a week at home before I was to leave for Florida for two weeks, not counting three other trips.

I had just gotten home from Kenya when Holly hit me with one of her brainstorms, *"Let's move."*

"Move? Move where? Why would I want to move? My house is paid for, what are you talking about?"

She was quick to make her case, *"If you are going to marry Ray, you need to get to see him more often than Saturdays. You need to get to know him better."*

I was just as quick to disqualify her argument, *"I haven't said I was going to marry him yet. Besides, when would you like to move? I haven't even unpacked my suitcase from Kenya. When would you want us to find a house and when should I start packing? Should I do it between now and when I leave for Virginia in two days, or should I do it between Virginia and Missouri? Perhaps I could wait until I get back from Missouri and while I am packing to go to Florida. I could pack the dishes!"*

Remember, I told you she was like a pit bull. She was not about to let it go. *"Well, you might want to start packing now. I made an appointment in the morning to see an apartment in Cayce."*

Cayce is just outside Columbia, South Carolina where Ray lives. I knew arguing with her was fruitless. The next day, we drove to Cayce and accepted the apartment. I did insist on a short, six-month lease. I figured this would burn itself out and we would return to my home that was paid in full. It seemed ridiculous to pay rent when we had a paid home. Besides, I had never lived anywhere else, and I would have to tell Clairey—that was not going to be pleasant.

I went home, and, in between trips, I packed just enough to live there six months. We took Clairey out to dinner and I knew she was not going to be thrilled at my moving, but I didn't expect that sort of fall out. She was upset to the max! It broke my heart to see her so upset, but the decision had been made. We moved. I was struggling at leaving everything I knew. I didn't have any relationships in Cayce other than Ray. I had no foundation for ministry there. You must have some connections with a church or someone to build ministry. I was going to have no ministry, no friends, no life, poor me! What a cry baby. I got hold of myself and decided I would try to enjoy the journey. It was going to be exciting to see how God would build me a new life. Still, I missed my life back home. I should have known my life would not remain quiet for long. Neither Holly nor I ever lacked the ability to make friends. Life was busy trying to get settled. I was still Holly's caregiver, and now invested in developing my relationship with Ray and would soon plan my wedding. In the meantime, Holly was developing a relationship with someone she met online. She would go on to marry Tim not long after I married Ray.

Ray wanted me to meet his long-time friend and high school teacher, Sarah Jane. she invited us to church and then to her house for lunch after service. She attends a very liturgical church. I was not real sure about being at such an ordered and planned service as I was used to a more spontaneous church. We went. I can honestly say that, while it is not what I am called to and wouldn't want that structured order every Sunday, I learned some new things. I certainly felt the presence of the Holy Spirit there. We went to their house for lunch and Sarah Jane and I hit it off. We are very much alike and, while we have our differences, we have mutual respect for each other. I have come to love her and value her friendship. At one point, her husband said to Ray, *"Do we even need to be in the room?"* Ray replied, *"I knew it would be like this. They are like two peas in a pod."*

I had started losing weight before I met Ray, even though everyone thought that it was because I was in love. Becoming Holly's caregiver and the fact that we ate differently, the weight came off slowly. I hardly noticed it until Holly finally said, *"You have got to buy some new clothes. Those jeans are falling off you!"* By the time we moved to Cayce—you have to be specific and say "Cayce" and not "Columbia" because the Cayce people are very adamant about that, which has something to do with being on the right side of the river—I had lost enough weight that none of my clothes fit. I couldn't afford to replace them all. Holly also had lost some weight, so we went searching for someone to do alterations. It is expensive! We finally found a lady who does alterations out of her home, very reasonably priced, and, as we found out later, very efficient with her time. I made an appointment and knocked on her door. The minute she opened the door and we spoke, it was as if we had known each other a long time. She said, *"I think I have been waiting a long time for you."* That began a great friendship and we enjoyed spending time over lunch and bike riding.

Slowly, I was meeting people and building relationships. After Ray and I got married, he came home one day and said that one of his co-worker's asked him some questions. He told her he was unable to answer them, but he believed his wife could. A few days later, I took him a salad for lunch. I went into the break room and this lovely young woman was sitting there. Ray introduced me to Lyn; she was the one asking the questions. She started to talk, and I felt the Holy Spirit tell me not to let her tell me her issues. I asked Ray to leave the room so that Lyn and I could speak privately. The Holy Spirit showed me some things concerning her life. I shared them with her, and she was amazed at how the Holy Spirit works. That was the beginning of not only a deep friendship between her and me, but I have seen her relationship with the Lord grow exponentially. She has been a true blessing to me.

Then, there is Jenny. I was introduced to Jenny by my pastor friend, Robert. I call her my "Cayce Shelly." I really miss my friend from home. Shelly has been a unique presence in my life, and I see so much of her in my new friend, Jenny. I just appreciate her bluntness and honesty—they're both that way. We enjoy walking together on a regular basis. I still miss Shelly as no one can take her place, but it was sweet of our heavenly Father to give me someone like her.

Time and space will not allow me to mention all the relationships I have grown to love while making a life here. I teach a Bible study on Sunday afternoons and it is always changing, but the spiritual growth I see in each of its regular participants overwhelms my heart. I have already mentioned some within my little description of them, but there are a couple more that have a special place in my heart: Donald and Chris, thank you for your love and support of me and the Kingdom of God.

As I close this story, I want to say a word of gratitude for all the blessings of the Body of Christ and to our Savior, Jesus Christ, for allowing me to speak into your lives. I am so excited to be a part of His Kingdom.

My Aaron and Hur!

"But Moses' hands were heavy. Then they took a stone and put it under him, and he sat on it; and Aaron and Hur supported his hands, one on one side and one on the other...(Exodus 17:12)."

I once heard a minister say, *"Every ministry needs three things: a butler, a baker, and a pharaoh. A butler opens doors, a baker puts things together, and a pharaoh finances the journey."*

God has been so gracious to me. He has given me everything I need to do that which He has called me to do. He has sent me many 'pharaohs,' to finance this journey. The faithfulness of His people is phenomenal! I have had my share of bakers, those that are gifted in putting things together. I have had those who have opened doors for me; I give a special acknowledgement to my friend, Pastor Robert Reeves. He has a gift for connecting Kingdom people and opening doors of ministry. He has done that for me many times and is responsible for connecting me with someone who is currently a strong advocate in my life. Pastor Robert is a baker and a butler for many in the Body of Christ.

I also have had many pharaohs in my life. Remember, they are the ones who support ministries with finances. I have been blessed with seasonal providers, meaning they give for the season they are called to and move on. Each one is important in their faithfulness, no matter what the amount. I have a couple friends who are truly gifts from God. I will refer to them as "Ruth and Boaz" simply because their giving is unto the Lord, but they have been faithful in their giving and friendship for many years. They have no idea how they have sustained me and continue to do so.

While God has blessed me with those who have given of their time, money, and resources, there are two who stand out above the rest. One is Holly, about whom I have talked a lot throughout this book. Holly has many gifts and gives unselfishly. She promoted me and my ministry above her own. While she is a minister and awesome teacher in her own right, she always found ways to propel my ministry and gifts forward. She illustrated and published three of my books and she pushed me—and I mean pushed me hard to do things I would have never done on my own! I probably would not ever have met Ray had she not been a pit bull in my life. We lived together, traveled together, ministered together. We laughed, we cried, we argued, and we just did life together. But, as I said earlier, God does things in seasons and our season changed. She now lives in Georgia with her husband, Tim. Time marches on, but she had a tremendous impact on my life, and I am forever grateful and better for knowing her.

When she began going her own direction, I prayed and asked God for someone with her gifts to come alongside me. I am very limited in technology, and, if you are going to do ministry in today's world, you better know how. I don't. I wasn't just asking for someone to bless me, but someone with whom I could also be a blessing with my gifts. The Kingdom of God does not exist for consumers, but it thrives on participants. It is never about one person, but the Body of Christ collectively growing God's Kingdom.

Guess what? God sent me Alexys V. Wolf. Pastor Robert Reeves had met her through reading one of her books and contacted her.

He insisted that we connect. I called her just as she was about to call me. We met for lunch and, honestly, I'm not sure we really took to each other immediately. That's because, as I found out later, we are so much alike. We had to size each other up. We both are super strong in our personalities, although she might be a hair above me in that! We are both extraverts and have been in the ministry a long time. We know the pitfalls and we both have allowed God to clean our clocks! We speak the same things. We think alike. Scary, huh, I know. We don't completely agree on everything, but that is the beauty of individuality. We were never meant to be as if we were shaped by a cookie cutter.

Since knowing Alexys, she has gotten me on a television talk show, and we do a radio broadcast every Sunday morning called "*Better Together*." She is the reason this book is now a reality and is published under her publishing company, *The Fiery Sword Publications*. She has built me a new website, and, besides that, we have done other ministry together because we are better together! She is a great teacher, prophet, prayer warrior, and author. You will be blessed to get connected to her. You can find her on Facebook, YouTube, Amazon, Instagram, or go to her website, www.thefierysword.com. There you can find her many published books as she is a great writer.

Thank you, Alexys and Holly, for being my friends, ministry partners, and my Aaron and Hur when I needed you. I hope my life and ministry have been beneficial for both of you as well. I look forward to many years of great adventures. This is my last chapter, though I thought it would never get here, but here it is. I pray you will find hope, faith, and lots of love in this book. I pray you will be challenged in places you may be limiting God or yourself. We serve a God of impossibilities. Go for the goal of Christ Jesus, walk in freedom, and let the Holy Spirit heal and change you. Let God out of your box—He's not really in there anyway. Breathe and enjoy the journey!

Made in the USA
Middletown, DE
12 March 2023

26522490R00219